PRESENTING
SHAKESPEARE

PRESENTING SHAKESPEARE

WRITTEN AND ARRANGED

BY

R. C. PEAT M.A.

FORMER SECOND MASTER AND SENIOR ENGLISH MASTER HULL GRAMMAR SCHOOL

Nelson

Thomas Nelson and Sons Ltd
Nelson House   Mayfield Road
Walton-on-Thames   Surrey
KT12 5PL   UK

51 York Place
Edinburgh
EH1 3JD   UK

Thomas Nelson (Hong Kong) Ltd
Toppan Building 10/F
22A Westlands Road
Quarry Bay   Hong Kong

Distributed in Australia by
Thomas Nelson Australia
102 Dodds Street
South Melbourne   Victoria 3205
Australia

PREFACE

A BRIEF explanation of the purpose, arrangement, and method of this book is perhaps advisable.

Purpose

The book is an attempt to solve the problem of how and at what stage to introduce the plays of Shakespeare into the English syllabus of schools. That such a problem exists can hardly be doubted. The number of people who say that they were bored with Shakespeare at school, and who show no interest in his work after they have left school, is legion; it is impossible to avoid the conclusion that the presentment of the plays is not always satisfactory. I have tried here to put Shakespeare before the reader as a real figure, and to give as complete a picture as possible both of the man and of the age in which he lived and wrote.

Age of Pupils

In my own school, a city school of nearly seven hundred boys of widely varying types, it was the custom some years ago to read one of Shakespeare's plays—usually *The Merchant of Venice*—with the Third Forms, composed of boys about twelve years old. This was considered a failure and was abandoned. Our experience with boys a year older was similar; we found that many of them still took less interest in Shakespeare than in their other texts. This introduction to Shakespeare, therefore, is intended for pupils of about fourteen years of age. Most of them will have another year in which they can read two or three more plays before proceeding to the detailed study of one play which is at present necessary in the General Certificate year.

5

Contents

The main part of the book consists of four of Shakespeare's plays. Most teachers think that boys and girls who are beginning to read Shakespeare should learn something about the playhouses of the period; I have therefore included an introductory section dealing with the earliest English plays, with the Elizabethan theatre, and with Shakespeare himself. To help the pupils to form a picture of the theatres of the time I have added, in Part Three, some scenes from *The Knight of the Burning Pestle*, by Beaumont and Fletcher; and for the same purpose, in Part Four, some extracts from Sir A. T. Quiller-Couch's *Shakespeare's Christmas*. Maurice Baring's *The Rehearsal* also is given in Part Four, partly because it illustrates admirably the difficulties of play-production in Shakespeare's days, and partly because it is immensely popular with young people, either for reading in class or for producing at school concerts.

Choice of Plays

The choice of the first three plays seemed obvious; *A Midsummer Night's Dream* has been placed after *The Merchant of Venice* and *Twelfth Night* because of its somewhat more complicated construction. For the fourth play I have, after some hesitation, preferred *Macbeth* to *As You Like It*, partly because I have always found it to be the more popular play with young people, and partly because it illustrates another aspect of Shakespeare's work.

Treatment of Plays

In my student days it was my privilege to attend a series of lectures, given by a distinguished Professor of Education, on the teaching of Shakespeare in Grammar Schools. He spoke of the custom—at that time apparently not uncommon—of giving out copies of the play to be studied and then plunging *in medias res* by asking the pupils to read the parts in turn; his words, and his expression as he uttered them come back to me across the years: "That is the ass's way; you are not asses, and I trust you will never adopt that method." He suggested that the teacher should devote one or two lessons to telling the story of the play; meanwhile, for homework, the pupils should read some of the most important and most interesting scenes. The method adopted in this book is a modification of that suggestion. Because of the supreme importance of arousing and maintaining interest, use has been made of the perfectly natural and sensible plan of 'skipping' parts likely to prove dull to young readers. It is futile to pretend that boys and girls fourteen years old find much humour in the chatter of the Clown in *Twelfth Night* or that Malcolm's conversation with Macduff in England—whatever its dramatic importance—is anything but tedious to them. To make young people spend time reading scenes which they do not appreciate or even understand is merely to invite boredom, to arouse a distaste for Shakespeare, and to provide ammunition for the ungenerous and perhaps somewhat overrated "Eng. Lit." gibe. Further, four plays instead of only one or two can by this means be read in the year; there must surely be added interest, both for teacher and taught, in greater variety.

From each of the plays some parts have therefore been omitted, but it will be found that very few scenes of dramatic interest or literary worth have been left out. When scenes have been omitted necessary explanations have been given in order to maintain the continuity of the story. For these explanations I have, in places, used extracts from *Tales from Shakespeare*, by Charles and Mary Lamb. These *Tales*, however, are in some ways insufficient. There is, for example, no mention of the casket story or of the Lorenzo and Jessica story in *The Merchant of Venice*, no mention of the trick played on Malvolio in *Twelfth Night*, and no mention of the comic interlude in *A Midsummer Night's Dream*. All these sub-plots, in addition to their importance, are of interest to young readers. Some additional explanations have therefore been necessary, but they have been kept as few and as short as possible.

It will be seen that this scheme of work ensures that even pupils who leave school immediately after their General Certificate year have read seven or eight of Shakespeare's plays. Their interest will, I believe, have been aroused. Perhaps best of all, they will have realized from the beginning that Shakespeare was—to borrow a phrase from Arnold Bennett—a man, not a book.

R. C. P.

ACKNOWLEDGMENTS

ACKNOWLEDGMENTS are due to Messrs William Heinemann, Ltd., for permission to use *The Rehearsal*, from *Diminutive Dramas*, by Major the Hon. Maurice Baring. Permission had been granted by Major Baring also before his death. Extracts from *Shakespeare's Christmas*, by the late Sir Arthur Quiller-Couch, are included by permission of LadyQuiller-Couch and Messrs J. M. Dent and Sons, Ltd.

CONTENTS

PART ONE
THE BEGINNINGS

PART TWO
SOME PLAYS BY SHAKESPEARE

A*

PART ONE

THE BEGINNINGS

THE purpose of this book is to introduce to you the work
of William Shakespeare, the greatest poet and dramatist
ever born in England—perhaps, indeed, the greatest ever
born anywhere. In working through the book you will
study four of his most famous plays. You will also read
some extracts from a play, written by two dramatists who
lived at the same time as Shakespeare, which gives a fine
picture of the playhouse of those days; some extracts from
a story which tells how the Globe Theatre, the famous
theatre where many of Shakespeare's plays were produced,
came to be built; and a one-act play which shows in a
very amusing way the difficulties of producing plays in the
sixteenth and early seventeenth centuries. Shakespeare,
you must remember, lived more than three hundred years
ago. Fashions and manners then were very different from
those of to-day. Plays were at that time only gradually
developing an established form, and play-production, as
we know it, was still in its infancy. Some features of
Shakespeare's plays, therefore, may seem to you crude and
amateurish—even absurd. If you are to understand and
appreciate the plays you should know something about
the earlier English plays, about Shakespeare himself, about
the people for whom he wrote, and about the theatre as
it was in the days when he was writing.

I. THE EARLIEST ENGLISH PLAYS

(a) **Miracle Plays**

Origin. Although no doubt most of you attend church
services and pay occasional visits to the theatre, you have
probably never realized that there is any connexion between
the two. It was in the churches, however, that English plays
began. There were theatres in Britain when the Romans

were here, but for many centuries after the departure of the Romans the only forms of entertainment were puppet shows and mummers' shows, the songs of wandering minstrels, pageants, and acrobatic performances. The clergy were hostile to theatres because of the degrading nature of some of the Roman shows, but in the churches little ceremonies were performed as part of the ritual or to arouse interest in the Bible. Thus, a veil might be dropped at the words: "The veil of the temple was rent in twain," or a linen cloth torn at the words: "They parted my raiment among them." Sometimes a tomb was erected in the church, with a cross to represent the body of Jesus Christ. Short plays were constructed round famous biblical episodes such as the stories of the Creation, of Adam and Eve, of Cain and Abel, and of the Flood. Other plays dealt with the lives of saints. The parts were taken by the priests; dialogue, in Latin, was introduced. The favourite stories were those connected with Easter, such as the visit of the disciples to the tomb, and Jesus Christ's meeting with Mary Magdalene; Christmas stories were also much liked, and developed on similar lines. These plays were very popular during the eleventh, twelfth, and early thirteenth centuries. So many people wished to see them that in the course of time the performances had to be given out of doors, at first on scaffolds erected in the churchyards, but later—because of the trampling on the graves—in the streets and market-places. This removal took place about the middle of the thirteenth century; it is noteworthy because it led to many far-reaching developments in the plays during the next hundred years.

Results of the Removal to the Streets. While the plays were given in the churches and the churchyards they were arranged and acted by the clergy; laymen took no part. The clergy, however, were not allowed to act in the streets. The plays thus gradually passed out of the hands of the Church. They were taken over by the town authorities, and in many towns a performance of the plays became a yearly event. The acting was usually done by members of the trade guilds, English being used instead of Latin for the dialogue.

We have seen that the most popular stories were those connected with Christmas and Easter. Christmas and Easter, however, are not always suitable seasons for performances out-of-doors. Once again the Church, although it now looked on the plays with disfavour, helped in the cause of dramatic development. In the year 1264 the Pope had instituted the Festival of Corpus Christi. This festival came in June; it was a general holiday, and became the most magnificent celebration in the Church year. Splendid processions were held, and to take part in them was a privilege much prized. Places were allotted to the various trade guilds, and in time dramatic performances came to be a recognized part of the festivities. Many scenes were now in existence, and they were acted by the most suitable guilds; thus the shipbuilders presented the building of the ark, the mariners and fishermen the story of Noah and his family, the bakers the Last Supper, and the butchers the Crucifixion. The various episodes were gradually combined into continuous stories; thus the Easter play consisted of a long series of incidents beginning with the setting of the watch and ending with the incredulity of St Thomas. These plays were called miracle plays. More and more scenes were added, until there was in existence a series of plays representing an unbroken story from the Creation to the Day of Judgment. Such a series of plays was called a "cycle."

Method of Presentment. The plays were performed on scaffolds. Beneath the floor on which the plays were acted was a space which served the actors as a dressing room, and was used in the plays to represent Hell. The entrance to this space was at the back of the stage, and was hidden by a curtain. Above the stage was a roof, on which the angels took up their positions; when they were required on the stage they were let down by means of ropes. Later on you will be reading a description of the playhouses of Elizabethan days, and you will notice with interest that many features were apparently taken from the scaffolds of the miracle plays.

The stages, which were often called "pageants," were usually on wheels, so that they could be moved from one street to another. One scene was given on each pageant. The first pageant presented the story of the Creation, and then moved on to repeat it somewhere else. Meanwhile, another pageant had come to the first pitch and was giving the story of Adam and Eve. Then this second pageant followed the first, which had gone to give a third performance in another place. Other pageants came in turn to play the story of Cain and Abel, the story of the Flood, the story of Abraham and Isaac, and all the other scenes. Thus many plays were going on simultaneously, and the whole cycle was acted in various parts of the town. In some places the performances were completed in one day, but in others two or three days were required.

Features of the Plays. While the plays were controlled by the Church they were essentially religious, but when they passed into the hands of laymen they were produced as much for entertainment as for religious purposes. A humorous element was introduced, and spread rapidly. The Devil was shown as a comic character. He appeared "in most horrible wise to deter men from sin"; he lived beneath the stage, in Hell, and he sometimes rushed out to drag away his victims or to "make a sally among the people." King Herod was a blustering tyrant; he raged about the stage—and also among the spectators—tearing his beard and brandishing a sword. Pontius Pilate was another tyrant; after one pageant had moved on, he and Herod kept the spectators in order until the next scene began. Cain was an uncouth fellow, and Joseph the carpenter was an elderly man who complained about marriage and warned the audience against it. Most of the female characters were gentle and womanly, but Noah's wife was a termagant who refused to enter the ark. The shepherds who "watched their flocks by night" were always humorously treated, and sometimes an amusing story—entirely without biblical foundation—was introduced immediately before the angel appeared to announce the birth of Jesus Christ. The following is an example of such a story.

Three shepherds were visited by a man called Mak, who was suspected of sheep-stealing. He was allowed to spend the night with them, but while they were asleep he stole a sheep and took it home to his wife Gill. When the shepherds came to look for it Mak and Gill pretended it was a child, and put it in a cradle. The trick was discovered when the shepherds wished to greet the child, and Mak was tossed in a blanket.

The plays were expensively produced. The players were elaborately dressed, but their costumes were not suited to the characters represented—a curious fault which, as you will read later, was repeated by the Elizabethans. The dresses worn by the actors in the miracle plays were probably copied from pictures in the churches or from representations of the various characters in stained glass windows. Herod and Pilate were always grotesquely dressed; St Peter had a gilt beard; the angels wore surplices. It is amusing to us to read in the accounts of the plays that twopence was paid for a pair of gloves for God; that buckram for the Holy Ghost's coat cost two shillings and a penny; and that the stage properties included "Hell-mouth, the head of a whale with jaws worked by two men, out of which devil boys run." You must not think, however, that there was any intentional irreverence. The plays were thought to be an excellent means of spreading scriptural knowledge, and were taken very seriously; it is recorded at Beverley that on one occasion a weaver was fined for not knowing his part. Further, some of the scenes, far from being comic, were full of tenderness and pathos. The most noteworthy of these are a scene in which Abraham prepares to sacrifice his only son Isaac, and another in which the Virgin Mary lies at the foot of the Cross on which Jesus Christ has died.

The Influence of Miracle Plays on Later Plays. The chief importance of miracle plays is that they developed in the people an interest in dramatic performances. Their influence can be seen in many of the features of later plays. We have already noticed that the stages of Elizabethan playhouses resembled in some ways the scaffolds on which the miracle plays were performed, and that elaborate— though inappropriate—costumes were characteristic of both periods. The introduction of characters not taken from the Bible, such as Mak, prepared the way for plays introducing men and women taken from real life. Similarly, the representation of devils and angels was a forerunner of the use of supernatural agencies, such as the fairies in *A Midsummer Night's Dream* and Banquo's ghost in *Macbeth*. Both the villain of modern melodrama and the bold, bad baron of the pantomime are descendants of Herod and Pontius Pilate. Finally, there is in many of Shakespeare's plays—as in many modern plays—the mingling of the comic and the tragic that we noticed in the miracle plays; in *Macbeth*, for example, you will find a scene introducing a comic drunken porter immediately after a terrible scene in which the king is murdered and immediately before the discovery of the murder.

(b) Other Very Early Plays

Besides the miracle plays, plays dealing with the lives of saints were also in existence during this period. They were not as popular as the miracles, but they played a part in the development of the drama by establishing an interest in shorter plays.

There were also plays based on country customs and legends, and on folk festivals. Dances round the maypole, sword dances, and morris dances were very common. Sometimes a Fool was introduced, dressed in the skin of a fox or of some other animal. Other plays dealt with Robin Hood and his followers. The influence of these plays on later drama, however, was small in comparison with that of the miracle plays.

(c) **Morality Plays, Interludes, Masks, and Chronicle Plays**

Miracle plays had a long run; they were popular for nearly three centuries, and were still being produced late in the sixteenth century. Before that time, however, they had begun to lose favour. Perhaps they were too long; perhaps the spectators began to wish for new characters and new plots. About the middle of the fifteenth century plays of a new type, called morality plays, came into fashion. The characters in these new plays were representations of vices and virtues, such as Avarice, Ignorance, Mischief, Repentance, Forgiveness, and Knowledge. The plots were concerned with the struggle in a man's soul between good and evil. Such plots were probably rather dull, and to counteract any tendency towards tediousness the comic element of the miracle plays was retained and became even more pronounced. The Devil still appeared, but he was accompanied—and finally superseded—by a new character called the Vice. The Vice was a great favourite; he was partly clown and partly devil, and his share in the play was to provide merriment and to lead men astray. He carried a wooden sword, and his chief occupation was tormenting the Devil. He belaboured the Devil with his sword, rode on the Devil's back, and cut the Devil's nails with his wooden sword. At the end of the play he was carried off by the Devil to Hell. There are many references in literature to the Vice; you will find this song in Shakespeare's *Twelfth Night*:

> I am gone, sir,
> And anon, sir,
> I'll be with you again,
> In a trice,
> Like to the old Vice,
> Your need to sustain;
>
> Who, with dagger of lath,
> In his rage and his wrath,
> Cries, ah, ha! to the devil:
> Like a mad lad,
> Pare thy nails, dad;
> Adieu, goodman devil.

The Vice of the morality plays became the fool and jester of later plays. He was the ancestor of such characters as the Clown in *Twelfth Night* and Launcelot Gobbo in *The Merchant of Venice*, and the scenes of revelry in *Twelfth Night* reflect some of his antics.

We have seen that the religious motive was less pronounced in the morality plays than in the miracles. This movement away from religion was even more marked in plays called interludes, which came into fashion early in the sixteenth century. Interludes were short comedies or farces which were usually played at the houses of great lords at times of festivity, between the courses at banquets or between the acts of longer plays. It was common for the noblemen to keep companies of players under their patronage—a custom still prevalent in the days of Shakespeare—and it was often by these players that the interludes were acted. The play given by the Athenian rustics in Shakespeare's *A Midsummer Night's Dream* was really an interlude. Interludes, like morality plays, frequently taught moral lessons; nevertheless, they represent the final stage of the separation of the drama from religion.

Other plays of the period were called masks. They were

originally only spectacular processions or pageants, but later music and dialogue were added. The fairy scenes in *A Midsummer Night's Dream*, with their singing and dancing, are reminiscent of the mask.

At this time, too, chronicle plays became popular. These plays—in the words of a writer of the period—dealt with

> our English chronicles, wherein our forefathers' valiant acts, that have lien long buried in rusty brass and worm-eaten books, are revived, and they themselves raised from the grave of oblivion and brought to plead their aged honours in open presence.

(d) The Rise of Regular Drama

You will have read in your history lessons about the Renaissance, and you will know that in the fifteenth and sixteenth centuries men studied with much enthusiasm the literature of ancient Greece and Rome. Italian plays, too, were widely read. These two factors—the Renaissance and contemporary Italian literature—had a marked effect on the development of English drama. Young men who had studied classical tragedy and comedy at the Universities blended the action and humour of the early English plays with the dignity and form of classical drama and the romance and imagination of Italian plays. These men are sometimes called the 'University Wits'; one of them, Thomas Nashe, plays a part in the story *Shakespeare's Christmas* which you will find in Part Four of this book. The most important of them was Christopher Marlowe, who was a forerunner of William Shakespeare. Before we pass on to the plays of Shakespeare, however, it will be well for us to consider the playhouses of the time and the conditions under which the plays were performed.

II. THE ELIZABETHAN PLAYHOUSE

(a) Its Development

We have seen that the miracle and the morality plays of the thirteenth and fourteenth centuries were performed in the churchyard, in the street, in the market-place, and in any other public place where a scaffold could be erected and a crowd assembled. Plays were often given in inn-yards, and by the middle of the sixteenth century the inn-yard had become a recognized ready-made theatre. The Elizabethan inn often consisted of buildings of two storeys set along the sides of a rectangular central yard, with a balcony—which connected the upper rooms—running round the yard and overlooking it. The stage was built on trestles in the middle of the yard. The poorer people watched the play from the floor of the yard, and the richer people looked on from the balcony.

This was the usual setting for plays until the year 1576; in that year the first playhouse was built, by James Burbage. Plays were not allowed in London because they caused crowds to gather and sometimes led to rowdiness, and Burbage built his theatre at Shoreditch outside the boundary of the city. It was of wood and modelled on the inn-yard, but was circular in shape. Burbage called his playhouse The Theatre, and it was here that Shakespeare's first plays were acted. Other theatres followed; the Curtain, the Rose, the Swan, and several others were in existence before the end of the century. The most famous of all was the Globe, built in the year 1599 by James Burbage's sons, Richard and Cuthbert, from the timber of the old Theatre, which was now taken down, carried across the Thames, and re-erected in a disreputable quarter known as the Bankside. You will read about this notable incident in the story *Shakespeare's Christmas*. Shakespeare had a share in the venture, and many of his plays were performed at the Globe. You will notice that in *The Rehearsal*, given in Part Four of this book, the scene is laid at the Globe Theatre in the year 1606; Richard Burbage was a popular tragic actor, and he is presumably the Mr Burbage who took the part of Macbeth. The Globe Theatre was destroyed by fire in 1613, and it is possible that some of Shakespeare's manuscripts were lost in the flames. Another famous producer of the period was Philip Henslowe; he built three theatres—the Rose, the Fortune, and the Hope—and left a diary and various documents which give us much information about the theatres of those days.

(b) What It was Like

The Elizabethan playhouse, like the bull-baiting and bear-baiting rings, was usually circular. It was very small; the diameter of the inside space was less than the length of a cricket pitch. The stage was movable because many of the theatres were used for bull-baiting and bear-baiting as well as for plays; it projected from one side almost into the middle of the theatre. Round the theatre ran three tiers of galleries, like the balconies of the inn-yards, and from these the richer people watched the performances; the most expensive seats were behind the stage, in a part of the gallery called the lords' room. The poorer people watched from the floor of the theatre, which was called then—as it still is—the pit. The occupants of the pit were known as the groundlings. The stage and the galleries were covered, but the rest of the playhouse was open to the sky. The plays were performed in daylight, usually in the afternoons, and lasted two or three hours.

At the back of the stage were two doors opening into the players' dressing-room. Between these doors was a third door which was hidden by a curtain; this door led to a space which was used by players who were 'concealed behind the arras' and by the prompter. The part of the gallery above this space served as an upper stage; it enabled the actors to 'enter above,' and could be used as a balcony, as the battlements of a castle, or as a bedroom. It would be used, for example, in *The Merchant of Venice*, when Jessica threw down Shylock's jewels to Lorenzo, who was standing below. Above this upper room there was a turret from which a flag was flown when a play was being performed. A trap-door in the floor of the stage—or perhaps two, one in the front part and another behind the arras—gave access to a space which could be used as a dungeon or for similar purposes.

Only the back of the stage could be used for scenery. Crudely painted cloths—perhaps black for tragedies—were hung there. Sometimes, too, boards were used to describe the scenes; for example, "A Street in Venice," or "A Wood near Athens," or "The Duke's Palace." On the other hand, the actors' costumes were expensive and magnificent. There was no attempt, however, to show the period of the play; the same costumes might be used for Venetians, Athenians, or thanes of Scotland. There were no actresses; female parts were taken by boys and young men. The theatre was considered hardly respectable, and ladies who attended often wore masks. This attitude to the theatre is emphasized in the story *Shakespeare's Christmas*.

The Elizabethans were fond of noise. Trumpets were very popular; they were used to announce from the turret the beginning of the performance, and again in the course of the play for 'tuckets,' 'sennets,' 'alarums,' and 'flourishes.' The spectators were often rowdy and quarrelsome. Clappers were hired to lead the applause; displeasure was shown by hissing, shouting, and mewing like a cat.

(c) How the Plays were affected by the Conditions

From the brief description you have just read you will realize how much the Elizabethan playhouse differed from the theatre of to-day. Because of the conditions under which they were produced, the plays of the period have some features which will seem very strange to you. You will understand the plays better if some of these features are pointed out.

(i) Since there was little or no scenery, the writer could change the scene more frequently than is usual to-day. This explains the very short scenes you will find in some of Shakespeare's plays. The division into acts and scenes has been made by later editors, who have been guided by the principle that when all the actors have left the stage the scene has ended. You will notice that although Shakespeare usually wrote in unrhymed verse many scenes end with rhyming couplets. This was probably done to give warning to the actors of the next scene to be ready.

(ii) In the absence of scenery, information about the time and place of the action is sometimes given in the play itself. One scene in *Twelfth Night* opens with these words:

> VIOLA. What country, friends, is this?
> CAPTAIN. This is Illyria, lady.

Again, since the plays were performed in daylight, the audience had to be reminded when it was supposed to be dark. Jessica, in *The Merchant of Venice*, escaping by night in the disguise of a boy from her father's house, said to Lorenzo:

> Here, catch this casket; it is worth the pains.
> I am glad 'tis night, you do not look on me,
> For I am much asham'd of my exchange:

and Lorenzo replied:

> Descend, for you must be my torch-bearer.

(iii) Since they had no scenery to help them, the dramatists had to give the actors words which would arouse the emotions of the audience. The actors themselves had to make full use of their powers of rhetoric. It is noteworthy that many modern producers have chosen to give Shakespeare's plays with little scenery, in order to focus the attention of the spectators on the words of the play and on the actors.

(iv) There were not many boys or young men available for playing female parts. In many of the plays of the period there are few female characters. Female characters often masquerade as men; for example, Jessica in *The Merchant of Venice* and Viola in *Twelfth Night*.

(v) You will notice that many of the characters of Shakespeare's plays use soliloquies—that is, utter their thoughts aloud. These soliloquies may seem foolish to you, but Elizabethan playgoers saw nothing ususual in them. When an actor advanced to the front of the stage he was close to the spectators and almost surrounded by them; it seemed natural for him to speak to them in confidence.

(vi) Since there was no curtain for the front of the stage, the dramatist had to arrange for all his characters to leave the stage at the end of the play. A play often ends with the death of the hero or of the villain, and it would have been ludicrous for a dead man to get up and walk off as soon as the play was over. The dramatist had therefore to be careful to arrange for the corpse or corpses to be carried off at the close, as in *Julius Cæsar* and *Hamlet*.

The scenes from *The Knight of the Burning Pestle* which are given in Part Three of this book and the extracts from *Shakespeare's Christmas* given in Part Four will help you to form a picture of the appearance of an Elizabethan playhouse. Maurice Baring's burlesque *The Rehearsal*, also given in Part Four, shows cleverly the shortcomings of the actors and the crudities of the play-production of the time.

III. WILLIAM SHAKESPEARE

(a) At Stratford

William Shakespeare was born at Stratford-on-Avon in the year 1564. Stratford is in one of the most beautiful districts of England, and Shakespeare's boyhood and youth there gave him the intimate knowledge of the countryside and its people which is shown in *A Midsummer Night's Dream* and other plays. According to the records of Holy Trinity Church, Stratford, he was baptized on the 26th of April, and it is assumed from this that he was born on the 23rd of April. His father, John Shakespeare, was a dealer in wool, gloves, corn, and other commodities, and during William's boyhood was both a prosperous merchant and a prominent citizen; he was chief citizen of Stratford in 1571. During his year of office a company of travelling players visited Stratford, and this was perhaps the first occasion on which young William Shakespeare saw a play. The boy was probably educated at the Free Grammar School. Unfortunately John Shakespeare's business seems to have failed soon after his year of mayoralty, and the family fell on bad times; probably William had to leave school sooner than he would have done in more favourable circumstances. Stratford records show that he married Anne Hathaway in 1582, but the marriage was apparently a failure. We do not know how he lived during these years; he may have fallen into bad ways, for there is a story that he was punished for deer-stealing in the park of Sir Thomas Lucy at Charlecote, that in revenge he wrote some satirical verses about Sir Thomas, and that he had to escape to London to avoid further punishment. According to another story he left Stratford, where he was not happy, with a company of players who had been visiting the town. Whatever the cause, soon after his marriage he left Stratford and went to London to seek his fortune there.

(b) In London

Of Shakespeare's early years in London we know little. It is said that he used to hold the horses of the people who came to visit the playhouses, which—as you will remember —were outside the city. Later, he probably found work inside the theatre, perhaps as prompter's assistant. Still later, he took minor acting parts; you will find a reference to this in *The Rehearsal*. Then he began to write. At first he merely adapted old plays; then he took legends, old stories, and well-known events in history, and made plays about them. He was associated for many years with the Lord Chamberlain's Company of players—afterwards adopted by James the First and called the King's Men— and most of his plays were written for them. Before the end of the sixteenth century he was becoming famous and wealthy. As we have seen, he had a share in the Globe Theatre; he bought a big house called New Place at Stratford, and he had other property; he knew and was on friendly terms with the best writers and the most prominent people of the period.

In spite of his prosperity, there is reason to believe that Shakespeare was at this time very unhappy. His early plays are full of fun and high spirits; you will notice this in the pranks of Sir Toby Belch and his friends in *Twelfth Night* and in the rich comedy of the interlude in *A Midsummer Night's Dream*. But his later plays are of a very different kind; he wrote many gloomy tragedies, like *Macbeth*, as though he had found that after all the world is full of evil, and life full of bitterness.

(c) At Stratford Again

About the year 1611 Shakespeare returned to Stratford, and there he recovered some of his peace of mind. In the plays he wrote during these last years—sometimes called the romances—there is not the brooding sense of evil which is to be found in his great tragedies. With *The Tempest* he said farewell to his work:

> Be cheerful, sir.
> Our revels now are ended. These our actors,
> As I foretold you, were all spirits and
> Are melted into air, into thin air:
> And, like the baseless fabric of this vision,
> The cloud-capp'd towers, the gorgeous palaces,
> The solemn temples, the great globe itself,
> Yea, all which it inherit, shall dissolve
> And, like this insubstantial pageant faded,
> Leave not a rack behind. We are such stuff
> As dreams are made on, and our little life
> Is rounded with a sleep.

He died in the year 1616. He was buried in Stratford Church on the 25th of April, and it is therefore possible that he died on his birthday, the 23rd of April.

PART TWO
SOME PLAYS BY SHAKESPEARE

In this part of the book you will read four of Shakespeare's best-known plays. They were not written in the order in which they are given here; *A Midsummer Night's Dream* was written before both *The Merchant of Venice* and *Twelfth Night*. From each of the plays some scenes have been omitted, but explanations have been given so that there may be no breaks in the stories. Many of these explanations —those followed by the words *Tales from Shakespeare*— were written by the famous essayist Charles Lamb and his sister Mary, more than a hundred years ago. These *Tales* still provide a useful way of introducing the work of Shakespeare to boys and girls.

These are the plays which will be given:

   I. *The Merchant of Venice*
  II. *Twelfth Night*
 III. *A Midsummer Night's Dream*
 IV. *Macbeth*

THE MERCHANT OF VENICE

Characters

THE DUKE OF VENICE
ANTONIO, *a merchant of Venice*
BASSANIO, *his friend, suitor to Portia*
SALANIO
SALARINO
GRATIANO } *Friends to Antonio and Bassanio*
SALERIO
LORENZO, *in love with Jessica*
SHYLOCK, *a rich Jew*
TUBAL, *a Jew, his friend*
LAUNCELOT GOBBO, *servant to Shylock*

PORTIA, *a rich heiress, the Lady of Belmont*
NERISSA, *her waiting-maid*
JESSICA, *daughter to Shylock*

Shylock, the Jew, lived at Venice: he was an usurer, who had amassed an immense fortune by lending money at great interest to Christian merchants. Shylock, being a hard-hearted man, exacted the payment of the money he lent with such severity that he was much disliked by all good men, and particularly by Antonio, a young merchant of Venice; and Shylock as much hated Antonio, because he used to lend money to people in distress, and would never take any interest for the money he lent; therefore there was great enmity between this covetous Jew and the generous merchant Antonio. Whenever Antonio met Shylock on the Rialto (or Exchange), he used to reproach him with his usuries and hard dealings, which the Jew would bear with seeming patience, while he secretly meditated revenge.

Antonio was the kindest man that lived, the best conditioned, and had the most unwearied spirit in doing courtesies; indeed, he was one in whom the ancient Roman honour more appeared than in any that drew breath in Italy. He was greatly beloved by all his fellow-citizens; but the friend who was nearest and dearest to his heart was Bassanio, a noble Venetian, who, having but a small patrimony, had nearly exhausted his little fortune by living in too expensive a manner for his slender means, as young men of high rank with small fortunes are too apt to do. Whenever Bassanio wanted money, Antonio assisted him; and it seemed as if they had but one heart and one purse between them.

One day Bassanio came to Antonio, and told him that he wished to repair his fortune by a wealthy marriage with a lady whom he dearly loved, whose father, that was lately dead, had left her sole heiress to a large estate;

and that in her father's lifetime he used to visit at her house, when he thought he had observed this lady had sometimes from her eyes sent speechless messages, that seemed to say he would be no unwelcome suitor; but not having money to furnish himself with an appearance befitting the lover of so rich an heiress, he besought Antonio to add to the many favours he had shown him, by lending him three thousand ducats.

Tales from Shakespeare

SCENE: *Venice. A street.*

ANTONIO. Well, tell me now what lady is the same
To whom you swore a secret pilgrimage,
That you to-day promised to tell me of?

BASSANIO. 'Tis not unknown to you, Antonio,
How much I have disabled mine estate,
By something showing a more swelling port
Than my faint means would grant continuance:
Nor do I now make moan to be abridg'd
From such a noble rate; but my chief care
Is to come fairly off from the great debts,
Wherein my time, something too prodigal,
Hath left me gaged. To you, Antonio,
I owe the most, in money and in love;
And from your love I have a warranty
To unburden all my plots and purposes
How to get clear of all the debts I owe.

ANTONIO. I pray you, good Bassanio, let me know it;
And if it stand, as you yourself still do,
Within the eye of honour, be assur'd,
My purse, my person, my extremest means,
Lie all unlock'd to your occasions.

BASSANIO. In my school-days, when I had lost one shaft
I shot his fellow of the self-same flight
The self-same way with more advised watch,

To find the other forth, and by adventuring both,
I oft found both: I urge this childhood proof,
Because what follows is pure innocence.
I owe you much, and, like a wilful youth,
That which I owe is lost; but if you please
To shoot another arrow that self way
Which you did shoot the first, I do not doubt,
As I will watch the aim, or to find both,
Or bring your latter hazard back again,
And thankfully rest debtor for the first.

ANTONIO. You know me well, and herein spend but time
To wind about my love with circumstance;
And out of doubt you do me now more wrong
In making question of my uttermost
Than if you had made waste of all I have:
Then do but say to me what I should do
That in your knowledge may by me be done,
And I am prest unto it: therefore, speak.

BASSANIO. In Belmont is a lady richly left;
And she is fair, and, fairer than that word,
Of wondrous virtues: sometimes from her eyes
I did receive fair speechless messages:
Her name is Portia, nothing undervalu'd
To Cato's daughter, Brutus' Portia:
Nor is the wide world ignorant of her worth,
For the four winds blow in from every coast
Renowned suitors; and her sunny locks
Hang on her temples like a golden fleece;
Which makes her seat of Belmont Colchos' strand,
And many Jasons come in quest of her.
O my Antonio, had I but the means
To hold a rival place with one of them,
I have a mind presages me such thrift,
That I should questionless be fortunate.

ANTONIO. Thou know'st that all my fortunes are at sea;
Neither have I money, nor commodity

To raise a present sum: therefore go forth;
Try what my credit can in Venice do:
That shall be rack'd, even to the uttermost,
To furnish thee to Belmont, to fair Portia.
Go, presently inquire, and so will I,
Where money is, and I no question make
To have it of my trust, or for my sake.

> Thus, on Antonio's suggestion, Bassanio used Antonio's good name to borrow the money necessary for his visit to Belmont.

SCENE: *Venice. A public place.*

Enter BASSANIO *and* SHYLOCK.

SHYLOCK. Three thousand ducats; well.

BASSANIO. Ay, sir, for three months.

SHYLOCK. For three months; well.

BASSANIO. For the which, as I told you, Antonio shall be bound.

SHYLOCK. Antonio shall become bound; well.

BASSANIO. May you stead me? will you pleasure me? shall I know your answer?

SHYLOCK. Three thousand ducats for three months, and Antonio bound.

BASSANIO. Your answer to that.

SHYLOCK. Antonio is a good man.

BASSANIO. Have you heard any imputation to the contrary?

SHYLOCK. Oh, no, no, no, no: my meaning in saying he is a good man is to have you understand me that he is sufficient. Yet his means are in supposition: he hath an argosy bound to Tripolis, another to the Indies; I understand, moreover, upon the Rialto, he hath a third at Mexico, a fourth for England, and other ventures he hath, squander'd abroad. But ships are but boards, sailors but men: there be land-rats and water-rats, water-thieves and land-thieves, I mean pirates: and then there is the peril of waters, winds, and rocks. The man is, notwithstanding, sufficient. Three thousand ducats; I think I may take his bond.

BASSANIO. Be assur'd you may.

SHYLOCK. I will be assur'd I may; and, that I may be assur'd, I will bethink me. May I speak with Antonio?

BASSANIO. If it please you to dine with us.

SHYLOCK. Yes, to smell pork; to eat of the habitation which your prophet the Nazarite conjured the devil into. I will buy with you, sell with you, talk with you, walk with you, and so following; but I will not eat with you, drink with you, nor pray with you. What news on the Rialto? Who is he comes here?

Enter ANTONIO.

BASSANIO. This is Signior Antonio.

SHYLOCK [*aside*]. How like a fawning publican he looks!
I hate him for he is a Christian;
But more for that in low simplicity
He lends out money gratis and brings down
The rate of usance here with us in Venice.
If I can catch him once upon the hip,
I will feed fat the ancient grudge I bear him.
He hates our sacred nation, and he rails,
Even there where merchants most do congregate,
On me, my bargains, and my well-won thrift,
Which he calls interest. Cursed be my tribe,
If I forgive him!

BASSANIO. Shylock, do you hear?

SHYLOCK. I am debating of my present store,
And, by the near guess of my memory,
I cannot instantly raise up the gross
Of full three thousand ducats. What of that?
Tubal, a wealthy Hebrew of my tribe,
Will furnish me. But soft! how many months
Do you desire? [*To* ANT.] Rest you fair, good signior;

Your worship was the last man in our mouths.

ANTONIO. Shylock, although I neither lend nor borrow
By taking nor by giving of excess,
Yet, to supply the ripe wants of my friend,
I'll break a custom. Is he yet possess'd
How much ye would?

SHYLOCK. Ay, ay, three thousand ducats.

ANTONIO. And for three months.

SHYLOCK. I had forgot; three months; you told me so.
Well then, your bond; and, let me see; but hear you;
Methought you said you neither lend nor borrow
Upon advantage.

ANTONIO. I do never use it.

SHYLOCK. When Jacob graz'd his uncle Laban's sheep—
This Jacob from our holy Abram was,
As his wise mother wrought in his behalf,
The third possessor; ay, he was the third—

ANTONIO. And what of him? did he take interest?

SHYLOCK. No, not take interest; not, as you would say,
Directly interest: mark what Jacob did.
When Laban and himself were compromis'd
That all the eanlings which were streak'd and pied
Should fall as Jacob's hire.
This was a way to thrive, and he was blest:
And thrift is blessing, if men steal it not.

ANTONIO. This was a venture, sir, that Jacob serv'd for;
A thing not in his power to bring to pass,
But sway'd and fashion'd by the hand of heaven.
Was this inserted to make interest good?
Or is your gold and silver ewes and rams?

SHYLOCK. I cannot tell; I make it breed as fast:
But note me, signior.

ANTONIO. Mark you this, Bassanio,
The devil can cite Scripture for his purpose.
An evil soul, producing holy witness,
Is like a villain with a smiling cheek;

A goodly apple rotten at the heart:
O, what a goodly outside falsehood hath !

SHYLOCK. Three thousand ducats; 'tis a good round sum.

Three months from twelve, then, let me see; the rate——

ANTONIO. Well, Shylock, shall we be beholding to you?

SHYLOCK. Signior Antonio, many a time and oft
In the Rialto you have rated me
About my moneys and my usances:
Still have I borne it with a patient shrug,
For sufferance is the badge of all our tribe.
You call me misbeliever, cut-throat dog,
And spit upon my Jewish gaberdine,
And all for use of that which is mine own.
Well then, it now appears you need my help:
Go to, then; you come to me, and you say,
'Shylock, we would have moneys:' you say so;
You, that did void your rheum upon my beard,
And foot me as you spurn a stranger cur
Over your threshold: moneys is your suit.
What should I say to you? Should I not say,
'Hath a dog money? Is it possible
A cur can lend three thousand ducats?' Or
Shall I bend low, and in a bondman's key,
With bated breath and whispering humbleness,
Say this:
'Fair sir, you spit on me on Wednesday last;
You spurn'd me such a day; another time
You call'd me dog; and for these courtesies
I'll lend you thus much moneys'?

ANTONIO. I am as like to call thee so again,
To spit on thee again, to spurn thee too.
If thou wilt lend this money, lend it not
As to thy friends; for when did friendship take
A breed of barren metal of his friend?
But lend it rather to thine enemy;

Who, if he break, thou mayst with better face
Exact the penalty.

SHYLOCK. Why, look you, how you storm!
I would be friends with you, and have your love,
Forget the shames that you have stain'd me with,
Supply your present wants, and take no doit
Of usance for my moneys, and you'll not hear me.
This is kind I offer.

BASSANIO. This were kindness.

SHYLOCK. This kindness will I show:
Go with me to a notary, seal me there
Your single bond; and, in a merry sport,
If you repay me not on such a day,
In such a place, such sum or sums as are
Express'd in the condition, let the forfeit
Be nominated for an equal pound
Of your fair flesh, to be cut off and taken
In what part of your body pleaseth me.

ANTONIO. Content, i' faith: I'll seal to such a bond,
And say there is much kindness in the Jew.

BASSANIO. You shall not seal to such a bond for me:
I'll rather dwell in my necessity.

ANTONIO. Why, fear not, man; I will not forfeit it:
Within these two months, that's a month before
This bond expires, I do expect return
Of thrice three times the value of this bond.

SHYLOCK. O father Abram, what these Christians are,
Whose own hard dealings teaches them suspect
The thoughts of others! Pray you, tell me this:
If he should break his day, what should I gain
By the exaction of the forfeiture?
A pound of man's flesh taken from a man
Is not so estimable, profitable neither,
As flesh of muttons, beefs, or goats. I say,
To buy his favour, I extend this friendship:
If he will take it, so; if not, adieu;

And, for my love, I pray you wrong me not.

ANTONIO. Yes, Shylock, I will seal unto this bond.

SHYLOCK. Then meet me forthwith at the notary's;
Give him direction for this merry bond,
And I will go and purse the ducats straight,
See to my house, left in the fearful guard
Of an unthrifty knave, and presently
I will be with you.

ANTONIO. Hie, thee, gentle Jew.   [*Exit* SHYLOCK.
The Hebrew will turn Christian: he grows kind.

BASSANIO. I like not fair terms and a villain's mind.

ANTONIO. Come on: in this there can be no dismay;
My ships come home a month before the day.   [*Exeunt.*

Shylock had living with him his daughter, Jessica,
and a man-servant, Launcelot Gobbo, the "unthrifty
knave" to whom Shylock had referred when speaking
with Antonio and Bassanio. Jessica was loved by a
young Venetian called Lorenzo, and she returned his
love. She was ashamed to be the daughter of so un-
popular a man as Shylock, and had made up her mind
to run away with Lorenzo. Launcelot Gobbo was
leaving Shylock's service in order to work for Bassanio,
and she asked him to take a letter for her to Lorenzo.
Here, in Shakespeare's words, is the story of the
elopement.

SCENE: *Venice. A room in Shylock's house.*

Enter JESSICA *and* LAUNCELOT.

JESSICA. I am sorry thou wilt leave my father so:
Our house is hell, and thou, a merry devil,
Didst rob it of some taste of tediousness.
But fare thee well; there is a ducat for thee:
And, Launcelot, soon at supper shalt thou see
Lorenzo, who is thy new master's guest:
Give him this letter; do it secretly;

And so farewell: I would not have my father
See me in talk with thee.

LAUNCELOT. Adieu! tears exhibit my tongue. Most
beautiful pagan, most sweet Jew, adieu: these foolish drops
do something drown my manly spirit: adieu.

JESSICA. Farewell, good Launcelot.   [*Exit* LAUNCELOT.
Alack, what heinous sin is it in me
To be asham'd to be my father's child!
But though I am a daughter to his blood,
I am not to his manners. O Lorenzo,
If thou keep promise, I shall end this strife,
Become a Christian, and thy loving wife.   [*Exit.*

SCENE: *Venice. A street.*

Enter GRATIANO, LORENZO, SALARINO, *and* SALANIO.

LORENZO. Nay, we will slink away in supper-time,
Disguise us at my lodging, and return
All in an hour.

GRATIANO. We have not made good preparation.

SALARINO. We have not spoke us yet of torch-bearers.

SALANIO. 'Tis vile, unless it may be quaintly order'd,
And better in my mind not undertook.

LORENZO. 'Tis now but four o'clock: we have two hours
To furnish us.

Enter LAUNCELOT, *with a letter.*
               Friend Launcelot, what's the news?

LAUNCELOT. An it shall please you to break up this, it
shall seem to signify.

LORENZO. I know the hand: in faith, 'tis a fair hand;
And whiter than the paper it writ on
Is the fair hand that writ.

GRATIANO. Love-news, in faith.

LAUNCELOT. By your leave, sir.

LORENZO. Whither goest thou?

LAUNCELOT. Marry, sir, to bid my old master the Jew
to sup to-night with my new master the Christian.

LORENZO. Hold here, take this: tell gentle Jessica
I will not fail her; speak it privately; go.
Gentlemen,   [*Exit* LAUNCELOT.
Will you prepare you for this masque to-night?
I am provided of a torch-bearer.

SALARINO. Ay, marry, I'll be gone about it straight.

SALANIO. And so will I.

LORENZO. Meet me and Gratiano
At Gratiano's lodging some hour hence.

SALARINO. 'Tis good we do so.
                         [*Exeunt* SALARINO *and* SALANIO.

GRATIANO. Was not that letter from fair Jessica?

LORENZO. I must needs tell thee all. She hath directed
How I shall take her from her father's house,
What gold and jewels she is furnish'd with,
What page's suit she hath in readiness.
If e'er the Jew her father come to heaven,
It will be for his gentle daughter's sake;
And never dare misfortune cross her foot,
Unless she do it under this excuse,
That she is issue to a faithless Jew.
Come, go with me: peruse this as thou goest.
Fair Jessica shall be my torch-bearer.   [*Exeunt.*

SCENE: *Venice. Before* SHYLOCK'S *house.*

Enter SHYLOCK *and* LAUNCELOT.

SHYLOCK. Well, thou shalt see, thy eyes shall be thy
judge,
The difference of old Shylock and Bassanio:—
What, Jessica!—thou shalt not gormandize,
As thou hast done with me;—What, Jessica!—
And sleep and snore, and rend apparel out;—

B*

Why, Jessica, I say !

LAUNCELOT. Why, Jessica !

SHYLOCK. Who bids thee call? I do not bid thee call.

LAUNCELOT. Your worship was wont to tell me I could do nothing without bidding.

Enter JESSICA.

JESSICA. Call you? what is your will?

SHYLOCK. I am bid forth to supper, Jessica:
There are my keys. But wherefore should I go?
I am not bid for love; they flatter me:
But yet I'll go in hate, to feed upon
The prodigal Christian. Jessica, my girl,
Look to my house. I am right loath to go:
There is some ill a-brewing towards my rest,
For I did dream of money-bags to-night.

LAUNCELOT. I beseech you, sir, go: my young master doth expect your reproach.

SHYLOCK. So do I his.

LAUNCELOT. And they have conspir'd together, I will not say you shall see a masque; but if you do, then it was not for nothing that my nose fell a-bleeding on Black-Monday last at six o'clock i' the morning, falling out that year on Ash-Wednesday was four year, in the afternoon.

SHYLOCK. What, are there masques? Hear you me, Jessica:
Lock up my doors; and when you hear the drum,
And the vile squealing of the wry-neck'd fife,
Clamber not you up to the casements then,
Nor thrust your head into the public street
To gaze on Christian fools with varnish'd faces,
But stop my house's ears, I mean my casements:
Let not the sound of shallow foppery enter
My sober house. By Jacob's staff, I swear
I have no mind of feasting forth to-night;
But I will go. Go you before me, sirrah;
Say I will come.

LAUNCELOT. I will go before, sir. Mistress, look out at
window, for all this;
>There will come a Christian by,
>Will be worth a Jewess' eye. [*Exit.*

SHYLOCK. What says that fool of Hagar's offspring, ha?

JESSICA. His words were, 'Farewell, mistress'; nothing
else.

SHYLOCK. The patch is kind enough, but a huge feeder;
Snail-slow in profit, and he sleeps by day
More than the wild-cat: drones hive not with me;
Therefore I part with him, and part with him
To one that I would have him help to waste
His borrow'd purse. Well, Jessica, go in;
Perhaps I will return immediately:
Do as I bid you; shut doors after you:
Fast bind, fast find;
A proverb never stale in thrifty mind. [*Exit.*

JESSICA. Farewell; and if my fortune be not crost,
I have a father, you a daughter, lost. [*Exit.*

SCENE: *The same.*

Enter GRATIANO *and* SALARINO, *masqued.*

GRATIANO. This is the pent-house under which Lorenzo
Desir'd us to make stand.

SALARINO. His hour is almost past.

GRATIANO. And it is marvel he out-dwells his hour,
For lovers ever run before the clock.

SALARINO. O, ten times faster Venus' pigeons fly
To seal love's bonds new-made, than they are wont
To keep obliged faith unforfeited!

GRATIANO. That ever holds: who riseth from a feast
With that keen appetite that he sits down?
Where is the horse that doth untread again
His tedious measures with the unbated fire
That he did pace them first? All things that are,

Art with more spirit chased than enjoy'd.
How like a younker or a prodigal
The scarfed bark puts from her native bay,
Hugg'd and embraced by the strumpet wind!
How like the prodigal doth she return,
With over-weather'd ribs and ragged sails,
Lean, rent, and beggar'd by the strumpet wind!

SALARINO. Here comes Lorenzo more of this hereafter.

Enter LORENZO.

LORENZO. Sweet friends, your patience for my long abode;
Not I, but my affairs, have made you wait:
When you shall please to play the thieves for wives,
I'll watch as long for you then. Approach;
Here dwells my father Jew. Ho! who's within?

Enter JESSICA, *above, in boy's clothes.*

JESSICA. Who are you? Tell me, for more certainty,
Albeit I'll swear that I do know your tongue.

LORENZO. Lorenzo, and thy love.

JESSICA. Lorenzo, certain; and my love indeed,
For who love I so much? And now who knows
But you, Lorenzo, whether I am yours?

LORENZO Heaven and thy thoughts are witness that thou art.

JESSICA. Here, catch this casket; it is worth the pains.
I am glad 'tis night, you do not look on me,
For I am much asham'd of my exchange:
But love is blind, and lovers cannot see
The pretty follies that themselves commit;
For if they could, Cupid himself would blush
To see me thus transformed to a boy.

LORENZO. Descend, for you must be my torch-bearer.

JESSICA. What, must I hold a candle to my shames?
They in themselves, good sooth, are too too light.
Why, 'tis an office of discovery, love;
And I should be obscur'd.

LORENZO. So are you, sweet,
Even in the lovely garnish of a boy.
But come at once;
For the close night doth play the runaway,
And we are stay'd for at Bassanio's feast.

JESSICA. I will make fast the doors, and gild myself
With some more ducats, and be with you straight.
                                              [*Exit above.*

GRATIANO. Now, by my hood, a Gentile, and no Jew.

LORENZO Beshrew me but I love her heartily;
For she is wise, if I can judge of her;
And fair she is, if that mine eyes be true,
And true she is, as she hath prov'd herself;
And therefore, like herself, wise, fair, and true,
Shall she be placed in my constant soul.
                    Enter JESSICA, *below.*
What, art thou come? On, gentlemen; away!
Our masquing mates by this time for us stay.
                    [*Exit with* JESSICA *and* SALARINO
                    Enter ANTONIO.

ANTONIO. Who's there?

GRATIANO. Signior Antonio!

ANTONIO. Fie, fie, Gratiano! where are all the rest?
'Tis nine o'clock; our friends all stay for you.
No masque to-night: the wind is come about;
Bassanio presently will go aboard:
I have sent twenty out to seek for you.

GRATIANO. I am glad on't: I desire no more delight
Than to be under sail and gone to-night.   [*Exeunt.*

Having borrowed from Shylock the money for his
journey, Bassanio set sail for Belmont, the home of
Portia. Gratiano, the somewhat boisterous Venetian
who has already been introduced as a friend of
Lorenzo, begged to be allowed to go with him, and
after some hesitation Bassanio agreed to his request.

Portia, the lady of Belmont, was so beautiful and so wealthy that suitors came from all over Europe and even from North Africa to seek her hand in marriage. She was not, however, allowed to choose her own husband. Before his death, her father had arranged three caskets, one of gold, another of silver, and the third of lead. On each of them there was an inscription. On the gold casket the inscription read:

Who chooseth me shall gain what many men desire;

on the silver casket:

Who chooseth me shall get as much as he deserves;

on the lead casket:

Who chooseth me must give and hazard all he hath.

Every man who wished to marry Portia had to choose one of the caskets. In one of the caskets there was a portrait of Portia, and whoever chose that casket was to have her for his wife. Before any suitor chose he had to promise that if he chose wrongly he would never say which casket he had chosen, would never speak to any other maiden about marriage, and would go away from Belmont at once.

Many of the suitors, when they heard these terms, refused to choose and went back home. The Prince of Morocco, however, decided to try his luck. He chose the golden casket, but found inside it a skull and a scroll, bearing these words:

All that glisters is not gold;
Often have you heard that told:
Many a man his life hath sold
But my outside to behold:
Gilded timber do worms infold.
Had you been as wise as bold,
Young in limbs, in judgement old,
Your answer had not been inscroll'd:
Fare you well; your suit is cold.

Another suitor, the Prince of Arragon, chose the silver casket. Inside it he found only "the portrait of a blinking idiot," with these words:

> The fire seven times tried this:
> Seven times tried that judgement is,
> That did never choose amiss.
> Some there be that shadows kiss;
> Such have but a shadow's bliss:
> There be fools alive, I wis,
> Silver'd o'er; and so was this.
> Take what wife you will to bed,
> I will ever be your head:
> So be gone: you are sped.

Then Bassanio's turn came. He chose the leaden casket, and to his delight—and to that of Portia also, for she already loved him—when he opened it he found a portrait of Portia and a scroll bearing the words:

> You that choose not by the view,
> Chance as fair and choose as true!
> Since this fortune falls to you,
> Be content and seek no new.
> If you be well pleas'd with this
> And hold your fortune for your bliss,
> Turn you where your lady is
> And claim her with a loving kiss.

But while Bassanio was having such good fortune at Belmont, matters were going very badly for Antonio. News was received at Venice that one after another his ships were being wrecked, until it began to be doubtful whether, when it became due, he would be able to pay back the money he had borrowed from Shylock. Shylock, enraged by the desertion of his daughter and the loss of his money and jewels, seemed to hate Antonio more fiercely than ever, and was determined to exact the penalty if Antonio defaulted.

SCENE: *Venice. A street.*

Enter SALANIO *and* SALARINO.

SALANIO. Now, what news on the Rialto?

SALARINO. Why, yet it lives there uncheck'd that Antonio hath a ship of rich lading wreck'd on the narrow seas; the Goodwins, I think they call the place; a very dangerous flat and fatal, where the carcasses of many a tall ship lie buried, as they say, if my gossip Report be an honest woman of her word.

SALANIO. I would she were as lying a gossip in that as ever knapp'd ginger, or made her neighbours believe she wept for the death of a third husband. But it is true, without any slips of prolixity or crossing the plain highway of talk, that the good Antonio, the honest Antonio,—O, that I had a title good enough to keep his name company!——

SALARINO. Come, the full stop.

SALANIO. Ha! what sayest thou? Why, the end is, he hath lost a ship.

SALARINO. I would it might prove the end of his losses.

SALANIO. Let me say 'amen' betimes, lest the devil cross my prayer, for here he comes in the likeness of a Jew.

Enter SHYLOCK.

How now, Shylock! what news among the merchants?

SHYLOCK. You knew, none so well, none so well as you, of my daughter's flight.

SALARINO. That's certain: I, for my part, knew the tailor that made the wings she flew withal.

SALANIO. And Shylock, for his own part, knew the bird was fledg'd; and then it is the complexion of them all to leave the dam.

SHYLOCK. She is damn'd for it.

SALARINO. That's certain, if the devil may be her judge.

SHYLOCK. My own flesh and blood to rebel!

SALARINO. There is more difference between thy flesh and hers than between jet and ivory; more between your bloods than there is between red wine and rhenish. But tell us, do you hear whether Antonio have had any loss at sea or no?

SHYLOCK. There I have another bad match: a bankrupt, a prodigal, who dare scarce show his head on the Rialto; a beggar, that was us'd to come so smug upon the mart; let him look to his bond: he was wont to call me usurer; let him look to his bond: he was wont to lend money for a Christian courtesy; let him look to his bond.

SALARINO. Why, I am sure, if he forfeit, thou wilt not take his flesh: what's that good for?

SHYLOCK. To bait fish withal: if it will feed nothing else, it will feed my revenge. He hath disgrac'd me, and hinder'd me half a million; laugh'd at my losses, mock'd at my gains, scorn'd my nation, thwarted my bargains, cool'd my friends, heated mine enemies; and what's his reason? I am a Jew. Hath not a Jew eyes? hath not a Jew hands, organs, dimensions, senses, affections, passions? fed with the same food, hurt with the same weapons, subject to the same diseases, heal'd by the same means, warm'd and cool'd by the same winter and summer, as a Christian is? If you prick us, do we not bleed? if you tickle us, do we not laugh? if you poison us, do we not die? and if you wrong us, shall we not revenge? If we are like you in the rest, we will resemble you in that. If a Jew wrong a Christian, what is his humility? Revenge. If a Christian wrong a Jew, what should his sufferance be by Christian example? Why, revenge. The villainy you teach me, I will execute, and it shall go hard but I will better the instruction. [*Enter a Servant.*

SERVANT. Gentlemen, my master Antonio is at his house, and desires to speak with you both.

SALARINO. We have been up and down to seek him.

[*Enter* TUBAL.

SALANIO. Here comes another of the tribe: a third cannot be match'd, unless the devil himself turn Jew.

[*Exeunt* SALANIO, SALARINO, *and* Servant.

SHYLOCK. How now, Tubal! what news from Genoa? hast thou found my daughter?

TUBAL. I often came where I did hear of her, but cannot find her.

SHYLOCK. Why, there, there, there, there! a diamond gone, cost me two thousand ducats in Frankfort! The curse never fell upon our nation till now; I never felt it till now: two thousand ducats in that; and other precious, precious jewels. I would my daughter were dead at my foot, and the jewels in her ear! would she were hears'd at my foot, and the ducats in her coffin! No news of them? Why, so: and I know not what's spent in the search: why, thou loss upon loss! the thief gone with so much, and so much to find the thief; and no satisfaction, no revenge: nor no ill luck stirring but what lights on my shoulders; no sighs but of my breathing; no tears but of my shedding.

TUBAL. Yes, other men have ill luck too: Antonio, as I heard in Genoa,——

SHYLOCK. What, what, what? ill luck, ill luck?

TUBAL. Hath an argosy cast away, coming from Tripolis.

SHYLOCK. I thank God, I thank God!—Is't true, is't true?

TUBAL. I spoke with some of the sailors that escap'd the wreck.

SHYLOCK. I thank thee, good Tubal: good news, good news! ha, ha! where? in Genoa?

TUBAL. Your daughter spent in Genoa, as I heard, in one night fourscore ducats.

SHYLOCK. Thou stickest a dagger in me: I shall never see my gold again: fourscore ducats at a sitting! fourscore ducats!

TUBAL. There came divers of Antonio's creditors in my company to Venice, that swear he cannot choose but break.

SHYLOCK. I am very glad of it: I'll plague him; I'll torture him: I am glad of it.

TUBAL. One of them show'd me a ring that he had of your daughter for a monkey.

SHYLOCK. Out upon her! Thou torturest me, Tubal: it was my turquoise; I had it of Leah when I was a bachelor: I would not have given it for a wilderness of monkeys.

TUBAL. But Antonio is certainly undone.

SHYLOCK. Nay, that's true, that's very true. Go, Tubal, fee me an officer; bespeak him a fortnight before. I will have the heart of him, if he forfeit; for, were he out of Venice, I can make what merchandise I will. Go, go, Tubal, and meet me at our synagogue; go, good Tubal; at our synagogue, Tubal. [*Exeunt.*

While these events were taking place at Venice, Bassanio and Portia, at Belmont, were happily making arrangements for their marriage.

Bassanio confessed to Portia that he had no fortune, and that his high birth and noble ancestry was all that he could boast of; she, who loved him for his worthy qualities, and had riches enough not to regard wealth in a husband, answered with a graceful modesty that she would wish herself a thousand times more fair, and ten thousand times more rich, to be worthy of him; and then the accomplished Portia prettily dispraised herself and said she was an unlessoned girl, unschooled, unpractised, yet not so old but that she could learn, and that she would commit her gentle spirit to be directed and governed by him in all things; and she said, "Myself and what is mine, to you and yours is now converted. But yesterday, Bassanio, I was the lady of this fair mansion, queen of myself, and mistress over these servants; and now this house, these servants, and myself, are yours, my lord; I give them with this ring"; presenting a ring to Bassanio.

Bassanio was so overpowered with gratitude and wonder at the gracious manner in which the rich and noble Portia accepted of a man of his humble fortunes, that he could not express his joy and reverence to the dear lady who so honoured him, by anything but broken words of love and thankfulness; and taking the ring, he vowed never to part with it.

Gratiano and Nerissa, Portia's waiting-maid, were in attendance upon their lord and lady, when Portia so gracefully promised to become the obedient wife of Bassanio; and Gratiano, wishing Bassanio and the generous lady joy, desired permission to be married at the same time.

"With all my heart, Gratiano," said Bassanio, "if you can get a wife."

Gratiano then said that he loved the lady Portia's fair waiting gentlewoman, Nerissa, and that she had promised to be his wife, if her lady married Bassanio. Portia asked Nerissa if this was true. Nerissa replied, "Madam, it is so, if you approve of it." Portia willingly consenting, Bassanio pleasantly said, "Then our wedding-feast shall be much honoured by your marriage, Gratiano."

The happiness of these lovers was sadly crossed at this moment by the entrance of a messenger, who brought a letter from Antonio containing fearful tidings. When Bassanio read Antonio's letter, Portia feared it was to tell him of the death of some dear friend, he looked so pale; and inquiring what was the news which had so distressed him, he said, "O sweet Portia, here are a few of the unpleasantest words that ever blotted paper: gentle lady, when I first imparted my love to you, I freely told you all the wealth I had ran in my veins; but I should have told you that I had less than nothing, being in debt." Bassanio then told Portia what has been here related, of his borrowing the money of Antonio, and of Antonio's procuring it of Shylock the Jew, and of the bond by which Antonio had engaged to forfeit a pound of flesh, if it was not repaid by a certain day: and then Bassanio read Antonio's letter; the words of which were:

Sweet Bassanio, my ships are all lost, my bond to the Jew is forfeited, and since in paying it is impossible I should live, I could wish to see you at my death; notwithstanding, use your pleasure; if your love for me do not persuade you to come, let not my letter.

"O, my dear love," said Portia, "despatch all business, and begone; you shall have gold to pay the money twenty times over, before this kind friend shall lose a hair by my Bassanio's fault; and as you are so dearly bought, I will dearly love you." Portia then said she would be married to Bassanio before he set out, to give him a legal right to her money; and that same day they were married, and Gratiano was also married to Nerissa; and Bassanio and Gratiano, the instant they were married, set out in great haste for Venice, where Bassanio found Antonio in prison.

The day of payment being past, the cruel Jew would not accept of the money which Bassanio offered him, but insisted upon having a pound of Antonio's flesh. A day was appointed to try this shocking cause before the Duke of Venice, and Bassanio awaited in dreadful suspense the event of the trial.

When Portia parted with her husband, she spoke cheeringly to him, and bade him bring his dear friend along with him when he returned; yet she feared it would go hard with Antonio, and when she was left alone, she began to think and consider within herself, if she could by any means be instrumental in saving the life of her dear Bassanio's friend; and notwithstanding when she wished to honour her Bassanio, she had said to him with such a meek and wife-like grace, that she would submit in all things to be governed by his superior wisdom, yet being now called forth into action by the peril of her honoured husband's friend, she did nothing doubt her own powers, and by the sole guidance of her own true and perfect judgement, at once resolved to go herself to Venice, and speak in Antonio's defence.

Portia had a relation who was a cosunellor in the law; to this gentleman, whose name was Bellario, she wrote, and stating the case to him, desired his opinion, and that with his advice he would also send her the dress worn by a counsellor. When the messenger returned, he brought letters from Bellario of advice how to proceed, and also everything necessary for her equipment.

Portia dressed herself and her maid Nerissa in men's apparel, and putting on the robes of a counsellor, she took Nerissa along with her as her clerk; and setting out immediately, they arrived at Venice on the very day of the trial. The cause was just going to be heard before the duke and senators of Venice in the senate-house, when Portia entered this high court of justice, and presented a letter from Bellario, in which that learned counsellor wrote to the duke, saying, he would have come himself to plead for Antonio, but that he was prevented by sickness, and he requested that the learned young doctor Balthasar (so he called Portia) might be permitted to plead in his stead. This the duke granted, much wondering at the youthful appearance of the stranger, who was prettily disguised by her counsellor's robes and her large wig.

And now began this important trial.

Tales from Shakespeare

SCENE: *Venice. A court of justice.*

Enter the DUKE, *the* Magnificoes, ANTONIO, BASSANIO, GRATIANO, SALERIO, *and others.*

DUKE. What, is Antonio here?

ANTONIO. Ready, so please your grace.

DUKE. I am sorry for thee: thou art come to answer
A stony adversary, an inhuman wretch
Uncapable of pity, void and empty
From any dram of mercy.

ANTONIO.   I have heard

Your grace hath ta'en great pains to qualify
His rigorous course; but since he stands obdurate,
And that no lawful means can carry me
Out of his envy's reach, I do oppose
My patience to his fury, and am arm'd
To suffer, with a quietness of spirit,
The very tyranny ånd rage of his.

DUKE. Go one, and call the Jew into the court.

SALERIO. He is ready at the door: he comes, my lord.

Enter SHYLOCK.

DUKE. Make room, and let him stand before our face.
Shylock, the world thinks, and I think so too,
That thou but lead'st this fashion of thy malice
To the last hour of act; and then 'tis thought
Thou'lt show thy mercy and remorse more strange
Than is thy strange apparent cruelty;
And where thou now exact'st the penalty,
Which is a pound of this poor merchant's flesh,
Thou wilt not only loose the forfeiture,
But, touch'd with human gentleness and love,
Forgive a moiety of the principal;
Glancing an eye of pity on his losses,
That have of late so huddled on his back,
Enow to press a royal merchant down,
And pluck commiseration of his state
From brassy bosoms and rough hearts of flint,
From stubborn Turks and Tartars, never train'd
To offices of tender courtesy.
We all expect a gentle answer, Jew.

SHYLOCK. I have possess'd your grace of what I purpose;
And by our holy Sabbath have I sworn
To have the due and forfeit of my bond:
If you deny it, let the danger light
Upon your charter and your city's freedom.
You'll ask me, why I rather choose to have
A weight of carrion-flesh than to receive

Three thousand ducats: I'll not answer that:
But, say, it is my humour; is it answer'd?
What if my house be troubl'd with a rat,
And I be pleas'd to give ten thousand ducats
To have it ban'd! What, are you answer'd yet?
Some men there are love not a gaping pig;
Some, that are mad if they behold a cat;
And others, when the bag-pipe sings; affection,
Mistress of passion, sways it to the mood
Of what it likes or loathes. Now, for your answer:
As there is no firm reason to be render'd,
Why he cannot abide a gaping pig;
Why he, a harmless necessary cat;
Why he, a woollen bag-pipe, but of force
Must yield to such inevitable shame
As to offend, himself being offended;
So can I give no reason, nor I will not,
More than a lodg'd hate and a certain loathing
I bear Antonio, that I follow thus
A losing suit against him. Are you answer'd?

BASSANIO. This is no answer, thou unfeeling man,
To excuse the current of thy cruelty.

SHYLOCK. I am not bound to please thee with my
answers.

BASSANIO. Do all men kill the things they do not love?

SHYLOCK. Hates any man the thing he would not kill?

BASSANIO. Every offence is not a hate at first.

SHYLOCK. What, wouldst thou have a serpent sting thee
twice?

ANTONIO. I pray you, think you question with the Jew:
You may as well go stand upon the beach,
And bid the main flood bate his usual height;
You may as well use question with the wolf,
Why he hath made the ewe bleat for the lamb;
You may as well forbid the mountain pines
To wag their high tops, and to make no noise,

When they are fretten with the gusts of heaven;
You may as well do anything most hard,
As seek to soften that—than which what's harder?—
His Jewish heart: therefore, I do beseech you,
Make no more offers, use no farther means;
But with all brief and plain conveniency
Let me have judgement, and the Jew his will.

BASSANIO. For thy three thousand ducats here is six.

SHYLOCK. If every ducat in six thousand ducats
Were in six parts, and every part a ducat,
I would not draw them; I would have my bond.

DUKE. How shalt thou hope for mercy, rendering none?

SHYLOCK. What judgement shall I dread, doing no
wrong?
You have among you many a purchas'd slave,
Which, like your asses and your dogs and mules,
You use in abject and in slavish parts,
Because you bought them: shall I say to you,
Let them be free, marry them to your heirs?
Why sweat they under burthens? let their beds
Be made as soft as yours, and let their palates
Be season'd with such viands? You will answer,
'The slaves are ours': so do I answer you:
The pound of flesh, which I demand of him,
Is dearly bought; 'tis mine, and I will have it.
If you deny me, fie upon your law!
There is no force in the decrees of Venice.
I stand for judgement: answer; shall I have it?

DUKE. Upon my power I may dismiss this court,
Unless Bellario, a learned doctor,
Whom I have sent for to determine this,
Come here to-day.

SALERIO. My lord, here stays without
A messenger with letters from the doctor,
New come from Padua.

DUKE. Bring us the letters; call the messenger.

BASSANIO. Good cheer, Antonio! What, man, courage
  yet!
The Jew shall have my flesh, blood, bones, and all,
Ere thou shalt loose for me one drop of blood.

ANTONIO. I am a tainted wether of the flock,
Meetest for death: the weakest kind of fruit
Drops earliest to the ground; and so let me:
You cannot better be employ'd, Bassanio,
Than to live still, and write mine epitaph.

Enter NERISSA, *dressed like a lawyer's clerk.*

DUKE. Came you from Padua, from Bellario?

NERISSA. From both, my lord. Bellario greets your
  grace.   [*Presenting a letter.*

BASSANIO. Why dost thou whet thy knife so earnestly?

SHYLOCK. To cut the forfeiture from that bankrupt there.

GRATIANO. Not on thy sole, but on thy soul, harsh Jew,
Thou mak'st thy knife keen; but no metal can,
No, not the hangman's axe, bear half the keenness
Of thy sharp envy. Can no prayers pierce thee?

SHYLOCK. No, none that thou hast wit enough to make.

GRATIANO. O, be thou damn'd, inexecrable dog!
And for thy life let justice be accus'd.
Thou almost mak'st me waver in my faith
To hold opinion with Pythagoras,
That souls of animals infuse themselves
Into the trunks of men: thy currish spirit
Govern'd a wolf, who, hang'd for human slaughter,
Even from the gallows did his fell soul fleet,
And, whilst thou lay'st in thy unhallow'd dam,
Infus'd itself in thee; for thy desires
Are wolfish, bloody, starv'd, and ravenous.

SHYLOCK. Till thou canst rail the seal from off my bond,
Thou but offend'st thy lungs to speak so loud:
Repair thy wit, good youth, or it will fall
To cureless ruin. I stand here for law.

DUKE. This letter from Bellario doth commend

A young and learned doctor to our court.
Where is he?

NERISSA.   He attendeth here hard by,
To know your answer, whether you'll admit him.

DUKE. With all my heart. Some three or four of you
Go give him courteous conduct to this place.
Meantime the court shall hear Bellario's letter.

CLERK [*reads*].

"Your grace shall understand that at the receipt of your
letter I am very sick: but in the instant that your messenger
came, in loving visitation was with me a young doctor of
Rome; his name is Balthasar. I acquainted him with the
cause in controversy between the Jew and Antonio the
merchant: we turn'd o'er many books together: he is
furnish'd with my opinion; which, better'd with his own
learning, the greatness whereof I cannot enough commend,
comes with him, at my importunity, to fill up your grace's
request in my stead. I beseech you, let his lack of years
be no impediment to let him lack a reverend estimation;
for I never knew so young a body with so old a head. I
leave him to your gracious acceptance, whose trial shall
better publish his commendation."

DUKE. You hear the learn'd Bellario, what he writes:
And here, I take it, is the doctor come.

Enter PORTIA, *dressed like a doctor of laws.*

Give me your hand. Come you from old Bellario?

PORTIA. I did, my lord.

DUKE. You are welcome: take your place.
Are you acquainted with the difference
That holds this present question in the court?

PORTIA. I am informed throughly of the cause.
Which is the merchant here, and which the Jew?

DUKE. Antonio and old Shylock, both stand forth.

PORTIA. Is your name Shylock?

SHYLOCK.   Shylock is my name.

PORTIA. Of a strange nature is the suit you follow;

Yet in such rule that the Venetian law
Cannot impugn you as you do proceed.
You stand within his danger, do you not?

ANTONIO. Ay, so he says.

PORTIA.   Do you confess the bond ?

ANTONIO. I do.

PORTIA.   Then must the Jew be merciful.

SHYLOCK. On what compulsion must I? tell me that.

PORTIA. The quality of mercy is not strain'd,
It droppeth as the gentle rain from heaven
Upon the place beneath: it is twice blest;
It blesseth him that gives and him that takes:
'Tis mightiest in the mightiest: it becomes
The throned monarch better than his crown;
His sceptre shows the force of temporal power,
The attribute to awe and majesty,
Wherein doth sit the dread and fear of kings;
But mercy is above this sceptred sway;
It is enthroned in the hearts of kings,
It is an attribute to God himself;
And earthly power doth then show likest God's
When mercy seasons justice. Therefore, Jew,
Though justice be thy plea, consider this,
That, in the course of justice, none of us
Should see salvation: we do pray for mercy;
And that same prayer doth teach us all to render
The deeds of mercy. I have spoke thus much
To mitigate the justice of thy plea;
Which if thou follow, this strict court of Venice
Must needs give sentence 'gainst the merchant there.

SHYLOCK. My deeds upon my head! I crave the law,
The penalty and forfeit of my bond.

PORTIA. Is he not able to discharge the money?

BASSANIO. Yes, here I tender it for him in the court;
Yea, twice the sum: if that will not suffice,
I will be bound to pay it ten times o'er,

On forfeit of my hands, my head, my heart:
If this will not suffice, it must appear
That malice bears down truth. And I beseech you,
Wrest once the law to your authority
To do a great right, do a little wrong,
And curb this cruel devil of his will.

PORTIA. It must not be; there is no power in Venice
Can alter a decree established:
'Twill be recorded for a precedent,
And many an error by the same example
Will rush into the state: it cannot be.

SHYLOCK. A Daniel come to judgement! yea, a Daniel!
O wise young judge, how I do honour thee!

PORTIA. I pray you, let me look upon the bond.

SHYLOCK. Here 'tis, most reverend doctor; here it is.

PORTIA. Shylock, there's thrice thy money offer'd thee.

SHYLOCK. An oath, an oath, I have an oath in heaven:
Shall I lay perjury upon my soul?
No, not for Venice.

PORTIA. Why, this bond is forfeit;
And lawfully by this the Jew may claim
A pound of flesh, to be by him cut off
Nearest the merchant's heart. Be merciful:
Take thrice thy money; bid me tear the bond.

SHYLOCK. When it is paid according to the tenour.
It doth appear you are a worthy judge;
You know the law, your exposition
Hath been most sound: I charge you by the law,
Whereof you are a well-deserving pillar,
Proceed to judgement: by my soul I swear
There is no power in the tongue of man
To alter me: I stay here on my bond.

ANTONIO. Most heartily I do beseech the court
To give the judgement.

PORTIA.   Why then, thus it is:

You must prepare your bosom for his knife.

    SHYLOCK. O noble judge! O excellent young man!

    PORTIA. For the intent and purpose of the law
Hath full relation to the penalty,
Which here appeareth due upon the bond.

    SHYLOCK. 'Tis very true. O wise and upright judge!
How much more elder art thou than thy looks!

    PORTIA. Therefore lay bare your bosom.

    SHYLOCK.   Ay, his breast:
So says the bond: doth it not, noble judge?
'Nearest his heart': those are the very words.

    PORTIA. It is so. Are there balance here to weigh
The flesh?

    SHYLOCK. I have them ready.

    PORTIA. Have by some surgeon, Shylock, on your charge,
To stop his wounds, lest he do bleed to death.

    SHYLOCK. Is it so nominated in the bond?

    PORTIA. It is not so express'd; but what of that?
'Twere good you do so much for charity.

    SHYLOCK. I cannot find it; 'tis not in the bond.

    PORTIA. You, merchant, have you anything to say?

    ANTONIO. But little: I am arm'd and well prepar'd.
Give me your hand, Bassanio: fare you well!
Grieve not that I am fallen to this for you;
For herein Fortune shows herself more kind
Than is her custom: it is still her use
To let the wretched man outlive his wealth,
To view with hollow eye and wrinkled brow
An age of poverty; from which lingering penance
Of such misery doth she cut me off.
Commend me to your honourable wife:
Tell her the process of Antonio's end;
Say how I lov'd you, speak me fair in death;
And, when the tale is told, bid her be judge
Whether Bassanio had not once a love.
Repent but you that you shall lose your friend,

And he repents not that he pays your debt;
For if the Jew do cut but deep enough,
I'll pay it instantly with all my heart.

BASSANIO. Antonio, I am married to a wife
Which is as dear to me as life itself;
But life itself, my wife, and all the world,
Are not with me esteem'd above thy life:
I would lose all, ay, sacrifice them all
Here to this devil, to deliver you.

PORTIA. Your wife would give you little thanks for that,
If she were by, to hear you make the offer.

GRATIANO. I have a wife, whom, I protest, I love:
I would she were in heaven, so she could
Entreat some power to change this currish Jew.

NERISSA. 'Tis well you offer it behind her back;
The wish would make else an unquiet house.

SHYLOCK [aside]. These be the Christian husbands! I
have a daughter;
Would any of the stock of Barrabas
Had been her husband rather than a Christian!
[Aloud] We trifle time: I pray thee, pursue sentence.

PORTIA. A pound of that same merchant's flesh is thine:
The court awards it, and the law doth give it.

SHYLOCK. Most rightful judge!

PORTIA. And you must cut this flesh from off his breast:
The law allows it, and the court awards it.

SHYLOCK. Most learned judge! A sentence! Come,
prepare!

PORTIA. Tarry a little; there is something else.
This bond doth give thee here no jot of blood;
The words expressly are, 'a pound of flesh':
Take then thy bond, take thou thy pound of flesh;
But, in the cutting it, if thou dost shed
One drop of Christian blood, thy lands and goods
Are, by the laws of Venice, confiscate
Unto the state of Venice.

GRATIANO. O upright judge! Mark, Jew: O learned judge!

SHYLOCK. Is that the law?

PORTIA.   Thyself shalt see the act:
For, as thou urgest justice, be assur'd
Thou shalt have justice, more than thou desirest.

GRATIANO. O learned judge!—Mark, Jew: a learned judge!

SHYLOCK. I take this offer, then; pay the bond thrice,
And let the Christian go.

BASSANIO.   Here is the money.

PORTIA. Soft!
The Jew shall have all justice; soft! no haste:
He shall have nothing but the penalty.

GRATIANO. O Jew! an upright judge, a learned judge!

PORTIA. Therefore prepare thee to cut off the flesh.
Shed thou no blood, nor cut thou less nor more
But just a pound of flesh: if thou cut'st more
Or less than a just pound, be it but so much
As makes it light or heavy in the substance,
Or the division of the twentieth part
Of one poor scruple, nay, if the scale do turn
But in the estimation of a hair,
Thou diest and all thy goods are confiscate.

GRATIANO. A second Daniel, a Daniel, Jew!
Now, infidel, I have you on the hip.

PORTIA. Why doth the Jew pause? take thy forfeiture.

SHYLOCK. Give me my principal, and let me go.

BASSANIO. I have it ready for thee; here it is.

PORTIA. He hath refus'd it in the open court:
He shall have merely justice and his bond.

GRATIANO. A Daniel, still say I, a second Daniel!
I thank thee, Jew, for teaching me that word.

SHYLOCK. Shall I not have barely my principal?

PORTIA. Thou shalt have nothing but the forfeiture,
To be so taken at thy peril, Jew.

SHYLOCK. Why, then the devil give him good of it!
I'll stay no longer question.

PORTIA. Tarry, Jew:
The law hath yet another hold on you.
It is enacted in the laws of Venice,
If it be proved against an alien
That by direct or indirect attempts
He seek the life of any citizen,
The party 'gainst the which he doth contrive
Shall seize one half his goods; the other half
Comes to the privy coffer of the state;
And the offender's life lies in the mercy
Of the duke only, 'gainst all other voice.
In which predicament, I say, thou stand'st;
For it appears, by manifest proceeding,
That indirectly and directly too
Thou hast contriv'd against the very life
Of the defendant; and thou hast incurr'd
The danger formerly by me rehears'd.
Down therefore and beg mercy of the duke.

GRATIANO. Beg that thou mayst have leave to hang
thyself,
And yet, thy wealth being forfeit to the state,
Thou hast not left the value of a cord;
Therefore thou must be hang'd at the state's charge.

DUKE. That thou shalt see the difference of our spirits,
I pardon thee thy life before thou ask it:
For half thy wealth, it is Antonio's;
The other half comes to the general state,
Which humbleness may drive unto a fine.

PORTIA. Ay, for the state; not for Antonio.

SHYLOCK. Nay, take my life and all; pardon not that:
You take my house, when you do take the prop
That doth sustain my house; you take my life
When you do take the means whereby I live.

PORTIA. What mercy can you render him, Antonio?

GRATIANO. A halter gratis; nothing else, for God's sake.

ANTONIO. So please my lord the duke and all the court
To quit the fine for one half of his goods,
I am content; so he will let me have
The other half in use, to render it,
Upon his death, unto the gentleman
That lately stole his daughter:
Two things provided more, that, for this favour,
He presently become a Christian;
The other, that he do record a gift,
Here in the court, of all he dies possess'd,
Unto his son Lorenzo and his daughter.

DUKE. He shall do this, or else I do recant
The pardon that I late pronounced here.

PORTIA. Art thou contented, Jew? what dost thou say?

SHYLOCK. I am content.

PORTIA. Clerk, draw a deed of gift.

SHYLOCK. I pray you, give me leave to go from hence;
I am not well: send the deed after me,
And I will sign it.

DUKE. Get thee gone, but do it.

GRATIANO. In christening shalt thou have two god-
fathers:
Had I been judge, thou shouldst have had ten more,
To bring thee to the gallows, not the font.

[*Exit* SHYLOCK.

DUKE. Sir, I entreat you home with me to dinner.

PORTIA. I humbly do desire your grace of pardon:
I must away this night toward Padua,
And it is meet I presently set forth.

DUKE. I am sorry that your leisure serves you not.
Antonio, gratify this gentleman,
For, in my mind, you are much bound to him.

[*Exeunt the* DUKE *and his train.*

BASSANIO. Most worthy gentleman, I and my friend
Have by your wisdom been this day acquitted

Of grievous penalties; in lieu whereof,
Three thousand ducats, due unto the Jew,
We freely cope your courteous pains withal.

ANTONIO.   And stand indebted, over and above,
In love and service to you evermore.

PORTIA.   He is well paid that is well satisfied;
And I, delivering you, am satisfied,
And therein do account myself well paid:
My mind was never yet more mercenary.
I pray you, know me when we meet again:
I wish you well, and so I take my leave.

BASSANIO.   Dear sir, of force I must attempt you further:
Take some remembrance of us, as a tribute,
Not as a fee: grant me two things, I pray you,
Not to deny me, and to pardon me.

PORTIA.   You press me far, and therefore I will yield.
[To ANTONIO]   Give me your gloves, I'll wear them for
    your sake;
[To BASSANIO]   And, for your love, I'll take this ring from
    you.
Do not draw back your hand; I'll take no more;
And you in love shall not deny me this.

BASSANIO.   This ring, good sir, alas, it is a trifle!
I will not shame myself to give you this.

PORTIA.   I will have nothing else but only this;
And now methinks I have a mind to it.

BASSANIO.   There's more depends on this than on the
    value.
The dearest ring in Venice will I give you,
And find it out by proclamation:
Only for this, I pray you, pardon me.

PORTIA.   I see, sir, you are liberal in offers:
You taught me first to beg; and now methinks
You teach me how a beggar should be answer'd.

BASSANIO.   Good sir, this ring was given me by my wife;
And when she put it on, she made me vow

That I should neither sell nor give nor lose it.

PORTIA. That 'scuse serves many men to save their gifts.
An if your wife be not a mad-woman,
And know how well I have deserv'd the ring,
She would not hold out enemy for ever,
For giving it to me. Well, peace be with you !

[*Exeunt* PORTIA *and* NERISSA.

ANTONIO. My Lord Bassanio, let him have the ring:
Let his deservings and my love withal
Be valued 'gainst your wife's commandment.

BASSANIO. Go, Gratiano, run and overtake him;
Give him the ring, and bring him, if thou canst,
Unto Antonio's house. Away ! make haste.

[*Exit* GRATIANO.

Come, you and I will thither presently;
And in the morning early will we both
Fly toward Belmont: come, Antonio.

[*Exeunt.*

Gratiano overtook Portia in the street, and gave
back to her the ring she had given to Bassanio.
Nerissa asked for—and obtained—the ring which she
herself had given to Gratiano. Portia and Nerissa then
returned to Belmont, where Lorenzo and Jessica—who
had arrived at Belmont with the messenger who
brought Antonio's letter—had been in charge during
Portia's absence.

Portia, when she returned, was in that happy temper of
mind which never fails to attend the consciousness of
having performed a good action; her cheerful spirits
enjoyed everything she saw: the moon never seemed to
shine so bright before; and when that pleasant moon was
hid behind a cloud, then a light which she saw from her
house at Belmont as well pleased her charmed fancy, and
she said to Nerissa, "That light we see is burning in my
hall; how far that little candle throws its beams, so shines
a good deed in a naughty world"; and hearing the sound

of music from her house, she said, "Methinks that music sounds much sweeter than by day."

And now Portia and Nerissa entered the house, and dressing themselves in their own apparel, they awaited the arrival of their husbands, who soon followed them with Antonio; and Bassanio presenting his dear friend to the lady Portia, the congratulations and welcomings of that lady were hardly over, when they perceived Nerissa and her husband quarrelling in a corner of the room. "A quarrel already?" said Portia. "What is the matter?" Gratiano replied, "Lady, it is about a paltry gilt ring that Nerissa gave me, with words upon it like the poetry on a cutler's knife: *Love me, and leave me not.*"

"What does the poetry or the value of the ring signify?" said Nerissa. "You swore to me when I gave it to you, that you would keep it till the hour of death; and now you say you gave it to the lawyer's clerk. I know you gave it to a woman." "By this hand," replied Gratiano, "I gave it to a youth, a kind of boy, a little scrubbed boy, no higher than yourself; he was clerk to the young counsellor that by his wise pleading saved Antonio's life: this prating boy begged it for a fee, and I could not for my life deny him." Portia said, "You were to blame, Gratiano, to part with your wife's first gift. I gave my lord Bassanio a ring, and I am sure he would not part with it for all the world." Gratiano, in excuse for his fault, now said, "My lord Bassanio gave his ring away to the counsellor, and then the boy, his clerk, that took some pains in writing, he begged my ring."

Portia, hearing this, seemed very angry, and reproached Bassanio for giving away her ring; and she said, Nerissa had taught her what to believe, and that she knew some woman had the ring. Bassanio was very unhappy to have so offended his dear lady, and he said with great earnestness, "No, by my honour, no woman had it, but a civil doctor, who refused three thousand ducats of me, and begged the ring, which when I denied him, he went displeased away. What could I do, sweet Portia? I was so beset with shame for my seeming ingratitude, that I was forced to send the ring after him. Pardon me, good lady; had you been there, I think you would have begged the ring of me to give the worthy doctor."

"Ah!" said Antonio, "I am the unhappy cause of these quarrels."

Portia bid Antonio not to grieve at that, for that he was welcome notwithstanding; and then Antonio said, "I once did lend my body for Bassanio's sake; and but for him to whom your husband gave the ring, I should have now been dead. I dare be bound again, my soul upon the forfeit, your lord will never more break his faith with you."—"Then you shall be his surety," said Portia; "give him this ring, and bid him keep it better than the other."

When Bassanio looked at this ring, he was strangely surprised to find it was the same he gave away; and then Portia told him how she was the young counsellor, and Nerissa was her clerk; and Bassanio found, to his unspeakable wonder and delight, that it was by the noble courage and wisdom of his wife that Antonio's life was saved.

And Portia again welcomed Antonio, and gave him letters which by some chance had fallen into her hands, which contained an account of Antonio's ships, that were supposed lost, being safely arrived in the harbour. So these tragical beginnings of this rich merchant's story were all forgotten in the unexpected good fortune which ensued; and there was leisure to laugh at the comical adventure of the rings, and the husbands that did not know their own wives: Gratiano merrily swearing, in a sort of rhyming speech, that

while he lived, he'd fear no other thing
So sore, as keeping safe Nerissa's ring.

Tales from Shakespeare

TWELFTH NIGHT; OR, WHAT YOU WILL

Characters

ORSINO, DUKE OF ILLYRIA
CURIO
VALENTINE } *his gentlemen*
SIR TOBY BELCH, *uncle to Olivia*
SIR ANDREW AGUECHEEK
MALVOLIO, *steward to Olivia*
SEBASTIAN, *Viola's brother*
ANTONIO, *a sea captain, friend to Sebastian*
A SEA CAPTAIN, *friend to Viola*
FABIAN
FESTE, *a Clown* } *servants to Olivia*
A PRIEST
OLIVIA
VIOLA
MARIA, *Olivia's gentlewoman*

SEBASTIAN and his sister Viola, a young gentleman and lady of Messaline, were twins, and (which was accounted a great wonder) from their birth they so much resembled each other, that, but for the difference in their dress, they could not be known apart. They were both born in one hour, and in one hour they were both in danger of perishing, for they were shipwrecked on the coast of Illyria, as they were making a sea-voyage together. The ship, on board of which they were, split on a rock in a violent storm, and a very small number of the ship's company escaped with their lives. The captain of the vessel, with a few of the sailors that were saved, got to land in a small boat, and with them they brought Viola safe on shore, where she, poor lady, instead of rejoicing at her own deliverance, began to lament her brother's loss.

Tales from Shakespeare

SCENE: *The sea-coast.*

Enter VIOLA, *a* CAPTAIN, *and* SAILORS.

VIOLA. What country, friends, is this?

CAPTAIN. This is Illyria, lady.

VIOLA. And what should I do in Illyria?
My brother he is in Elysium.
Perchance he is not drown'd: what think you, sailors?

CAPTAIN. It is perchance that you yourself were sav'd.

VIOLA. O my poor brother! and so perchance may he be.

CAPTAIN. True, madam: and, to comfort you with
    chance,
Assure yourself, after our ship did split,
When you and those poor number sav'd with you
Hung on our driving boat, I saw your brother,
Most provident in peril, bind himself,
Courage and hope both teaching him the practice,
To a strong mast that liv'd upon the sea;
Where, like Arion on the dolphin's back,
I saw him hold acquaintance with the waves
So long as I could see.

VIOLA. For saying so, there's gold:
Mine own escape unfoldeth to my hope,
Whereto thy speech serves for authority,
The like of him. Know'st thou this country?

CAPTAIN. Ay, madam, well; for I was bred and born
Not three hours' travel from this very place.

VIOLA. Who governs here?

CAPTAIN. A noble duke, in nature as in name.

VIOLA. What is his name?

CAPTAIN. Orsino.

VIOLA. Orsino! I have heard my father name him;
He was a bachelor then.

CAPTAIN. And so is now, or was so very late;
For but a month ago I went from hence,
And then t'was fresh in murmur—as, you know,

What great ones do the less will prattle of—
That he did seek the love of fair Olivia.

    VIOLA. What's she?

    CAPTAIN. A virtuous maid, the daughter of a count
That died some twelvemonth since, then leaving her
In the protection of his son, her brother,
Who shortly also died; for whose dear love,
They say, she hath abjur'd the company
And sight of men.

    VIOLA. O that I serv'd that lady,
And might not be deliver'd to the world,
Till I had made mine own occasion mellow,
What my estate is!

    CAPTAIN. That were hard to compass;
Because she will admit no kind of suit,
No, not the duke's.

    VIOLA. There is a fair behaviour in thee, captain;
And though that nature with a beauteous wall
Doth oft close in pollution, yet of thee
I will believe thou hast a mind that suits
With this thy fair and outward character.
I prithee, and I'll pay thee bounteously,
Conceal me what I am, and be my aid
For such disguise as haply shall become
The form of my intent. I'll serve this duke:
Thou shalt present me as an eunuch to him:
It may be worth thy pains; for I can sing
And speak to him in many sorts of music
That will allow me very worth his service.
What else may hap to time I will commit;
Only shape thou thy silence to my wit.

    CAPTAIN. Be you his eunuch, and your mute I'll be:
When my tongue blabs, then let mine eyes not see.

    VIOLA. I thank thee; lead me on.   [*Exeunt.*

Viola's good friend, the captain, when he had transformed this pretty lady into a gentleman, having some interest at court, got her presented to Orsino under the feigned name of Cesario. The duke was wonderfully pleased with the address and graceful deportment of this handsome youth, and made Cesario one of his pages, that being the office Viola wished to obtain: and she so well fulfilled the duties of her new station, and showed such a ready observance and faithful attachment to her lord, that she soon became his most favoured attendant. To Cesario Orsino confided the whole history of his love for the lady Olivia. To Cesario he told the long and unsuccessful suit he had made to one who, rejecting his long services, and despising his person, refused to admit him to her presence; and for the love of this lady who had so unkindly treated him, the noble Orsino, forsaking the sports of the field and all manly exercises in which he used to delight, passed his hours in ignoble sloth, listening to the effeminate sounds of soft music, gentle airs, and passionate love-songs; and neglecting the company of the wise and learned lords with whom he used to associate, he was now all day long conversing with young Cesario. Unmeet companion, no doubt, his grave courtiers thought Cesario was for their once noble master, the great duke Orsino.

It is a dangerous matter for young maidens to be the confidants of handsome young dukes; which Viola too soon found to her sorrow, for all that Orsino told her he endured for Olivia, she presently perceived she suffered for the love of him; and much it moved her wonder, that Olivia could be so regardless of this her peerless lord and master, whom she thought no one could behold without the deepest admiration.

Tales from Shakespeare

SCENE: *The* DUKE's *palace.*

Enter VALENTINE, *and* VIOLA *in man's attire.*

VALENTINE. If the duke continue these favours towards you, Cesario, you are like to be much advanc'd: he hath known you but three days, and already you are no stranger.

VIOLA. You either fear his humour or my negligence, that you call in question the continuance of his love. Is he inconstant, sir, in his favours?

VALENTINE. No, believe me.

VIOLA. I thank you. Here comes the count.

Enter DUKE, CURIO, *and* Attendants.

DUKE. Who saw Cesario, ho?

VIOLA. On your attendance, my lord; here.

DUKE. Stand you awhile aloof. Cesario,
Thou know'st no less but all; I have unclasp'd
To thee the book even of my secret soul:
Therefore, good youth, address thy gait unto her;
Be not denied access, stand at her doors,
And tell them, there thy fixed foot shall grow
Till thou have audience.

VIOLA. Sure, my noble lord,
If she be so abandon'd to her sorrow
As it is spoke, she never will admit me.

DUKE. Be clamorous and leap all civil bounds
Rather than make unprofited return.

VIOLA. Say I do speak with her, my lord, what then?

DUKE. O, then unfold the passion of my love,
Surprise her with discourse of my dear faith:
It shall become thee well to act my woes;
She will attend it better in thy youth
Than in a nuncio's of more grave aspect.

VIOLA. I think not so, my lord.

DUKE.   Dear lad, believe it:
For they shall yet belie thy happy years,
That say thou art a man: Diana's lip

Is not more smooth and rubious; thy small pipe
Is as the maiden's organ, shrill and sound,
And all is semblative a woman's part.
I know thy constellation is right apt
For this affair. Some four or five attend him;
All, if you will; for I myself am best
When least in company. Prosper well in this,
And thou shalt live as freely as thy lord,
To call his fortunes thine.

    VIOLA. I'll do my best
To woo your lady: [*aside*] yet, a barful strife !
Whoe'er I woo, myself would be his wife.   [*Exeunt.*

The members of Olivia's household included a clown or jester, a somewhat pert waiting-woman called Maria, a drunken knight called Sir Toby Belch, who was Olivia's uncle, and a rather foolish knight called Sir Andrew Aguecheek. Sir Toby hoped that the countess would marry his friend Sir Andrew. Olivia had also in her household a vain and rather Puritanical steward called Malvolio, who had hopes of winning the countess's hand in marriage. Sir Toby and his friends were fond of revelry, and were a source of much annoyance to Malvolio. On one occasion, when Olivia had been amused by some of the clown's comments, she said to Malvolio: "What think you of this fool, Malvolio?"; but Malvolio replied sourly: "I marvel your ladyship takes delight in such a barren rascal; I saw him put down the other day with an ordinary fool that has no more brain than a stone." Malvolio himself was much disliked by the other characters because of his officious manner.

When Viola arrived at Olivia's house she was announced first by Maria and then by Malvolio. After some hesitation, Olivia decided to see her.

SCENE: OLIVIA's *house*.

OLIVIA. Give me my veil; come, throw it o'er my face. We'll once more hear Orsino's embassy.

Enter VIOLA, *and* Attendants.

VIOLA. The honourable lady of the house, which is she?

OLIVIA. Speak to me; I shall answer for her. Your will?

VIOLA. Most radiant, exquisite, and unmatchable beauty,—I pray you, tell me if this be the lady of the house, for I never saw her: I would be loth to cast away my speech; for besides that it is excellently well penn'd, I have taken great pains to con it. Good beauties, let me sustain no scorn; I am very comptible, even to the least sinister usage.

OLIVIA. Whence came you, sir?

VIOLA. I can say little more than I have studied, and that question's out of my part. Good gentle one, give me modest assurance if you be the lady of the house, that I may proceed in my speech.

OLIVIA. Are you a comedian?

VIOLA. No, my profound heart; and yet, by the very fangs of malice I swear, I am not that I play. Are you the lady of the house?

OLIVIA. If I do not usurp myself, I am.

VIOLA. Most certain, if you are she, you do usurp yourself; for what is yours to bestow is not yours to reserve. But this is from my commission: I will on with my speech in your praise, and then show you the heart of my message.

OLIVIA. Come to what is important in't: I forgive you the praise.

VIOLA. Alas, I took great pains to study it, and 'tis poetical.

OLIVIA. It is the more like to be feign'd: I pray you, keep it in. I heard you were saucy at my gates, and allow'd your approach rather to wonder at you than to hear you. If you be not mad, be gone; if you have reason, be brief: 'tis not that time of moon with me to make one in so skipping a dialogue.

MARIA. Will you hoist sail, sir? here lies your way.

VIOLA. No, good swabber; I am to hull here a little longer. Some mollification for your giant, sweet lady. Tell me your mind; I am a messenger.

OLIVIA. Sure, you have some hideous matter to deliver, when the courtesy of it is so fearful. Speak your office.

VIOLA. It alone concerns your ear. I bring no overture of war, no taxation of homage: I hold the olive in my hand; my words are as full of peace as matter.

OLIVIA. Yet you began rudely. What are you? what would you?

VIOLA. The rudeness that hath appear'd in me have I learn'd from my entertainment. What I am, and what I would, are as secret as maidenhead; to your ears, divinity; to any other's, profanation.

OLIVIA. Give us the place alone; we will hear this divinity. [*Exeunt* MARIA *and* Attendants.] Now, sir, what is your text?

VIOLA. Most sweet lady,——

OLIVIA. A comfortable doctrine, and much may be said of it. Where lies your text?

VIOLA. In Orsino's bosom.

OLIVIA. In his bosom! In what chapter of his bosom?

VIOLA. To answer by the method, in the first of his heart.

OLIVIA. O, I have read it: it is heresy. Have you no more to say?

VIOLA. Good madam, let me see your face.

OLIVIA. Have you any commission from your lord to negotiate with my face? You are now out of your text: but we will draw the curtain and show you the picture. Look you, sir, such a one I was this present: is't not well done? [*Unveiling*.

VIOLA. Excellently done, if God did all.

OLIVIA. 'Tis in grain, sir; 'twill endure wind and weather.

VIOLA. 'Tis beauty truly blent, whose red and white
Nature's own sweet and cunning hand laid on:
Lady, you are the cruell'st she alive,
If you will lead these graces to the grave
And leave the world no copy.

OLIVIA. O, sir, I will not be so hard-hearted; I will give out divers schedules of my beauty: it shall be inventoried, and every particle and utensil labell'd to my will: as, item, two lips, indifferent red; item, two grey eyes, with lids to them; item, one neck, one chin, and so forth. Were you sent hither to praise me?

VIOLA. I see you what you are, you are too proud;
But, if you were the devil, you are fair.
My lord and master loves you. O, such love
Could be but recompens'd, though you were crown'd
The nonpareil of beauty!

OLIVIA.   How does he love me?

VIOLA. With adorations, fertile tears,
With groans that thunder love, with sighs of fire.

OLIVIA. Your lord does know my mind; I cannot love him:
Yet I suppose him virtuous, know him noble,
Of great estate, of fresh and stainless youth;
In voices well divulg'd, free, learn'd, and valiant;
And in dimension and the shape of nature
A gracious person: but yet I cannot love him;
He might have took his answer long ago.

VIOLA. If I did love you in my master's flame,
With such a suffering, such a deadly life,
In your denial I would find no sense;
I would not understand it.

OLIVIA.   Why, what would you?

VIOLA. Make me a willow cabin at your gate,
And call upon my soul within the house;

Write loyal cantons of contemned love,
And sing them loud even in the dead of night;
Halloo your name to the reverberate hills,
And make the babbling gossip of the air
Cry out 'Olivia!' O, you should not rest
Between the elements of air and earth,
But you should pity me!

OLIVIA. You might do much. What is your parentage?

VIOLA. Above my fortunes, yet my state is well:
I am a gentleman.

OLIVIA.   Get you to your lord;
I cannot love him: let him send no more;
Unless, perchance, you come to me again,
To tell me how he takes it. Fare you well:
I thank you for your pains: spend this for me.

VIOLA. I am no fee'd post, lady; keep your purse:
My master, not myself, lacks recompense.
Love make his heart of flint that you shall love;
And let your fervour, like my master's, be
Plac'd in contempt! Farewell, fair cruelty.

When Viola was gone, Olivia repeated the words,
Above my fortunes, yet my state is well: I am a gentleman. And
she said aloud, "I will be sworn he is; his tongue, his
face, his limbs, action, and spirit, plainly show he is a
gentleman." And then she wished Cesario was the duke;
and perceiving the fast hold he had taken on her affections,
she blamed herself for her sudden love: but the gentle
blame which people lay upon their own faults has no
deep root; and presently the noble lady Olivia so far
forgot the inequality between her fortunes and those of
this seeming page, as well as the maidenly reserve which
is the chief ornament of a lady's character, that she resolved
to court the love of young Cesario, and sent a servant
after him with a diamond ring, under the pretence that
he had left it with her as a present from Orsino. She

hoped by thus artfully making Cesario a present of the ring, she should give him some intimation of her design. And truly it did make Viola suspect; for knowing that Orsino had sent no ring by her, she began to recollect that Olivia's looks and manner were expressive of admiration, and she presently guessed her master's mistress had fallen in love with her. "Alas," said she, "the poor lady might as well love a dream. Disguise I see is wicked, for it has caused Olivia to breathe as fruitless sighs for me as I do for Orsino."

Viola returned to Orsino's palace, and related to her lord the ill success of the negotiation, repeating the command of Olivia, that the duke should trouble her no more. Yet still the duke persisted in hoping that the gentle Cesario would in time be able to persuade her to show some pity, and therefore he bade him he should go to her again the next day. In the meantime, to pass away the tedious interval, he commanded a song which he loved to be sung.

Tales from Shakespeare

SCENE: *The* DUKE'S *palace.*

Enter DUKE, VIOLA, CURIO, *and others.*

DUKE. Give me some music. Now, good morrow, friends.

Now, good Cesario, but that piece of song,
That old and antique song we heard last night;
Methought it did relieve my passion much,
More than light airs and recollected terms
Of these most brisk and giddy-paced times:
Come, but one verse.

CURIO. He is not here, so please your lordship, that should sing it.

DUKE. Who was it?

CURIO. Feste, the jester, my lord; a fool that the lady

Olivia's father took much delight in. He is about the
house.

DUKE. Go seek him out, and play the tune the while.

[*Exit* CURIO. *Music plays.*

Come hither, boy: if ever thou shalt love,
In the sweet pangs of it remember me;
For such as I am all true lovers are,
Unstaid and skittish in all motions else,
Save in the constant image of the creature
That is belov'd. How dost thou like this tune?

VIOLA. It gives a very echo to the seat
Where love is thron'd.

DUKE. Thou dost speak masterly:
My life upon't, young though thou art, thine eye
Hath stay'd upon some favour that it loves;
Hath it not, boy?

VIOLA. A little, by your favour.

DUKE. What kind of woman is't?

VIOLA.   Of your complexion.

DUKE. She is not worth thee, then. What years, i'
faith?

VIOLA. About your years, my lord.

DUKE. Too old, by heaven: let still the woman take
An elder than herself; so wears she to him,
So sways she level in her husband's heart:
For, boy, however we do praise ourselves,
Our fancies are more giddy and unfirm,
More longing, wavering, sooner lost and worn,
Than women's are.

VIOLA.   I think it well, my lord.

DUKE. Then let thy love be younger than thyself,
Or thy affection cannot hold the bent;
For women are as roses, whose fair flower
Being once display'd, doth fall that very hour.

VIOLA. And so they are: alas, that they are so;
To die, even when they to perfection grow!

Re-enter CURIO *and* CLOWN.

DUKE. O, fellow, come, the song we had last night.
Mark it, Cesario, it is old and plain;
The spinsters and the knitters in the sun,
And the free maids that weave their thread with bones,
Do use to chant it: it is silly sooth,
And dallies with the innocence of love,
Like the old age.

CLOWN. Are you ready, sir?

DUKE. Ay; prithee, sing.

SONG

CLOWN.
    Come away, come away, death,
      And in sad cypress let me be laid;
    Fly away, fly away, breath;
      I am slain by a fair cruel maid.
    My shroud of white, stuck all with yew,
        O, prepare it!
    My part of death, no one so true
        Did share it.

    Not a flower, not a flower sweet,
      On my black coffin let there be strown;
    Not a friend, not a friend greet
      My poor corpse, where my bones shall be thrown
    A thousand thousand sighs to save,
        Lay me, O, where
    Sad true lover never find my grave,
        To weep there!

DUKE. There's for thy pains.

CLOWN. No pains, sir; I take pleasure in singing, sir.

DUKE. I'll pay thy pleasure then.

CLOWN. Truly, sir, and pleasure will be paid, one time
or another.

DUKE. Give me now leave to leave thee.

CLOWN. Now, the melancholy god protect thee; and the tailor make thy doublet of changeable taffeta, for thy mind is a very opal. I would have men of such constancy put to sea, that their business might be every thing and their intent every where; for that's it that always makes a good voyage of nothing. Farewell.   [*Exit.*

DUKE. Let all the rest give place.

[CURIO *and* Attendants *retire*

Once more, Cesario,
Get thee to yond same sovereign cruelty.
Tell her, my love, more noble than the world,
Prizes not quantity of dirty lands;
The parts that fortune hath bestow'd upon her,
Tell her, I hold as giddily as fortune;
But 'tis that miracle and queen of gems
That nature pranks her in attracts my soul.

VIOLA. But if she cannot love you, sir?

DUKE. I cannot be so answer'd.

VIOLA.   Sooth, but you must.
Say that some lady, as perhaps there is,
Hath for your love as great a pang of heart
As you have for Olivia: you cannot love her;
You tell her so; must she not then be answer'd?

DUKE. There is no woman's sides
Can bide the beating of so strong a passion
As love doth give my heart; no woman's heart
So big, to hold so much; they lack retention.
Alas, their love may be call'd appetite,
No motion of the liver, but the palate,
That suffer surfeit, cloyment, and revolt;
But mine is all as hungry as the sea,
And can digest as much: make no compare
Between that love a woman can bear me
And that I owe Olivia.

VIOLA.   Ay, but I know—

DUKE. What dost thou know?

VIOLA. Too well what love women to men may owe,
In faith, they are as true of heart as we.
My father had a daughter lov'd a man,
As it might be, perhaps, were I a woman,
I should your lordship.

DUKE.   And what's her history?

VIOLA. A blank, my lord. She never told her love,
But let concealment, like a worm i' the bud,
Feed on her damask cheek: she pin'd in thought,
And with a green and yellow melancholy,
She sat like patience on a monument,
Smiling at grief. Was not this love indeed?
We men may say more, swear more; but indeed
Our shows are more than will; for still we prove
Much in our vows, but little in our love.

DUKE. But died thy sister of her love, my boy?

VIOLA. I am all the daughters of my father's house,
And all the brothers too; and yet I know not.
Sir, shall I to this lady?

DUKE.   Ay, that's the theme.
To her in haste; give her this jewel; say
My love can give no place, bide no denay.   [Exeunt.

While this was happening at Orsino's palace,
trouble had arisen at the house of Olivia. Singing
and drinking, Sir Toby and his friends one night
made so much noise that Malvolio, sent by Olivia,
reprimanded them severely for their riotous behaviour.
In revenge Maria, taking advantage of Malvolio's
conceit and of his dreams of winning Olivia's hand
in marriage, set a cunning trap for him.

SCENE: OLIVIA'S *house*.

Enter SIR TOBY *and* SIR ANDREW.

SIR TOBY. Approach, Sir Andrew: not to be a-bed after
midnight is to be up betimes; and 'diluculo surgere,' thou
know'st,——

SIR ANDREW. Nay, by my troth, I know not; but I know, to be up late is to be up late.

SIR TOBY. A false conclusion; I hate it as an unfill'd can. To be up after midnight and to go to bed then, is early; so that to go to bed after midnight is to go bed betimes. Does not our life consist of the four elements?

SIR ANDREW. Faith, so they say; but I think it rather consists of eating and drinking.

SIR TOBY. Thou'rt a scholar; let us therefore eat and drink. Marian, I say! a stoup of wine!

Enter CLOWN.

SIR ANDREW. Here comes the fool, i' faith.

CLOWN. How now, my hearts! did you never see the picture of 'We Three'?

SIR TOBY. Welcome, ass. Now let's have a catch.

SIR ANDREW. By my troth, the fool has an excellent breast. I had rather than forty shillings I had such a leg, and so sweet a breath to sing, as the fool has. In sooth, thou wast in very gracious fooling last night, when thou spokest of Pigrogromitus, of the Vapians passing the equinoctial of Queuebus: 'twas very good, i' faith. I sent thee sixpence for thy leman: hadst it?

CLOWN. I did impeticos thy gratillity; for Malvolio's nose is no whipstock; my lady has a white hand, and the Myrmidons are no bottle-ale houses.

SIR ANDREW. Excellent! why, this is the best fooling when all is done. Now, a song.

SIR TOBY. Come on; there is sixpence for you: let's have a song.

SIR ANDREW. There's a testril of me too: if one knight give a——

CLOWN. Would you have a love-song, or a song of good life?

SIR TOBY. A love-song, a love-song.

SIR ANDREW. Ay, ay; I care not for good life.

CLOWN [*sings*].

O mistress mine, where are you roaming?
O, stay and hear; your true-love's coming,
That can sing both high and low:
Trip no further, pretty sweeting;
Journeys end in lovers meeting,
Every wise man's son doth know.

SIR ANDREW. Excellent good, i' faith.

SIR TOBY. Good, good.

CLOWN [sings].

What is love? 'Tis not hereafter;
Present mirth hath present laughter;
What's to come is still unsure:
In delay there lies no plenty;
Then come kiss me, sweet and twenty,
Youth's a stuff will not endure.

SIR ANDREW. A mellifluous voice, as I am a true knight.

SIR TOBY. A contagious breath.

SIR ANDREW. Very sweet and contagious, i' faith.

SIR TOBY. To hear by the nose, it is dulcet in contagion. But shall we make the welkin dance indeed? shall we rouse the night-owl in a catch that will draw three souls out of one weaver? shall we do that?

SIR ANDREW. An you love me, let's do't; I am a dog at a catch.

CLOWN. By'r lady, sir, and some dogs will catch well.

SIR ANDREW. Most certain. Let our catch be, 'Thou knave.'

CLOWN. 'Hold thy peace, thou knave,' knight? I shall be constrain'd in't to call thee knave, knight.

SIR ANDREW. 'Tis not the first time I have constrain'd one to call me knave. Begin, fool: it begins, 'Hold thy peace.'

CLOWN. I shall never begin if I hold my peace.

SIR ANDREW. Good, i' faith. Come, begin. [Catch sung.

Enter MARIA.

MARIA. What a caterwauling do you keep here! If my

lady have not call'd up her steward Malvolio and bid him turn you out of doors, never trust me.

SIR TOBY. My lady's a Cataian, we are politicians, Malvolio's a Peg-a-Ramsey, and 'Three merry men be we.' Am not I consanguineous? am I not of her blood? Tillyvally. Lady! [*Sings*] 'There dwelt a man in Babylon, lady, lady!'

CLOWN. Beshrew me, the knight's in admirable fooling.

SIR ANDREW. Ay, he does well enough if he be dispos'd, and so do I too: he does it with a better grace, but I do it more natural.

SIR TOBY [*sings*]. 'O, the twelfth day of December,'——

MARIA. For the love o' God, peace!

Enter MALVOLIO.

MALVOLIO. My masters, are you mad? or what are you? Have you no wit, manners, nor honesty, but to gabble like tinkers at this time of night? Do ye make an alehouse of my lady's house, that ye squeak out your coziers' catches without any mitigation or remorse of voice? Is there no respect of place, persons, nor time in you?

SIR TOBY. We did keep time, sir, in our catches. Sneck up!

MALVOLIO. Sir Toby, I must be round with you. My lady bade me tell you, that, though she harbours son as her kinsman, she's nothing allied to your disorders. If you can separate yourself and your misdemeanours, you are welcome to the house: if not, and it would please you to take leave of her, she is very willing to bid you farewell.

SIR TOBY. 'Farewell, dear heart, since I must needs be gone.'

MARIA. Nay, good Sir Toby.

CLOWN. 'His eyes do show his days are almost done.'

MALVOLIO. Is't even so?

SIR TOBY. 'But I will never die.'

CLOWN. Sir Toby, there you lie.

MALVOLIO. This is much credit to you.

SIR TOBY. 'Shall I bid him go?'

CLOWN. 'What an if you do?'

SIR TOBY. 'Shall I bid him go, and spare not?'

CLOWN. 'O, no, no, no, no, you dare not.'

SIR TOBY. Out o' tune, sir? ye lie. Art any more than a steward? Dost thou think, because thou art virtuous, there shall be no more cakes and ale?

CLOWN. Yes, by Saint Anne, and ginger shall be hot i' the mouth too.

SIR TOBY. Thou'rt i' the right. Go, sir, rub your chain with crumbs. A stoup of wine, Maria!

MALVOLIO. Mistress Mary, if you priz'd my lady's favour at any thing more than contempt, you would not give means for this uncivil rule: she shall know of it, by this hand.   [*Exit.*

MARIA. Go shake your ears.

SIR ANDREW. 'Twere as good a deed as to drink when a man's a-hungry, to challenge him the field, and then to break promise with him and make a fool of him.

SIR TOBY. Do't, knight: I'll write thee a challenge; or I'll deliver thy indignation to him by word of mouth.

MARIA. Sweet Sir Toby, be patient for to-night: since the youth of the count's was to-day with my lady, she is much out of quiet. For Monsieur Malvolio, let me alone with him: if I do not gull him into a nayword, and make him a common recreation, do not think I have wit enough to lie straight in my bed: I know I can do it.

SIR TOBY. Possess us, possess us; tell us something of him.

MARIA. Marry, sir, sometimes he is a kind of puritan.

SIR ANDREW. O, if I thought that, I'ld beat him like a dog!

SIR TOBY. What, for being a puritan? thy exquisite reason, dear knight?

SIR ANDREW. I have no exquisite reason for't, but I have reason good enough.

MARIA. The devil a puritan that he is, or any thing constantly, but a time-pleaser; an affection'd ass, that cons state without book, and utters it by great swarths: the best persuaded of himself, so cramm'd, as he thinks, with excellencies, that it is his grounds of faith that all that look on him love him; and on that vice in him will my revenge find notable cause to work.

SIR TOBY. What wilt thou do?

MARIA. I will drop in his way some obscure epistles of love; wherein, by the colour of his beard, the shape of his leg, the manner of his gait, the expressure of his eye, forehead, and complexion, he shall find himself most feelingly personated. I can write very like my lady, your niece; on a forgotten matter we can hardly make distinction of our hands.

SIR TOBY. Excellent! I smell a device.

SIR ANDREW. I have't in my nose, too.

SIR TOBY. He shall think, by the letters that thou wilt drop, that they come from my niece, and that she's in love with him.

MARIA. My purpose is, indeed, a horse of that colour.

SIR ANDREW. And your horse now would make him an ass.

MARIA. Ass, I doubt not.

SIR ANDREW. O, 'twill be admirable!

MARIA. Sport royal, I warrant you: I know my physic will work with him. I will plant you two, and let the fool make a third, where he shall find the letter; observe his construction of it. For this night, to bed, and dream on the event. Farewell. [Exit.

SIR TOBY. Good night, Penthesilea.

SIR ANDREW. Before me, she's a good wench.

SIR TOBY. She's a beagle, true-bred, and one that adores me: what o' that?

SIR ANDREW. I was ador'd once too.

SIR TOBY. Let's to bed, knight. Thou hadst need send for more money.

SIR ANDREW. If I cannot recover your niece, I am a foul way out.

SIR TOBY. Send for money, knight: if thou hast her not i' the end, call me cut.

SIR ANDREW. If I do not, never trust me, take it how you will.

SIR TOBY. Come, come, I'll go burn some sack; 'tis too late to go to bed now. Come, knight; come, knight.

[*Exeunt.*

SCENE: OLIVIA'S *garden.*

Enter SIR TOBY, SIR ANDREW, *and* FABIAN.

SIR TOBY. Come thy ways, Signior Fabian.

FABIAN. Nay, I'll come: if I lose a scruple of this sport, let me be boil'd to death with melancholy.

SIR TOBY. Would'st thou not be glad to have the niggardly rascally sheep-biter come by some notable shame?

FABIAN. I would exult, man; you know he brought me out o' favour with my lady about a bear-baiting here.

SIR TOBY. To anger him we'll have the bear again; and we will fool him black and blue: shall we not, Sir Andrew?

SIR ANDREW. An we do not, it is pity of our lives.

Enter MARIA.

SIR TOBY. Here comes the little villain. How now, my metal of India!

MARIA. Get ye all three into the box-tree: Malvolio's coming down this walk: he has been yonder i' the sun practising behaviour to his own shadow this half hour. Observe him, for the love of mockery; for I know this letter will make a contemplative idiot of him. Close, in the name of jesting! Lie thou there [*throws down a letter*], for here comes the trout that must be caught with tickling. [*Exit.*

Enter MALVOLIO.

MALVOLIO. 'Tis but fortune; all is fortune. Maria once told me she did affect me; and I have heard herself come thus near, that, should she fancy, it should be one of my complexion. Besides, she uses me with a more exalted respect than any one else that follows her. What should I think on't?

SIR TOBY. Here's an overweening rogue!

FABIAN. O, peace! Contemplation makes a rare turkey-cock of him: how he jets under his advanc'd plumes!

SIR ANDREW. 'Slight, I could so beat the rogue!

SIR TOBY. Peace, I say.

MALVOLIO. To be Count Malvolio!

SIR TOBY. Ah, rogue!

SIR ANDREW. Pistol him, pistol him.

SIR TOBY. Peace, peace!

MALVOLIO. There is example for't; the lady of the Strachy married the yeoman of the wardrobe.

SIR ANDREW. Fie on him, Jezebel!

FABIAN. O, peace! now he's deeply in; look how imagination blows him.

MALVOLIO. Having been three months married to her, sitting in my state,——

SIR TOBY. O, for a stone-bow, to hit him in the eye!

MALVOLIO. Calling my officers about me, in my branch'd velvet gown; having come from a day-bed, where I have left Olivia sleeping,——

SIR TOBY. Fire and brimstone!

FABIAN. O, peace, peace!

MALVOLIO. And then to have the humour of state; and, after a demure travel of regard, telling them I know my place, as I would they should do theirs, to ask for my kinsman Toby,——

SIR TOBY. Bolts and shackles!

FABIAN. O, peace, peace, peace! now, now.

MALVOLIO. Seven of my people, with an obedient start, make out for him: I frown the while; and perchance wind up my watch, or play with my—some rich jewel. Toby approaches; courtesies there to me,——

SIR TOBY. Shall this fellow live?

FABIAN. Though our silence be drawn from us with cars, yet peace.

MALVOLIO. I extend my hand to him thus, quenching my familiar smile with an austere regard of control,——

SIR TOBY. And does not Toby take you a blow o' the lips, then?

MALVOLIO. Saying, 'Cousin Toby, my fortunes having cast me on your niece give me this prerogative of speech,'——

SIR TOBY. What, what?

MALVOLIO. 'You must amend your drunkenness.'

SIR TOBY. Out, scab!

MALVOLIO. 'Besides, you waste the treasure of your time with a foolish knight,'——

SIR ANDREW. That's me, I warrant you.

MALVOLIO. 'One Sir Andrew,'——

SIR ANDREW. I knew 'twas I; for many do call me fool.

MALVOLIO. What employment have we here?

[*Taking up the letter.*

FABIAN. Now is the woodcock near the gin.

SIR TOBY. O, peace! and the spirit of humours intimate reading aloud to him.

MALVOLIO. By my life, this is my lady's hand: these be her very C's, her U's, and her T's; and thus makes she her great P's. It is, in contempt of question, her hand.

SIR ANDREW. Her C's, her U's, and her T's; why that?

MALVOLIO [*reads*].

"To the unknown beloved, this, and my good wishes:" —her very phrases! By your leave, wax. Soft! and the impressure her Lucrece, with which she uses to seal: 'tis my lady. To whom should this be?

FABIAN. This wins him, liver and all.

MALVOLIO [*reads*].

"Jove knows I love;
     But who?
Lips, do not move;
No man must know."

"No man must know." What follows? the numbers alter'd! "No man must know." If this should be thee, Malvolio!

SIR TOBY. Marry, hang thee, brock!

MALVOLIO [reads].

"I may command where I adore;
    But silence, like a Lucrece knife,
    With bloodless stroke my heart doth gore:
        M, O, A, I, doth sway my life."

FABIAN. A fustian riddle!

SIR TOBY Excellent wench, say I.

MALVOLIO. "M, O, A, I, doth sway my life." Nay, but first, let me see, let me see, let me see.

FABIAN. What dish o' poison has she dress'd him!

SIR TOBY. And with what wing the staniel checks at it!

MALVOLIO. "I may command where I adore." Why, she may command me: I serve her; she is my lady. Why, this is evident to any formal capacity; there is no obstruction in this: and the end,—what should that alphabetical position portend? if I could make that resemble something in me!—Softly! M, O, A, I,——

SIR TOBY. O, ay, make up that: he is now at a cold scent.

FABIAN. Sowter will cry upon't, for all this, though it be as rank as a fox.

MALVOLIO. M,—Malvolio; M,—why, that begins my name.

FABIAN. Did not I say he would work it out? the cur is excellent at faults.

MALVOLIO. M,—but then there is no consonancy in the sequel; that suffers under probation: A should follow, but O does.

FABIAN. And O shall end, I hope.

SIR TOBY. Ay, or I'll cudgel him, and make him cry O!

MALVOLIO. And then I comes behind.

FABIAN. Ay, an you had any eye behind you, you might see more detraction at your heels than fortunes before you.

MALVOLIO. M, O, A, I; this simulation is not as the former; and yet, to crush this a little, it would bow to me, for every one of these letters are in my name. Soft! here follows prose.

[*Reads*] "If this fall into thy hand, revolve. In my stars I am above thee; but be not afraid of greatness: some are born great, some achieve greatness, and some have greatness thrust upon 'em. Thy Fates open their hands; let thy blood and spirit embrace them; and, to inure thyself to what thou art like to be, cast thy humble slough and appear fresh. Be opposite with a kinsman, surly with servants; let thy tongue tang arguments of state; put thyself into the trick of singularity: she thus advises thee that sighs for thee. Remember who commended thy yellow stockings, and wish'd to see thee ever cross-garter'd: I say, remember. Go to, thou art made, if thou desirest to be so; if not, let me see thee a steward still, the fellow of servants, and not worthy to touch Fortune's fingers. Farewell. She that would alter services with thee,

THE FORTUNATE-UNHAPPY"

Daylight and champain discovers not more; this is open. I will be proud, I will read politic authors, I will baffle Sir Toby, I will wash off gross acquaintance, I will be point-devise the very man. I do not now fool myself, to let imagination jade me; for every reason excites to this, that my lady loves me. She did commend my yellow stockings of late, she did praise my leg being cross-garter'd; and in this she manifests herself to my love, and with a kind of injunction drives me to these habits of her liking. I thank my stars I am happy. I will be strange, stout, in yellow stockings, and cross-garter'd, even with the swiftness of putting on. Jove and my stars be praised! Here is yet a postscript.

[*Reads*] "Thou canst not choose but know who I am. If thou entertainest my love, let it appear in thy smiling; thy smiles become thee well; therefore in my presence still smile, dear my sweet, I prithee."

Jove, I thank thee: I will smile; I will do every thing that thou wilt have me.   [*Exit.*

FABIAN. I will not give my part of this sport for a pension of thousands to be paid from the Sophy.

SIR TOBY. I could marry this wench for this device.

SIR ANDREW. So could I too.

SIR TOBY. And ask no other dowry with her but such another jest.

SIR ANDREW. Nor I neither.

FABIAN. Here comes my noble gull-catcher.

Re-enter MARIA.

SIR TOBY. Wilt thou set thy foot o' my neck?

SIR ANDREW. Or o' mine either?

SIR TOBY. Shall I play my freedom at tray-trip, and become thy bond-slave?

SIR ANDREW. I' faith, or I either?

SIR TOBY. Why, thou hast put him in such a dream, that when the image of it leaves him he must run mad.

MARIA. If you will then see the fruits of the sport, mark his first approach before my lady: he will come to her in yellow stockings, and 'tis a colour she abhors; and cross-garter'd, a fashion she detests; and he will smile upon her, which will now be so unsuitable to her disposition, being addicted to a melancholy as she is, that it cannot but turn him into a notable contempt. If you will see it, follow me.

SIR TOBY. To the gates of Tartar, thou most excellent devil of wit!

SIR ANDREW. I'll make one too.   [*Exeunt.*

When Viola made her second visit to Olivia's house she was much more courteously received than she had been on the previous occasion. She met Sir Toby and Sir Andrew in the garden, and while she was speaking with them Olivia entered with Maria.

SCENE: OLIVIA's *garden.*

SIR TOBY. Save you, gentleman.

VIOLA. And you, sir.

SIR ANDREW. Dieu vous garde, monsieur.

VIOLA. Et vous aussi; votre serviteur.

SIR ANDREW. I hope, sir, you are; and I am yours.

SIR TOBY. Will you encounter the house? my niece is desirous you should enter, if your trade be to her.

VIOLA. I am bound to your niece, sir; I mean, she is the list of my voyage.

SIR TOBY. Taste your legs, sir; put them to motion.

VIOLA. My legs do better understand me, sir, than I understand what you mean by bidding me taste my legs.

SIR TOBY. I mean, to go, sir, to enter.

VIOLA. I will answer you with gait and entrance. But we are prevented.

Enter OLIVIA *and* MARIA.

Most excellent accomplish'd lady, the heavens rain odours on you.

SIR ANDREW. That youth's a rare courtier. 'Rain odours': well.

VIOLA. My matter hath no voice, lady, but to your own most pregnant and vouchsafed ear.

SIR ANDREW. 'Odours,' 'pregnant,' and 'vouchsafed': I'll get 'em all three all ready.

OLIVIA. Let the garden door be shut, and leave me to my hearing. [*Exeunt* SIR TOBY, SIR ANDREW, *and* MARIA. Give me your hand, sir.

VIOLA. My duty, madam, and most humble service.

OLIVIA. What is your name?

VIOLA. Cesario is your servant's name, fair princess.

OLIVIA. My servant, sir! 'Twas never merry world
Since lowly feigning was call'd compliment:
You're servant to the Count Orsino, youth.

VIOLA. And he is yours, and his must needs be yours:
Your servant's servant is your servant, madam.

OLIVIA. For him, I think not on him: for his thoughts,
Would they were blanks, rather than fill'd with me!

VIOLA. Madam, I come to whet your gentle thoughts
On his behalf.

OLIVIA. O, by your leave, I pray you,
I bade you never speak again of him:
But, would you undertake another suit,
I had rather hear you to solicit that
Than music from the spheres.

VIOLA.   Dear lady,——

OLIVIA. Give me leave, beseech you. I did send,
After the last enchantment you did here,
A ring in chase of you: so did I abuse
Myself, my servant, and, I fear me, you:
Under your hard construction must I sit,
To force that on you, in a shameful cunning,
Which you knew none of yours: what might you think?
Have you not set mine honour at the stake,
And baited it with all the unmuzzled thoughts
That tyrannous heart can think? To one of your receiving
Enough is shown: a cypress, not a bosom,
Hideth my heart. So, let me hear you speak.

VIOLA. I pity you.

OLIVIA.   That's a degree to love.

VIOLA. No, not a grize; for 'tis a vulgar proof,
That very oft we pity enemies.

OLIVIA. Why, then, methinks 'tis time to smile again.
O world, how apt the poor are to be proud!
If one should be a prey, how much the better
To fall before the lion than the wolf!   [Clock strikes.
The clock upbraids me with the waste of time.

Be not afraid, good youth, I will not have you:
And yet, when wit and youth is come to harvest,
Your wife is like to reap a proper man.
There lies your way, due west.

VIOLA. Then westward-ho! Grace and good disposition
Attend your ladyship!
You'll nothing, madam, to my lord by me?

OLIVIA. Stay:
I prithee, tell me what thou think'st of me.

VIOLA. That you do think you are not what you are.

OLIVIA. If I think so, I think the same of you.

VIOLA. Then think you right; I am not what I am.

OLIVIA. I would you were as I would have you be!

VIOLA. Would it be better, madam, than I am?
I wish it might, for now I am your fool.

OLIVIA. O, what a deal of scorn looks beautiful
In the contempt and anger of his lip!
A murderous guilt shows not itself more soon
Than love that would seem hid; love's night is noon.
Cesario, by the roses of the spring,
By maidhood, honour, truth, and every thing,
I love thee so, that, maugre all thy pride,
Nor wit nor reason can my passion hide.
Do not extort thy reasons from this clause,
For that I woo, thou therefore hast no cause;
But rather reason thus with reason fetter,
Love sought is good, but given unsought is better.

VIOLA. By innocence I swear, and by my youth,
I have one heart, one bosom, and one truth,
And that no woman has; nor never none
Shall mistress be of it, save I alone.
And so adieu, good madam: never more
Will I my master's tears to you deplore.

OLIVIA. Yet come again; for thou perhaps mayst move
That heart, which now abhors, to like his love.   [*Exeunt.*

SCENE: OLIVIA's *house*.

Enter SIR TOBY, SIR ANDREW, *and* FABIAN.

SIR ANDREW. No, faith, I'll not stay a jot longer.

SIR TOBY. Thy reason, dear venom, give thy reason.

FABIAN. You must needs yield your reason, Sir Andrew.

SIR ANDREW. Marry, I saw your niece do more favours to the count's serving-man than ever she bestow'd upon me; I saw't i' the orchard.

SIR TOBY Did she see thee the while, old boy? tell me that

SIR ANDREW. As plain as I see you now.

FABIAN. This was a great argument of love in her toward you.

SIR ANDREW. 'Slight, will you make an ass o' me?

FABIAN I will prove it legitimate, sir, upon the oaths of judgement and reason.

SIR TOBY. And they have been grand-jurymen since before Noah was a sailor.

FABIAN. She did show favour to the youth in your sight only to exasperate you, to awake your dormouse valour, to put fire in your heart, and brimstone in your liver. You should then have accosted her; and with some excellent jests, fire-new from the mint, you should have banged the youth into dumbness. This was look'd for at your hand, and this was balk'd: the double gilt of this opportunity you let time wash off, and you are now sail'd into the north of my lady's opinion; where you will hang like an icicle on a Dutchman's beard, unless you do redeem it by some laudable attempt either of valour or policy.

SIR ANDREW. An 't be any way, it must be with valour; for policy I hate: I had as lief be a Brownist as a politician.

SIR TOBY. Why, then, build me thy fortunes upon the basis of valour. Challenge me the count's youth to fight with him; hurt him in eleven places: my niece shall take note of it; and assure thyself, there is no love-broker in the world can more prevail in man's commendation with woman than report of valour.

FABIAN. There is no way but this, Sir Andrew.

SIR ANDREW. Will either of you bear me a challenge to him?

SIR TOBY. Go, write it in a martial hand; be curst and brief; it is no matter how witty, so it be eloquent and full of invention: taunt him with the license of ink: if thou thou'st him some thrice, it shall not be amiss; and as many lies as will lie in thy sheet of paper, although the sheet were big enough for the bed of Ware in England, set 'em down: go, about it. Let there be gall enough in thy ink, though thou write with a goose-pen, no matter: about it.

SIR ANDREW. Where shall I find you?

SIR TOBY. We'll call thee at the cubiculo. Go.

[*Exit* SIR ANDREW.

FABIAN. This is a dear manakin to you, Sir Toby.

SIR TOBY. I have been dear to him, lad, some two thousand strong, or so.

FABIAN. We shall have a rare letter from him; but you'll not deliver't?

SIR TOBY. Never trust me, then; and by all means stir on the youth to an answer. I think oxen and wain-ropes cannot hale them together. For Andrew, if he were open'd, and you find so much blood in his liver as will clog the foot of a flea, I'll eat the rest of the anatomy.

FABIAN. And his opposite, the youth, bears in his visage no great presage of cruelty.

SIR TOBY. Look, where the youngest wren of nine comes.

Enter MARIA.

MARIA. If you desire the spleen, and will laugh your-selves into stitches, follow me. Yond gull Malvolio is turn'd heathen, a very renegado; for there is no Christian, that means to be sav'd by believing rightly, can ever believe such impossible passages of grossness. He's in yellow stockings.

SIR TOBY. And cross-garter'd?

MARIA. Most villanously; like a pedant that keeps a school i' the church. I have dogg'd him, like his murderer. He does obey every point of the letter that I dropp'd to betray him: he does smile his face into more lines than is in the new map with the augmentation of the Indies: you have not seen such a thing as 'tis. I can hardly forbear hurling things at him. I know my lady will strike him: if she do, he'll smile and take't for a great favour.

SIR TOBY. Come, bring us, bring us where he is. [*Exeunt.*

SCENE: OLIVIA'S *garden.*

Enter OLIVIA *and* MARIA.

OLIVIA. I have sent after him: he says he'll come;
How shall I feast him? what bestow of him?
For youth is bought more oft than begg'd or borrow'd.
I speak too loud.
Where is Malvolio? he is sad and civil,
And suits well for a servant with my fortunes:
Where is Malvolio?

MARIA. He's coming, madam; but in very strange manner. He is, sure, possess'd, madam.

OLIVIA. Why, what's the matter? does he rave?

MARIA. No, madam, he does nothing but smile: your ladyship were best to have some guard about you, if he come; for, sure, the man is tainted in's wits.

OLIVIA. Go call him hither. [*Exit* MARIA.] I am as mad as he,
If sad and merry madness equal be.
                         Re-enter MARIA, *with* MALVOLIO.
How now, Malvolio!

MALVOLIO. Sweet lady, ho, ho.

OLIVIA. Smilest thou?
I sent for thee upon a sad occasion.

MALVOLIO. Sad, lady! I could be sad: this does make some obstruction in the blood, this cross-gartering: but what of that? if it please the eye of one, it is with me as the very true sonnet is, 'Please one, and please all.'

OLIVIA. Why, how dost thou, man? what is the matter with thee?

MALVOLIO. Not black in my mind, though yellow in my legs. It did come to his hands, and commands shall be executed: I think we do know the sweet Roman hand.

OLIVIA. Wilt thou go to bed, Malvolio?

MALVOLIO. To bed! ay, sweetheart.

OLIVIA. God comfort thee! Why dost thou smile so and kiss thy hand so oft?

MARIA. How do you, Malvolio?

MALVOLIO. At your request! yes; nightingales answer daws.

MARIA. Why appear you with this ridiculous boldness before my lady?

MALVOLIO. 'Be not afraid of greatness:' 'twas well writ.

OLIVIA. What meanest thou by that, Malvolio?

MALVOLIO. 'Some are born great'——

OLIVIA. Ha!

MALVOLIO. 'Some achieve greatness'——

OLIVIA. What sayest thou?

MALVOLIO. 'And some have greatness thrust upon them.'

OLIVIA. Heaven restore thee!

MALVOLIO. 'Remember who commended thy yellow stockings'——

OLIVIA. Thy yellow stockings!

MALVOLIO. 'And wish'd to see thee cross-garter'd.'

OLIVIA. Cross-garter'd!

MALVOLIO. 'Go to, thou art made, if thou desirest to be so'——

OLIVIA. Am I made?

MALVOLIO. 'If not, let me see thee a servant still.'

OLIVIA. Why, this is very midsummer madness.

Enter SERVANT.

SERVANT. Madam, the young gentleman of the Count Orsino's is return'd: I could hardly entreat him back: he attends your ladyship's pleasure.

OLIVIA. I'll come to him. [*Exit* SERVANT.] Good Maria, let this fellow be look'd to. Where's my cousin Toby? Let some of my people have a special care of him: I would not have him miscarry for the half of my dowry.

[*Exeunt* OLIVIA *and* MARIA.

MALVOLIO. O, ho! do you come near me now? no worse man than Sir Toby to look to me! This concurs directly with the letter: she sends him on purpose, that I may appear stubborn to him; for she incites me to that in the letter. 'Cast thy humble slough,' says she; 'be opposite with a kinsman, surly with servants; let thy tongue tang with arguments of state; put thyself into the trick of singularity;' and consequently sets down the manner how; as, a sad face, a reverend carriage, a slow tongue, in the habit of some sir of note, and so forth. I have lim'd her; but it is Jove's doing, and Jove make me thankful! And, when she went away now, 'Let this fellow be look'd to:' fellow! not Malvolio, nor after my degree, but fellow. Why, every thing adheres together, that no dram of a scruple, no scruple of a scruple, no obstacle, no incredulous or unsafe circumstance—— What can be said? Nothing that can be can come between me and the full prospect of my hopes. Well, Jove, not I, is the doer of this, and he is to be thank'd.

Re-enter MARIA *with* SIR TOBY *and* FABIAN.

SIR TOBY. Which way is he, in the name of sanctity? If all the devils of hell be drawn in little, and Legion himself possessed him, yet I'll speak to him.

FABIAN. Here he is, here he is. How is't with you, sir? how is't with you, man?

MALVOLIO. Go off; I discard you: let me enjoy my private; go off.

MARIA. Lo, how hollow the fiend speaks within him! did not I tell you? Sir Toby, my lady prays you to have a care of him.

MALVOLIO. Ah, ha! does she so?

SIR TOBY. Go to, go to; peace, peace; we must deal gently with him: let me alone. How do you do, Malvolio? how is't with you? What, man! defy the devil; consider, he's an enemy to mankind.

MALVOLIO. Do you know what you say?

MARIA. La you, and you speak ill of the devil, how he takes it at heart! Pray God, he be not bewitch'd! My lady would not lose him for more than I'll say.

MALVOLIO. How now, mistress!

MARIA. O Lord!

SIR TOBY. Prithee, hold thy peace; this is not the way: do you not see you move him? let me alone with him.

FABIAN. No way but gentleness; gently, gently: the fiend is rough, and will not be roughly us'd.

SIR TOBY. Why, how now, my bawcock! how dost thou, chuck?

MALVOLIO. Sir!

SIR TOBY. Ay, Biddy, come with me. What, man! 'tis not for gravity to play at cherry-pit with Satan: hang him, foul collier!

MARIA. Get him to say his prayers, good Sir Toby, get him to pray.

MALVOLIO. My prayers, minx!

MARIA. No, I warrant you, he will not hear of godliness.

MALVOLIO. Go, hang yourselves all! you are idle shallow things. I am not of your element; you shall know more hereafter.   [*Exit.*

SIR TOBY. Is't possible?

FABIAN. If this were play'd upon a stage now, I could condemn it as an improbable fiction.

SIR TOBY. His very genius hath taken the infection of the device. man.

MARIA. Nay, pursue him now, lest the device take air and taint.

FABIAN. Why, we shall make him mad indeed.

MARIA. The house will be the quieter.

SIR TOBY. Come, we'll have him in a dark room and bound. My niece is already in the belief that he's mad: we may carry it thus, for our pleasure and his penance, till our very pastime, tired out of breath, prompt us to have mercy on him; at which time we will bring the device to the bar, and crown thee for a finder of madmen. But see, but see.

Enter SIR ANDREW.

FABIAN. More matter for a May morning.

SIR ANDREW. Here's the challenge, read it: I warrant there's vinegar and pepper in't.

FABIAN. Is't so saucy?

SIR ANDREW. Ay, is't, I warrant him; do but read.

SIR TOBY. Give me. [*Reads*] "Youth, whatsoever thou art, thou art but a scurvy fellow."

FABIAN. Good, and valiant.

SIR TOBY [*reads*]. "Wonder not, nor admire not in thy mind, why I do call thee so, for I will show thee no reason for't."

FABIAN. A good note; that keeps you from the blow of the law.

SIR TOBY [*reads*]. "Thou comest to the lady Olivia, and in my sight she uses thee kindly: but thou liest in thy throat; that is not the matter I challenge thee for."

FABIAN. Very brief, and to exceeding good sense—less.

SIR TOBY [*reads*]. "I will waylay thee going home; where if it be thy chance to kill me——"

FABIAN. Good.

SIR TOBY [*reads*]. "Thou killest me like a rogue and a villain."

FABIAN. Still you keep o' the windy side of the law: good.

SIR TOBY [*reads*]. "Fare thee well; and God have mercy upon one of our souls! He may have mercy upon mine; but my hope is better, and so look to thyself. Thy friend, as thou usest him, and thy sworn enemy,

ANDREW AGUECHEEK."

If this letter move him not, his legs cannot: I'll give't him.

MARIA. You may have very fit occasion for't: he is now in some commerce with my lady, and will by and by depart.

SIR TOBY. Go, Sir Andrew; scout me for him at the corner of the orchard, like a bum-baily: so soon as ever thou seest him, draw; and, as thou drawest, swear horrible; for it comes to pass oft that a terrible oath, with a swaggering accent sharply twang'd off, gives manhood more approbation than ever proof itself would have earn'd him. Away!

SIR ANDREW. Nay, let me alone for swearing.   [*Exit.*

SIR TOBY. Now will not I deliver his letter; for the behaviour of the young gentleman gives him out to be of good capacity and breeding; his employment between his lord and my niece confirms no less: therefore this letter, being so excellently ignorant, will breed no terror in the youth; he will find it comes from a clodpole. But, sir, I will deliver his challenge by word of mouth; set upon Aguecheek a notable report of valour; and drive the gentleman, as I know his youth will aptly receive it, into a most hideous opinion of his rage, skill, fury, and impetuosity. This will so fright them both that they will kill one another by the look, like cockatrices.

Re-enter OLIVIA, *with* VIOLA.

FABIAN. Here he comes with your niece: give them way till he take leave, and presently after him.

SIR TOBY. I will meditate the while upon some horrid message for a challenge.

[*Exeunt* SIR TOBY, FABIAN, *and* MARIA.

OLIVIA. I have said too much unto a heart of stone,
And laid mine honour too unchary out:
There's something in me that reproves my fault;
But such a headstrong potent fault it is,
That it but mocks reproof.

VIOLA. With the same 'haviour that your passion bears
Goes on my master's grief.

OLIVIA. Here, wear this jewel for me, 'tis my picture:
Refuse it not: it hath no tongue to vex you;
And I beseech you come again to-morrow.
What shall you ask of me that I'll deny,
That honour sav'd may upon asking give?

VIOLA. Nothing but this: your true love for my master.

OLIVIA. How with mine honour may I give him that
Which I have given to you?

VIOLA.   I will acquit you.

OLIVIA. Well, come again to-morrow: fare thee well:
A fiend like thee might bear my soul to hell.   [*Exit.*

Re-enter SIR TOBY *and* FABIAN.

SIR TOBY. Gentleman, God save thee.

VIOLA. And you, sir.

SIR TOBY. That defence thou hast, betake thee to't: of
what nature the wrongs are thou hast done him, I know
not; but thy intercepter, full of despite, bloody as the
hunter, attends thee at the orchard-end. Dismount thy
tuck, be yare in thy preparation, for thy assailant is quick,
skilful, and deadly.

VIOLA. You mistake, sir; I am sure no man hath any
quarrel to me: my remembrance is very free and clear
from any image of offence done to any man.

SIR TOBY. You'll find it otherwise, I assure you: therefore, if you hold your life at any price, betake you to your
guard; for your opposite hath in him what youth, strength,
skill, and wrath can furnish man withal.

VIOLA. I pray you, sir, what is he?

SIR TOBY. He is knight, dubb'd with unhatch'd rapier

and on carpet consideration; but he is a devil in private brawl: souls and bodies hath he divorc'd three; and his incensement at this moment is so implacable that satisfaction can be none but by pangs of death and sepulchre. Hob, nob, is his word; give't or take't.

VIOLA. I will return again into the house and desire some conduct of the lady. I am no fighter. I have heard of some kind of men that put quarrels purposely on others, to taste their valour; belike this is a man of that quirk.

SIR TOBY. Sir, no; his indignation derives itself out of a very competent injury: therefore, get you on and give him his desire. Back you shall not to the house, unless you undertake that with me which with as much safety you might answer him: therefore, on, or strip your sword stark naked; for meddle you must, that's certain, or forswear to wear iron about you.

VIOLA. This is as uncivil as strange. I beseech you, do me this courteous office, as to know of the knight what my offence to him is; it is something of my negligence, nothing of my purpose.

SIR TOBY. I will do so. Signior Fabian, stay you by this gentleman till my return.   [*Exit.*

VIOLA. Pray you, sir, do you know of this matter?

FABIAN. I know the knight is incens'd against you, even to a mortal arbitrement; but nothing of the circumstance more.

VIOLA. I beseech you, what manner of man is he?

FABIAN. Nothing of that wonderful promise, to read him by his form, as you are like to find him in the proof of his valour. He is, indeed, sir, the most skilful, bloody, and fatal opposite that you could possibly have found in any part of Illyria. Will you walk towards him? I will make your peace with him, if I can.

VIOLA. I shall be much bound to you for't. I am one that had rather go with sir priest than sir knight; I care not who knows so much of my mettle.   [*Exeunt*

Re-enter SIR TOBY, *with* SIR ANDREW.

SIR TOBY. Why, man, he's a very devil; I have not seen such a firago. I had a pass with him, rapier, scabbard and all, and he gives me the stuck-in with such a mortal motion that it is inevitable; and, on the answer, he pays you as surely as your feet hit the ground they step on. They say he has been fencer to the Sophy.

SIR ANDREW. Plague on't, I'll not meddle with him.

SIR TOBY. Ay, but he will not now be pacified: Fabian can scarce hold him yonder.

SIR ANDREW. Plague on't, and I thought he had been valiant and so cunning in fence, I'd have seen him damn'd ere I'd have challeng'd him. Let him let the matter slip, and I'll give him my horse, grey Capilet.

SIR TOBY. I'll make the motion. Stand here, make a good show on't: this shall end without the perdition of souls. [*Aside*] Marry, I'll ride your horse as well as I ride you.

Re-enter FABIAN *and* VIOLA.

[*To* FABIAN] I have his horse to take up the quarrel: I have persuaded him the youth's a devil.

FABIAN. He is as horribly conceited of him; and pants and looks pale, as if a bear were at his heels.

SIR TOBY [*to* VIOLA]. There's no remedy, sir; he will fight with you for's oath sake. Marry, he hath better bethought him of his quarrel, and he finds that now scarce to be worth talking of: therefore draw, for the supportance of his vow; he protests he will not hurt you.

VIOLA [*aside*]. Pray God defend me! A little thing would make me tell them how much I lack of a man.

FABIAN. Give ground, if you see him furious.

SIR TOBY. Come, Sir Andrew, there's no remedy; the gentleman will, for his honour's sake, have one bout with you; he cannot by the duello avoid it: but he has promis'd me, as he is a gentleman and a soldier, he will not hurt you. Come on; to't.

SIR ANDREW. Pray God, he keep his oath !
VIOLA. I do assure you 'tis against my will. [*They draw.*

When she saw her formidable rival advancing towards
her with his sword drawn, Viola began to think of confessing
that she was a woman; but she was relieved at once from
her terror, and the shame of such a discovery, by a stranger
that was passing by, who made up to them, and as if he
had been long known to her, and were her dearest friend,
said to her opponent, "If this young gentleman has done
offence, I will take the fault on me; and if you offend
him, I will for his sake defy you." Before Viola had time
to thank him for his protection, or to inquire the reason
of his kind interference, her new friend met with an enemy
where his bravery was of no use to him; for the officers
of justice coming up in that instant, apprehended the
stranger in the duke's name, to answer for an offence he
had committed some years before; and he said to Viola,
"This comes with seeking you": and then he asked her
for a purse, saying, "Now my necessity makes me ask
for my purse, and it grieves me much more for what I
cannot do for you, than for what befalls myself. You
stand amazed, but be of comfort." His words did indeed
amaze Viola, and she protested she knew him not, nor
had ever received a purse from him; but for the kindness
he had just shown her, she offered him a small sum of
money, being nearly the whole she possessed. And now
the stranger spoke severe things, charging her with ingratitude and unkindness. He said, "This youth, whom
you see here, I snatched from the jaws of death, and for
his sake alone I came to Illyria, and have fallen into this
danger." But the officers cared little for hearkening to
the complaints of their prisoner, and they hurried him off,
saying, "What is that to us?" And as he was carried away,
he called Viola by the name of Sebastian, reproaching
the supposed Sebastian for disowning his friend, as long

as he was within hearing. When Viola heard herself called Sebastian, though the stranger was taken away too hastily for her to ask an explanation, she conjectured that this seeming mystery might arise from her being mistaken for her brother; and she began to cherish hopes that it was her brother whose life this man said he had preserved. And so indeed it was. The stranger, whose name was Antonio, was a sea-captain. He had taken Sebastian up into his ship, when, almost exhausted with fatigue, he was floating on the mast to which he had fastened himself in the storm. Antonio conceived such a friendship for Sebastian, that he resolved to accompany him whithersoever he went; and when the youth expressed a curiosity to visit Orsino's court, Antonio, rather than part from him, came to Illyria, though he knew, if his person should be known there, his life would be in danger, because in a sea-fight he had once dangerously wounded the duke Orsino's nephew. This was the offence for which he was now made a prisoner.

Antonio and Sebastian had landed together but a few hours before Antonio met Viola. He had given his purse to Sebastian, desiring him to use it freely if he saw anything he wished to purchase, telling him he would wait at the inn, while Sebastian went to view the town; but Sebastian not returning at the time appointed, Antonio had ventured out to look for him, and Viola being dressed the same, and in face so exactly resembling her brother, Antonio drew his sword (as he thought) in defence of the youth he had saved, and when Sebastian (as he supposed) disowned him, and denied him his own purse, no wonder he accused him of ingratitude.

Viola, when Antonio was gone, fearing a second invitation to fight, slunk home as fast as she could. She had not been long gone, when her adversary thought he saw her return; but it was her brother Sebastian, who happened to arrive at this place, and he said, "Now, sir, have

I met with you again? There's for you"; and struck him
a blow. Sebastian was no coward; he returned the blow
with interest, and drew his sword.

A lady now put a stop to this duel, for Olivia came out
of the house, and she too mistaking Sebastian for Cesario,
invited him to come into her house, expressing much sorrow
at the rude attack he had met with. Though Sebastian
was as much surprised at the courtesy of this lady as at
the rudeness of his unknown foe, yet he went very willingly
into the house, and Olivia was delighted to find Cesario
(as she thought him) become more sensible of her attentions; for though their features were exactly the same,
there was none of the contempt and anger to be seen in
his face, which she had complained of when she told her
love to Cesario.

Sebastian did not at all object to the fondness the lady
lavished on him. He seemed to take it in very good part,
yet he wondered how it had come to pass, and he was
rather inclined to think Olivia was not in her right senses;
but perceiving that she was mistress of a fine house, and
that she ordered her affairs and seemed to govern her
family discreetly, and that in all but her sudden love for
him she appeared in the full possession of her reason, he
well approved of the courtship; and Olivia finding Cesario
in this good humour, and fearing he might change his
mind, proposed that, as she had a priest in the house, they
should be instantly married. Sebastian assented to this
proposal; and when the marriage ceremony was over,
he left his lady for a short time, intending to go and
tell his friend Antonio the good fortune that he had met
with.

Tales from Shakespeare

While Olivia's time was thus occupied Maria and
Sir Toby, with the help of the clown, made and carried
out further plans for tormenting Malvolio

SCENE: OLIVIA's *house.*

Enter MARIA *and* CLOWN.

MARIA. Nay, I prithee, put on this gown and this beard; make him believe thou art Sir Topas the curate: do it quickly; I'll call Sir Toby the whilst.   [*Exit.*

CLOWN. Well, I'll put it on, and I will dissemble myself in't; and I would I were the first that ever dissembl'd in such a gown. I am not tall enough to become the function well, nor lean enough to be thought a good student; but to be said an honest man and a good housekeeper goes as fairly as to say a careful man and a great scholar. The competitors enter.

Enter SIR TOBY *and* MARIA.

SIR TOBY. Jove bless thee, master parson!

CLOWN. Bonos dies, Sir Toby: for, as the old hermit of Prague, that never saw pen and ink, very wittily said to a niece of King Gorboduc, 'That that is is'; so I, being master parson, am master parson; for, what is 'that' but 'that', and 'is' but 'is'?

SIR TOBY. To him, Sir Topas.

CLOWN. What, ho, I say, peace in this prison!

SIR TOBY. The knave counterfeits well; a good knave.

MALVOLIO [*within*]. Who calls there?

CLOWN. Sir Topas, the curate, who comes to visit Malvolio the lunatic.

MALVOLIO. Sir Topas, Sir Topas, good Sir Topas, go to my lady.

CLOWN. Out, hyperbolical fiend! how vexest thou this man! talkest thou nothing but of ladies?

SIR TOBY. Well said, master parson.

MALVOLIO. Sir Topas, never was man thus wrong'd: good Sir Topas, do not think I am mad: they have laid me here in hideous darkness.

CLOWN. Fie, thou dishonest Satan! I call thee by the most modest terms; for I am one of those gentle ones that will use the devil himself with courtesy. Sayest thou that house is dark?

MALVOLIO. As hell, Sir Topas.

CLOWN. Why, it hath bay-windows transparent as barricadoes, and the clerestories toward the south north are as lustrous as ebony; and yet complainest thou of obstruction?

MALVOLIO. I am not mad, Sir Topas: I say to you, this house is dark.

CLOWN. Madman, thou errest: I say, there is no darkness but ignorance; in which thou art more puzzled than the Egyptians in their fog.

MALVOLIO. I say, this house is as dark as ignorance, though ignorance were as dark as hell; and I say, there was never man thus abus'd. I am no more mad than you are: make the trial of it in any constant question.

CLOWN. What is the opinion of Pythagoras concerning wild fowl?

MALVOLIO. That the soul of our grandam might haply inhabit a bird.

CLOWN. What thinkest thou of his opinion?

MALVOLIO. I think nobly of the soul, and no way approve his opinion.

CLOWN. Fare thee well. Remain thou still in darkness: thou shalt hold the opinion of Pythagoras ere I will allow of thy wits, and fear to kill a woodcock, lest thou dispossess the soul of thy grandam. Fare thee well.

MALVOLIO. Sir Topas, Sir Topas!

SIR TOBY. My most exquisite Sir Topas!

CLOWN. Nay, I am for all waters.

MARIA. Thou might'st have done this without thy beard and gown: he sees thee not.

SIR TOBY. To him in thine own voice, and bring me word how thou findest him: I would we were well rid of this knavery. If he may be conveniently deliver'd, I would he were, for I am now so far in offence with my niece that I cannot pursue with any safety this sport to the upshot. Come by and by to my chamber.

[*Exeunt* SIR TOBY *and* MARIA.

CLOWN [*singing*].

'Hey, Robin, jolly Robin,
    Tell me how thy lady does.'

MALVOLIO. Fool!

CLOWN.   'My lady is unkind, perdy.'

MALVOLIO. Fool!

CLOWN.   'Alas, why is she so?'

MALVOLIO. Fool, I say!

CLOWN.   'She loves another'——
Who calls, ha?

MALVOLIO. Good fool, as ever thou wilt deserve well at my hand, help me to a candle, and pen, ink, and paper: as I am a gentleman, I will live to be thankful to thee for't.

CLOWN. Master Malvolio?

MALVOLIO. Ay, good fool.

CLOWN. Alas, sir, how fell you besides your five wits?

MALVOLIO. Fool, there was never man so notoriously abus'd: I am as well in my wits, fool, as thou art.

CLOWN. But as well? then you are mad indeed, if you be no better in your wits than a fool.

MALVOLIO. They have here propertied me; keep me in darkness, send ministers to me, asses, and do all they can to face me out of my wits.

CLOWN. Advise you what you say; the minister is here. Malvolio, Malvolio, thy wits the heavens restore! endeavour thyself to sleep, and leave thy vain bibble babble.

MALVOLIO. Sir Topas!

CLOWN. Maintain no words with him, good fellow. Who, I, sir? not I, sir. God be wi' you, good Sir Topas! Marry, amen. I will, sir, I will.

MALVOLIO. Fool, fool, fool, I say!·

CLOWN. Alas, sir, be patient. What say you, sir? I am shent for speaking to you.

MALVOLIO. Good fool, help me to some light and some paper: I tell thee, I am as well in my wits as any man in Illyria.

CLOWN. Well-a-day that you were, sir!

MALVOLIO. By this hand, I am. Good fool, some ink, paper, and light; and convey what I will set down to my lady: it shall advantage thee more than ever the bearing of letter did.

CLOWN. I will help you to't. But tell me true, are you not mad indeed, or do you but counterfeit?

MALVOLIO. Believe me, I am not; I tell thee true.

CLOWN. Nay, I'll ne'er believe a madman till I see his brains. I will fetch you light and paper and ink.

MALVOLIO. Fool, I'll requite it in the highest degree; I prithee, be gone.

CLOWN [singing].

> I am gone, sir,
> And anon, sir,
> I'll be with you again,
> In a trice,
> Like to the old Vice,
> Your need to sustain;
>
> Who, with dagger of lath,
> In his rage and his wrath,
> Cries, ah, ha! to the devil:
> Like a mad lad,
> Pare thy nails, dad;
> Adieu, goodman devil.   [Exit.

In the meantime Orsino came to visit Olivia; and at the moment he arrived before Olivia's house, the officer. of justice brought their prisoner, Antonio, before the dukes Viola was with Orsino, her master; and when Antonio saw Viola, whom he still imagined to be Sebastian, he told the duke in what manner he had rescued this youth from the perils of the sea; and after fully relating all the kindness he had really shown to Sebastian, he ended his complaint with saying, that for three months, both day and night, this ungrateful youth had been with him. But now the lady Olivia coming forth from her house, the duke could no longer attend to Antonio's story.

Tales from Shakespeare

SCENE: *Before* OLIVIA'S *house.*

DUKE. Here comes the countess: now heaven walks on
    earth.
But for thee, fellow; fellow, thy words are madness:
Three months this youth hath tended upon me;
But more of that anon. Take him aside.

OLIVIA. What would my lord, but that he may not have,
Wherein Olivia may seem serviceable?
Cesario, you do not keep promise with me.

VIOLA. Madam!

DUKE. Gracious Olivia,——

OLIVIA. What do you say, Cesario? Good my lord,—

VIOLA. My lord would speak; my duty hushes me.

OLIVIA. If it be aught to the old tune, my lord,
It is as fat and fulsome to mine ear
As howling after music.

DUKE.   Still so cruel?

OLIVIA. Still so constant, lord.

DUKE. What, to perverseness? you uncivil lady,
To whose ingrate and unauspicious altars
My soul the faithfull'st offerings hath breath'd out
That e'er devotion tender'd! What shall I do?

OLIVIA. Even what it please my lord, that shall become
    him.

DUKE. Why should I not, had I the heart to do it.
Like to the Egyptian thief at point of death,
Kill what I love?—a savage jealousy

That sometime savours nobly. But hear me this:
Since you to non-regardance cast my faith,
And that I partly know the instrument
That screws me from my true place in your favour,
Live you the marble-breasted tyrant still;
But this your minion, whom I know you love,
And whom, by heaven I swear, I tender dearly,
Him will I tear out of that cruel eye,
Where he sits crowned in his master's spite.
Come, boy, with me; my thoughts are ripe in mischief;
I'll sacrifice the lamb that I do love,
To spite a raven's heart within a dove.

    VIOLA. And I, most jocund, apt, and willingly,
To do you rest, a thousand deaths would die.

    OLIVIA. Where goes Cesario?

    VIOLA.   After him I love
More than I love these eyes, more than my life,
More, by all mores, than e'er I shall love wife.
If I do feign, you witnesses above
Punish my life for tainting of my love!

    OLIVIA. Ay me, detested! how am I beguil'd!

    VIOLA. Who does beguile you? who does do you
       wrong?

    OLIVIA. Hast thou forgot thyself? is it so long?
Call forth the holy father.

    DUKE.   Come, away!

    OLIVIA. Whither, my lord? Cesario, husband, stay.

    DUKE. Husband!

    OLIVIA.   Ay, husband: can he that deny?

    DUKE. Her husband, sirrah!

    VIOLA.   No, my lord, not I.

    OLIVIA. Alas, it is the baseness of thy fear
That makes thee strangle thy propriety.
Fear not, Cesario; take thy fortunes up;
Be that thou know'st thou art, and then thou art
As great as that thou fear'st.

Enter PRIEST.

                 O, welcome, father!
Father, I charge thee, by thy reverence,
Here to unfold, though lately we intended
To keep in darkness what occasion now
Reveals before 'tis ripe, what thou dost know
Hath newly pass'd between this youth and me.

    PRIEST. A contract of eternal bond of love,
Confirm'd by mutual joinder of your hands,
Attested by the holy close of lips,
Strengthen'd by interchangement of your rings;
And all the ceremony of this compact
Seal'd in my function, by my testimony:
Since when, my watch hath told me, toward my grave
I have travell'd but two hours.

    DUKE. O thou dissembling cub! what wilt thou be
When time hath sow'd a grizzle on thy case?
Or will not else thy craft so quickly grow
That thine own trip shall be thine overthrow?
Farewell, and take her; but direct thy feet
Where thou and I henceforth may never meet.

    VIOLA. My lord, I do protest,——

    OLIVIA.   O, do not swear!
Hold little faith,.though thou hast too much fear.

Enter SIR ANDREW.

    SIR ANDREW. For the love of God, a surgeon! send one
presently to Sir Toby.

    OLIVIA. What's the matter?

    SIR ANDREW. Has broke my head across and has given
Sir Toby a bloody coxcomb too: for the love of God,
your help! I had rather than forty pound I were at
home.

    OLIVIA. Who has done this, Sir Andrew?

    SIR ANDREW. The count's gentleman, one Cesario: we
took him for a coward, but he's the very devil incardinate.

    DUKE. My gentleman, Cesario?

SIR ANDREW. 'Od's lifelings, here he is! You broke my
head for nothing; and that that I did, I was set on to do't
by Sir Toby.

VIOLA. Why do you speak to me? I never hurt you:
You drew your sword upon me without cause;
But I bespake you fair, and hurt you not.

SIR ANDREW. If a bloody coxcomb be a hurt, you have
hurt me; I think you set nothing by a bloody coxcomb.

Enter SIR TOBY *and* CLOWN.

Here comes Sir Toby halting; you shall hear more: but
if he had not been in drink, he would have tickl'd you
othergates than he did.

DUKE. How now, gentleman! how is't with you?

SIR TOBY. That's all one: has hurt me, and there's
the end on't. Sot, didst see Dick Surgeon, sot?

CLOWN. O, he's drunk, Sir Toby, an hour agone; his
eyes were set at eight i' the morning.

SIR TOBY. Then he's a rogue, and a passy measures
pavin. I hate a drunken rogue.

OLIVIA. Away with him! Who hath made this havoc
with them?

SIR ANDREW. I'll help you, Sir Toby, because we'll be
dress'd together.

SIR TOBY. Will you help? an ass-head and a coxcomb
and a knave, a thin-fac'd knave, a gull!

OLIVIA. Get him to bed, and let his hurt be look'd to.

[*Exeunt* CLOWN, FABIAN, SIR TOBY, *and* SIR ANDREW.
Enter SEBASTIAN.

SEBASTIAN. I am sorry, madam, I have hurt your kins-
man;
But, had it been the brother of my blood,
I must have done no less with wit and safety.
You throw a strange regard upon me, and by that
I do perceive it hath offended you:
Pardon me, sweet one, even for the vows
We made each other but so late ago.

DUKE. One face, one voice, one habit, and two persons,
A natural perspective, that is and is not!

SEBASTIAN. Antonio, O my dear Antonio!
How have the hours rack'd and tortur'd me,
Since I have lost thee!

ANTONIO. Sebastian are you?

SEBASTIAN.   Fear'st thou that, Antonio?

ANTONIO. How have you made division of yourself?
An apple cleft in two is not more twin
Than these two creatures. Which is Sebastian?

OLIVIA. Most wonderful!

SEBASTIAN. Do I stand there? I never had a brother;
Nor can there be that deity in my nature,
Of here and every where. I had a sister,
Whom the blind waves and surges have devour'd.
Of charity, what kin are you to me?
What countryman? what name? what parentage?

VIOLA. Of Messaline: Sebastian was my father;
Such a Sebastian was my brother too,
So went he suited to his watery tomb.
If spirits can assume both form and suit
You come to fright us.

SEBASTIAN. A spirit I am indeed;
But am in that dimension grossly clad
Which from my birth I did participate.
Were you a woman, as the rest goes even,
I should my tears let fall upon your cheek,
And say, 'Thrice-welcome, drown'd Viola!'

VIOLA. My father had a mole upon his brow.

SEBASTIAN. And so had mine.

VIOLA. And died that day when Viola from her birth
Had number'd thirteen years.

SEBASTIAN. O, that record is lively in my soul!
He finished indeed his mortal act
That day that made my sister thirteen years.

VIOLA. If nothing lets to make us happy both

But this my masculine usurp'd attire,
Do not embrace me till each circumstance
Of place, time, fortune, do cohere and jump
That I am Viola: which to confirm,
I'll bring you to a captain in this town,
Where lie my maiden weeds; by whose gentle help
I was preserv'd to serve this noble count.
All the occurrence of my fortune since
Hath been between this lady and this lord.

    SEBASTIAN [*to* OLIVIA]. So comes it, lady, you have been
But nature to her bias drew in that.   [mistook;
You would have been contracted to a maid;
Nor are you therein, by my life, deceiv'd,
You are betroth'd both to a maid and man.

    DUKE. Be not amaz'd; right noble is his blood.
If this be so, as yet the glass seems true,
I shall have share in this most happy wreck.
[*To* VIOLA] Boy, thou hast said to me a thousand times
Thou never shouldst love woman like to me.

    VIOLA. And all those sayings will I over-swear;
And all those swearings keep as true in soul
As doth that orbed continent the fire
That severs day from night.

    DUKE.   Give me thy hand;
And let me see thee in thy woman's weeds.

    VIOLA. The captain that did bring me first on shore
Hath my maid's garments: he upon some action
Is now in durance at Malvolio's suit,
A gentleman and follower of my lady's.

    OLIVIA. He shall enlarge him. Fetch Malvolio hither:
And yet, alas, now I remember me,
They say, poor gentleman, he's much distract.

    Re-enter CLOWN *with a letter, and* FABIAN
A most extracting frenzy of mine own
From my remembrance clearly banish'd his.
How does he, sirrah?

CLOWN. Truly, madam, he holds Belzebub at the stave's end as well as a man in his case may do. Has here writ a letter to you; I should have given't you to-day morning; but as a madman's epistles are no gospels, so it skills not much when they are deliver'd.

OLIVIA. Open't, and read it.

CLOWN. Look then to be well edified when the fool delivers the madman.

[*Reads*]. 'By the Lord, madam'——

OLIVIA. How now! art thou mad?

CLOWN. No, madam, I do but read madness: an your ladyship will have it as it ought to be, you must allow Vox.

OLIVIA. Prithee, read i' thy right wits.

CLOWN. So I do, madonna; but to read his right wits is to read thus: therefore perpend, my princess, and give ear.

OLIVIA [*to* FABIAN] Read it you, sirrah.

FABIAN [*reads*] "By the Lord, madam, you wrong me, and the world shall know it: though you have put me into darkness and given your drunken cousin rule over me, yet have I the benefit of my senses as well as your ladyship. I have your own letter that induc'd me to the semblance I put on; with the which I doubt not but to do myself much right, or you much shame. Think of me as you please. I leave my duty a little unthought of, and speak out of my injury.   THE MADLY US'D MALVOLIO."

OLIVIA. Did he write this?

CLOWN Ay, madam.

DUKE. This savours not much of distraction.

OLIVIA. See him deliver'd, Fabian; bring him hither.

[*Exit* FABIAN.

My lord, so please you, these things further thought on,
To think me as well a sister as a wife,
One day shall crown the alliance on't, so please you,
Here at my house and at my proper cost.

DUKE. Madam, I am most apt to embrace your offer.

[*To* VIOLA].   Your master quits you; and for your service
   done him,
So much against the mettle of your sex,
So far beneath your soft and tender breeding,
And since you call'd me master for so long,
Here is my hand; you shall from this time be
Your master's mistress.

   OLIVIA.   A sister! you are she.

          Re-enter FABIAN, *with* MALVOLIO.

   DUKE.   Is this the madman?

   OLIVIA.   Ay, my lord, this same.
How now, Malvolio!

   MALVOLIO.   Madam, you have done me wrong,
Notorious wrong.

   OLIVIA.   Have I, Malvolio? no.

   MALVOLIO.   Lady, you have. Pray you, peruse that letter.
You must not now deny it is your hand:
Write from it, if you can, in hand or phrase;
Or say 'tis not your seal, not your invention:
You can say none of this. Well, grant it then
And tell me, in the modesty of honour,
Why you have given me such clear lights of favour,
Bade me come smiling and cross-garter'd to you,
To put on yellow stockings, and to frown
Upon Sir Toby and the lighter people;
And, acting this in an obedient hope,
Why have you suffer'd me to be imprison'd,
Kept in a dark house, visited by the priest,
And made the most notorious geck and gull
That e'er invention play'd on? tell me why.

   OLIVIA.   Alas, Malvolio, this is not my writing,
Though, I confess, much like the character;
But out of question 'tis Maria's hand.
And now I do bethink me, it was she
First told me thou wast mad; then cam'st in smiling,
And in such forms which here were presuppos'd

Upon thee in the letter. Prithee, be content:
This practice hath most shrewdly pass'd upon thee;
But when we know the grounds and authors of it,
Thou shalt be both the plaintiff and the judge
Of thine own cause.

FABIAN.   Good madam, hear me speak,
And let no quarrel nor no brawl to come
Taint the condition of this present hour,
Which I have wonder'd at. In hope it shall not,
Most freely I confess, myself and Toby
Set this device against Malvolio here,
Upon some stubborn and uncourteous parts
We had conceiv'd against him. Maria writ
The letter at Sir Toby's great importance;
In recompense whereof he hath married her.
How with a sportful malice it was follow'd
May rather pluck on laughter than revenge;
If that the injuries be justly weigh'd
That have on both sides pass'd.

OLIVIA. Alas, poor fool, how have they baffled thee!

CLOWN. Why, 'some are born great, some achieve
greatness, and some have greatness thrown upon them.'
I was one, sir, in this interlude; one Sir Topas, sir; but
that's all one. 'By the Lord, fool, I am not mad'. But do
you remember? 'Madam, why laugh you at such a barren
rascal? an you smile not, he's gagg'd': and thus the
whirligig of time brings in his revenges.

MALVOLIO. I'll be reveng'd on the whole pack of you.

                                        [Exit.

OLIVIA. He hath been most notoriously abus'd.

DUKE. Pursue him, and entreat him to a peace.
He hath not told us of the captain yet:
When that is known and golden time convents,
A solemn combination shall be made
Of our dear souls. Meantime, sweet sister,
We will not part from hence. Cesario, come;

For so you shall be, while you are a man;
But when in other habits you are seen,
Orsino's mistress, and his fancy's queen.

> [*Exeunt all but the* CLOWN.

CLOWN [*sings*].

> When that I was and a little tiny boy,
>   With hey, ho, the wind and the rain,
> A foolish thing was but a toy,
>   For the rain it raineth every day.

> But when I came to man's estate,
>   With hey, ho, the wind and the rain,
> 'Gainst knaves and thieves men shut their gate,
>   For the rain it raineth every day.

> But when I came, alas! to wive,
>   With hey, ho, the wind and the rain,
> By swaggering could I never thrive,
>   For the rain it raineth every day.

> But when I came unto my beds,
>   With hey, ho, the wind and the rain,
> With toss-pots still had drunken heads,
>   For the rain it raineth every day.

> A great while ago the world begun,
>   With hey, ho, the wind and the rain,
> But that's all one, our play is done,
>   And we'll strive to please you every day.   [*Exit.*

A MIDSUMMER NIGHT'S DREAM

Characters

Mortals

THESEUS, DUKE OF ATHENS
LYSANDER
DEMETRIUS
PHILOSTRATE, *master of the revels*
EGEUS, *Hermia's father*
QUINCE, *a carpenter*
SNUG, *a joiner*
BOTTOM, *a weaver*
FLUTE, *a bellows-mender*
SNOUT, *a tinker*
STARVELING, *a tailor*
HIPPOLYTA, *betrothed to Theseus*
HERMIA
HELENA

Fairies

OBERON, *King of the Fairies*
TITANIA, *Queen of the Fairies*
PUCK
PEASEBLOSSOM
COBWEB
MOTH
MUSTARDSEED
OTHER FAIRIES

THERE was a law in the city of Athens which gave to its citizens the power of compelling their daughters to marry whomsoever they pleased; for upon a daughter's refusing to marry the man her father had chosen to be her husband, the father was empowered by this law to cause her to be put to death; but as fathers do not often desire the death of their own daughters, even though they do happen to prove a little refractory, this law was seldom or never put in execution, though perhaps the young ladies of that city were not unfrequently threatened by their parents with the terrors of it.

There was one instance, however, of an old man, whose name was Egeus, who actually did come before Theseus (at that time the reigning Duke of Athens), to complain that his daughter Hermia, whom he had commanded to marry Demetrius, a young man of a noble Athenian family, refused to obey him, because she loved another young Athenian, named Lysander. Egeus demanded justice of Theseus, and desired that this cruel law might be put in force against his daughter.

Hermia pleaded in excuse for her disobedience, that Demetrius had formerly professed love for her dear friend Helena, and that Helena loved Demetrius to distraction; but this honourable reason, which Hermia gave for not obeying her father's command, moved not the stern Egeus.

Theseus, though a great and merciful prince, had no power to alter the laws of his country; therefore he could only give Hermia four days to consider of it: and at the end of that time, if she still refused to marry Demetrius, she was to be put to death.

When Hermia was dismissed from the presence of the duke, she went to her lover Lysander, and told him the peril she was in, and that she must either give him up and marry Demetrius, or lose her life in four days.

Lysander was in great affliction at hearing these evil tidings; but recollecting that he had an aunt who lived at some distance from Athens, and that at the place where she lived the cruel law could not be put in force against Hermia (this law not extending beyond the boundaries of the city), he proposed to Hermia that she should steal out of her father's house that night, and go with him to his aunt's house, where he would marry her. "I will meet you," said Lysander, "in the wood a few miles without the city; in that delightful wood where we have so often walked with Helena in the pleasant month of May."

To this proposal Hermia joyfully agreed; and she told no one of her intended flight but her friend Helena. Helena (as maidens will do foolish things for love) very ungenerously resolved to go and tell this to Demetrius, though she could hope no benefit from betraying her friend's secret, but the poor pleasure of following her faithless lover to the wood; for she well knew that Demetrius would go thither in pursuit of Hermia.

Tales from Shakespeare

Four days after the events just described, the Duke was to be married to the lady Hippolyta. He had promised to marry her

With pomp, with triumph, and with revelling,

and among the festivities arranged to celebrate the wedding was a short play, or interlude, which was to be presented by a group of Athenian artisans. On the day when Egeus and Hermia appeared before Theseus, these amateur actors met at the house of one Peter Quince, a carpenter, to arrange for the production of their play.

SCENE: *Athens. A room in Quince's house.*

Enter QUINCE, SNUG, BOTTOM, FLUTE, SNOUT, *and*
STARVELING.

QUINCE. Is all our company here?

BOTTOM. You were best to call them generally, man by man, according to the scrip.

QUINCE. Here is the scroll of every man's name, which is thought fit, through all Athens, to play in our interlude before the duke and the duchess, on his wedding-day at night.

BOTTOM. First, good Peter Quince, say what the play treats on, then read the names of the actors, and so grow to a point.

QUINCE. Marry, our play is, The most lamentable comedy, and most cruel death of Pyramus and Thisby.

BOTTOM. A very good piece of work, I assure you, and a merry. Now, good Peter Quince, call forth your actors by the scroll. Masters, spread yourselves.

QUINCE. Answer as I call you. Nick Bottom, the weaver.

BOTTOM. Ready. Name what part I am for, and proceed.

QUINCE. You, Nick Bottom, are set down for Pyramus.

BOTTOM. What is Pyramus? a lover, or a tyrant?

QUINCE. A lover, that kills himself most gallant for love.

BOTTOM. That will ask some tears in the true performing of it: if I do it, let the audience look to their eyes; I will move storms, I will condole in some measure. To the rest: yet my chief humour is for a tyrant; I could play Ercles rarely, or a part to tear a cat in, to make all split.

> The raging rocks
> And shivering shocks
> Shall break the locks
>   Of prison gates;
> And Phibbus' car
> Shall shine from far,
> And make and mar
>   The foolish Fates.

This was lofty! Now name the rest of the players. This is Ercles' vein, a tyrant's vein; a lover is more condoling.

QUINCE. Francis Flute the bellows-mender.

FLUTE. Here, Peter Quince.

QUINCE. Flute, you must take Thisby on you.

FLUTE. What is Thisby? a wandering knight?

QUINCE. It is the lady that Pyramus must love.

FLUTE. Nay, faith, let me not play a woman; I have a beard coming.

QUINCE. That's all one: you shall play it in a mask, and you may speak as small as you will.

BOTTOM. An I may hide my face, let me play Thisby too. I'll speak in a monstrous little voice, 'Thisne, Thisne'; 'Ah, Pyramus, my lover dear! thy Thisby dear, and lady dear!'

QUINCE. No, no; you must play Pyramus, and, Flute, you Thisby.

BOTTOM. Well, proceed.

QUINCE. Robin Starveling, the tailor.

STARVELING. Here, Peter Quince.

QUINCE. Robin Starveling, you must play Thisby's mother. Tom Snout, the tinker.

SNOUT. Here, Peter Quince.

QUINCE. You, Pyramus' father: myself, Thisby's father. Snug, the joiner; you, the lion's part: and, I hope, here is a play fitted.

SNUG. Have you the lion's part written? pray you, if it be, give it me, for I am slow of study.

QUINCE. You may do it extempore, for it is nothing but roaring.

BOTTOM. Let me play the lion too. I will roar, that I will do any man's heart good to hear me; I will roar, that I will make the duke say, 'Let him roar again, let him roar again.'

QUINCE. An you should do it too terribly, you would fright the duchess and the ladies, that they would shriek; and that were enough to hang us all.

ALL. That would hang us, every mother's son.

BOTTOM. I grant you, friends, if that you should fright the ladies out of their wits, they would have no more discretion but to hang us; but I will aggravate my voice so that I will roar you as gently as any sucking dove; I will roar you an 'twere any nightingale.

QUINCE. You can play no part but Pyramus; for Pyramus is a sweet-fac'd man; a proper man as one shall see in a summer's day; a most lovely, gentleman-like man; therefore you must needs play Pyramus.

BOTTOM. Well, I will undertake it. What beard were I best to play it in?

QUINCE. Why, what you will.

BOTTOM. I will discharge it in either your straw-colour beard, your orange-tawny beard, your purple-in-grain beard, or your French-crown-colour beard, your perfect yellow.

QUINCE. Some of your French crowns have no hair at all, and then you will play bare-fac'd. But, masters, here are your parts: and I am to entreat you, request you, and desire you, to con them by to-morrow night; and meet me in the palace wood, a mile without the town, by moonlight: there will we rehearse; for if we meet in the city, we shall be dogg'd with company, and our devices known. In the meantime I will draw a bill of properties, such as our play wants. I pray you, fail me not.

BOTTOM. We will meet; and there may we rehearse most obscenely and courageously. Take pains; be perfect. Adieu.

QUINCE. At the duke's oak we meet.

BOTTOM. Enough; hold or cut bow-strings.   [*Exeunt.*

So it came about that, on the night when Lysander and Hermia arranged to meet in the wood, Bottom and his companions assembled there to rehearse in secrecy. But the lovers and the artisans were not alone in the wood, for it was haunted by fairies.

SCENE: *A wood near Athens.*

Enter, from opposite sides, a FAIRY *and* PUCK.

PUCK. How now, spirit! whither wander you?

FAIRY.   Over hill, over dale,
            Thorough bush, thorough brier,
        Over park, over pale,
            Thorough flood, thorough fire,

I do wander every where,
Swifter than the moon's sphere;
And I serve the fairy queen,
To dew her orbs upon the green.
The cowslips tall her pensioners be:
In their gold coats spots you see;
Those be rubies, fairy favours,
In those freckles live their savours:

I must go seek some dewdrops here,
And hang a pearl in every cowslip's ear.
Farewell, thou lob of spirits; I'll be gone:
Our queen and all her elves come here anon.

PUCK. The king doth keep his revels here to-night:
Take heed the queen come not within his sight;
For Oberon is passing fell and wrath,
Because that she as her attendant hath
A lovely boy, stol'n from an Indian king;
She never had so sweet a changeling;
And jealous Oberon would have the child
Knight of his train, to trace the forests wild;
But she perforce withholds the loved boy,
Crowns him with flowers, and makes him all her joy.
And now they never meet in grove or green,
By fountain clear or spangl'd starlight sheen,
But they do square, that all their elves for fear
Creep into acorn-cups and hide them there.

FAIRY. Either I mistake your shape and making quite,
Or else you are that shrewd and knavish sprite
Call'd Robin Goodfellow: are not you he
That frights the maidens of the villagery;
Skim milk, and sometimes labour in the quern,
And bootless make the breathless housewife churn;
And sometimes make the drink to bear no barm;
Mislead night-wanderers, laughing at their harm?
Those that Hobgoblin call you and sweet Puck,

You do their work, and they shall have good luck:
Are not you he?

PUCK.   Thou speak'st aright;
I am that merry wanderer of the night.
I jest to Oberon and make him smile
When I a fat and bean-fed horse beguile,
Neighing in likeness of a filly foal:
And sometime lurk I in a gossip's bowl,
In very likeness of a roasted crab,
And when she drinks, against her lips I bob
And on her wither'd dewlap pour the ale.
The wisest aunt, telling the saddest tale,
Sometime for three-foot stool mistaketh me;
Then slip I from her, and down topples she,
And 'tailor' cries, and falls into a cough;
And then the whole quire hold their hips and laugh,
And waxen in their mirth, and neeze, and swear
A merrier hour was never wasted there.
But room, fairy! Here comes Oberon.

FAIRY. And here my mistress. Would that he were gone!

"Ill met by moonlight, proud Titania," said the fairy
king. The queen replied, "What, jealous Oberon, is it
you? Fairies, skip hence; I have forsworn his company."
"Tarry, rash fairy," said Oberon; "am not I thy lord?
Why does Titania cross her Oberon? Give me your little
changeling boy to be my page."

"Set your heart at rest," answered the queen; "your
whole fairy kingdom buys not the boy of me." She then
left her lord in great anger. "Well, go your way," said
Oberon: "before the morning dawns I will torment you
for this injury."

Oberon then sent for Puck, his chief favourite and privy
counsellor. .

"Come hither, Puck," said Oberon to this little merry
wanderer of the night; "fetch me the flower which maids

call *Love in Idleness*; the juice of that little purple flower laid on the eyelids of those who sleep, will make them, when they awake, dote on the first thing they see. Some of the juice of that flower I will drop on the eyelids of my Titania when she is asleep; and the first thing she looks upon when she opens her eyes she will fall in love with, even though it be a lion or a bear, a meddling monkey, or a busy ape; and before I will take this charm from off her sight, which I can do with another charm I know of, I will make her give me that boy to be my page."

Puck, who loved mischief to his heart, was highly diverted with this intended frolic of his master, and ran to seek the flower; and while Oberon was waiting the return of Puck, he observed Demetrius and Helena enter the wood: he overheard Demetrius reproaching Helena for following him, and after many unkind words on his part, and gentle expostulations from Helena, reminding him of his former love and professions of true faith to her, he left her (as he said) to the mercy of the wild beasts, and she ran after him as swiftly as she could.

The fairy king, who was always friendly to true lovers, felt great compassion for Helena; and perhaps, as Lysander said they used to walk by moonlight in this pleasant wood, Oberon might have seen Helena in those happy times when she was beloved by Demetrius.

Tales from Shakespeare

OBERON. Fare thee well, nymph: ere he do leave this grove,
Thou shalt fly him, and he shall seek thy love.
Re-enter PUCK.
Hast thou the flower there? Welcome, wanderer.
PUCK. Ay, there it is.
OBERON.   I pray thee, give it me.
I know a bank where the wild thyme blows,
Where oxlips and the nodding violet grows,

Quite over-canopied with luscious woodbine,
With sweet musk-roses, and with eglantine:
There sleeps Titania sometime of the night,
Lull'd in these flowers with dances and delight;
And there the snake throws her enamell'd skin,
Weed wide enough to wrap a fairy in;
And with the juice of this I'll streak her eyes,
And make her full of hateful fantasies.
Take thou some of it, and seek through this grove:
A sweet Athenian lady is in love
With a disdainful youth: anoint his eyes;
But do it when the next thing he espies
May be the lady. Thou shalt know the man
By the Athenian garments he hath on.
Effect it with some care, that he may prove
More fond on her than she upon her love:
And look thou meet me ere the first cock crow.

    PUCK. Fear not, my lord, your servant shall do so.

                             [*Exeunt.*

      SCENE: *Another part of the wood.*
       Enter TITANIA, *with her train.*

    TITANIA. Come, now a roundel and a fairy song;
Then, for the third part of a minute, hence;
Some to kill cankers in the musk-rose buds,
Some war with rere-mice for their leathern wings,
To make my small elves coats, and some keep back
The clamorous owl, that nightly hoots and wonders
At our quaint spirits. Sing me now asleep;
Then to your offices, and let me rest.

             FAIRIES *sing.*

FIRST FAIRY.

      You spotted snakes with double tongue,
        Thorny hedgehogs, be not seen;
      Newts and blind-worms, do no wrong,
        Come not near our fairy queen.

CHORUS.

> Philomel, with melody;
> Sing in our sweet lullaby;
> Lulla, lulla, lullaby; lulla, lulla, lullaby:
> > Never harm,
> > Nor spell nor charm,
> Come our lovely lady nigh;
> So, good night. with lullaby.

SECOND FAIRY.

> Weaving spiders, come not here;
> > Hence, you long-legg'd spinners, hence!
> Beetles black, approach not near;
> > Worm nor snail, do no offence.

CHORUS.

> Philomel, with melody
> Sing in our sweet lullaby;
> Lulla, lulla, lullaby; lulla, lulla, lullaby:
> > Never harm,
> > Nor spell nor charm,
> Come our lovely lady nigh;
> So, good night, with lullaby.

FIRST FAIRY.

> Hence, away! now all is well:
> One aloof stand sentinel.

> > > > [*Exeunt* FAIRIES. TITANIA *sleeps.*

Enter OBERON, *and squeezes the flower* on TITANIA'S
eyelids.

OBERON.

> What thou seest when thou dost wake,
> Do it for thy true-love take;
> Love and languish for his sake:
> Be it ounce, or cat, or bear,
> Pard, or boar with bristl'd hair,
> In thy eye that shall appear
> When thou wak'st, it is thy dear:
> Wake when some vile thing is near.　　　　[*Exit.*

Enter QUINCE, SNUG, BOTTOM, FLUTE, SNOUT, *and*
STARVELING.

BOTTOM. Are we all met?

QUINCE. Pat, pat; and here's a marvellous convenient place for our rehearsal. This green plot shall be our stage, this hawthorn-brake our tiring-house; and we will do it in action as we will do it before the duke.

BOTTOM. Peter Quince,——

QUINCE. What sayest thou, bully Bottom?

BOTTOM. There are things in this comedy of Pyramus and Thisby that will never please. First, Pyramus must draw a sword to kill himself; which the ladies cannot abide. How answer you that?

SNOUT. By'r lakin, a parlous fear.

STARVELING. I believe we must leave the killing out, when all is done.

BOTTOM. Not a whit: I have a device to make all well. Write me a prologue; and let the prologue seem to say, we will do no harm with our swords, and that Pyramus is not kill'd indeed; and, for the more better assurance, tell them that I Pyramus am not Pyramus, but Bottom the weaver: this will put them out of fear.

QUINCE. Well, we will have such a prologue; and it shall be written in eight and six.

BOTTOM. No, make it two more; let it be written in eight and eight.

SNOUT. Will not the ladies be afeard of the lion?

STARVELING. I fear it, I promise you.

BOTTOM. Masters, you ought to consider with yourselves: to bring in—God shield us!—a lion among ladies, is a most dreadful thing; for there is not a more fearful wild-fowl than your lion living; and we ought to look to 't.

SNOUT. Therefore another prologue must tell he is not a lion.

BOTTOM. Nay, you must name his name, and half his face must be seen through the lion's neck; and he himself

must speak through, saying thus, or to the same defect,—
'Ladies,'—or, 'Fair ladies, I would wish you,'—or 'I
would request you,'—or, 'I would entreat you,—not to
fear, not to tremble: my life for yours. If you think I
come hither as a lion, it were pity of my life: no, I am no
such thing; I am a man as other men are'; and there,
indeed, let him name his name, and tell them plainly he
is Snug the joiner.

QUINCE. Well, it shall be so. But there is two hard
things; that is, to bring the moonlight into a chamber;
for, you know, Pyramus and Thisby meet by moonlight.

SNOUT. Doth the moon shine that night we play our
play?

BOTTOM. A calendar, a calendar! look in the almanac;
find out moonshine, find out moonshine.

QUINCE. Yes, it doth shine that night.

BOTTOM. Why, then may you leave a casement of the
great chamber-window, where we play, open, and the
moon may shine in at the casement.

QUINCE. Ay; or else one must come in with a bush of
thorns and a lantern, and say he comes to disfigure, or to
present, the person of Moonshine. Then, there is another
thing: we must have a wall in the great chamber; for
Pyramus and Thisby, says the story, did talk through the
chink of a wall.

SNOUT. You can never bring in a wall. What say you,
Bottom?

BOTTOM. Some man or other must present Wall: and
let him have some plaster, or some loam, or some rough-
cast about him, to signify wall; or let him hold his fingers
thus, and through that cranny shall Pyramus and Thisby
whisper.

QUINCE. If that may be, then all is well. Come, sit
down, every mother's son, and rehearse your parts.
Pyramus, you begin: when you have spoken your speech,
enter into that brake; and so every one according to his cue.

Enter PUCK *behind.*

PUCK. What hempen home-spuns have we swaggering here,
So near the cradle of the fairy queen?
What, a play toward! I'll be an auditor;
An actor too perhaps, if I see cause.

QUINCE. Speak, Pyramus. Thisby, stand forth.

BOTTOM. Thisby, the flowers of odious savours sweet,—

QUINCE. Odours, odours.

BOTTOM. —odours savours sweet:
So hath thy breath, my dearest Thisby dear.
But hark, a voice! stay thou but here awhile,
And by and by I will to thee appear.   [*Exit.*

PUCK. A stranger Pyramus than e'er play'd here. [*Exit.*

FLUTE. Must I speak now?

QUINCE. Ay, marry, must you; for you must understand he goes but to see a noise that he heard, and is to come again.

FLUTE. Most radiant Pyramus, most lily-white of hue,
Of colour like the red rose on triumphant brier,
Most brisky juvenal, and eke most lovely Jew,
As true as truest horse that yet would never tire,
I'll meet thee, Pyramus, at Ninny's tomb.

QUINCE. 'Ninus' tomb', man: why, you must not speak that yet; that you answer to Pyramus: you speak all your part at once, cues and all. Pyramus, enter: your cue is past; it is, 'never tire.'

FLUTE. O,—As true as truest horse, that yet would never tire.

Re-enter PUCK, *and* BOTTOM *with an ass's head.*

BOTTOM. If I were fair, Thisby, I were only thine.

QUINCE. O monstrous! O strange! we are haunted. Pray, masters! fly, masters! Help!

Exeunt QUINCE, SNUG, FLUTE, SNOUT, *and* STARVELING.

PUCK. I'll follow you, I'll lead you about a round,
Through bog, through bush, through brake, through brier:

Sometime a horse I'll be, sometime a hound,
  A hog, a headless bear, sometime a fire;
And neigh, and bark, and grunt, and roar, and burn,
Like horse, hound, hog, bear, fire, at every turn.   [*Exit.*

BOTTOM. Why do they run away? this is a knavery of
them to make me afeard.

Re-enter SNOUT.

SNOUT. O Bottom, thou art chang'd! what do I see
on thee?

BOTTOM. What do you see? you see an ass-head of your
own, do you?   [*Exit* SNOUT.

Re-enter QUINCE.

QUINCE. Bless thee, Bottom! bless thee! thou art
translated.   [*Exit.*

BOTTOM. I see their knavery: this is to make an ass of
me; to fright me, if they could. But I will not stir from
this place, do what they can: I will walk up and down
here, and I will sing, that they shall hear I am not afraid.
                                                [*Sings.*

The ousel-cock so black of hue,
  With orange-tawny bill,
The throstle with his note so true,
  The wren with little quill,—

TITANIA [*awaking*]. What angel wakes me from my
flowery bed?

BOTTOM [*sings*].

The finch, the sparrow, and the lărk,
  The plain-song cuckoo gray,
Whose note full many a man doth mark,
  And dares not answer nay;—

for, indeed, who would set his wit to so foolish a bird?
who would give a bird the lie, though he cry 'cuckoo'
never so?

TITANIA. I pray thee, gentle mortal, sing again:
Mine ear is much enamour'd of thy note;

So is mine eye enthralled to thy shape;
And thy fair virtue's force perforce doth move me,
On the first view, to say, to swear, I love thee.

BOTTOM. Methinks, mistress, you should have little
reason for that: and yet, to say the truth, reason and love
keep little company together now-a-days; the more the
pity that some honest neighbours will not make them
friends. Nay, I can gleek upon occasion.

TITANIA. Thou art as wise as thou art beautiful.

BOTTOM. Not so, neither; but if I had wit enough to get
out of this wood, I have enough to serve mine own turn.

TITANIA. Out of this wood do not desire to go;
Thou shalt remain here, whether thou wilt or no.
I am a spirit of no common rate:
The summer still doth tend upon my state;
And I do love thee: therefore, go with me;
I'll give thee fairies to attend on thee,
And they shall fetch thee jewels from the deep,
And sing while thou on pressed flowers dost sleep:
And I will purge thy mortal grossness so
That thou shalt like an airy spirit go.
Peaseblossom! Cobweb! Moth! and Mustardseed!

Enter PEASEBLOSSOM, COBWEB, MOTH, *and* MUSTARDSEED.

PEASEBLOSSOM. Ready.

COBWEB.   And I.

MOTH.   And I.

MUSTARDSEED.   And I.

ALL.   Where shall we go?

TITANIA. Be kind and courteous to this gentleman;
Hop in his walks, and gambol in his eyes;
Feed him with apricocks and dewberries,
With purple grapes, green figs, and mulberries;
The honey-bags steal from the humble-bees,
And for night-tapers crop their waxen thighs,
And light them at the fiery glow-worm's eyes,
To have my love to bed and to arise;

And pluck the wings from painted butterflies
To fan the moonbeams from his sleeping eyes:
Nod to him, elves, and do him courtesies.

PEASEBLOSSOM. Hail, mortal!

COBWEB. Hail!

MOTH. Hail!

MUSTARDSEED. Hail!

BOTTOM. I cry your worships mercy, heartily: I beseech your worship's name.

COBWEB. Cobweb.

BOTTOM. I shall desire you of more acquaintance, good Master Cobweb: if I cut my finger, I shall make bold with you. Your name, honest gentleman?

PEASEBLOSSOM. Peaseblossom.

BOTTOM. I pray you, commend me to Mistress Squash, your mother, and to Master Peascod, your father. Good Master Peaseblossom, I shall desire you of more acquaintance too. Your name, I beseech you, sir?

MUSTARDSEED. Mustardseed.

BOTTOM. Good Master Mustardseed, I know your patience well: that same cowardly, giant-like ox-beef hath devoured many a gentleman of your house. I promise you your kindred hath made my eyes water ere now. I desire your more acquaintance, good Master Mustardseed.

TITANIA. Come, wait upon him; lead him to my bower.
    The moon methinks looks with a watery eye;
And when she weeps, weeps every little flower,
    Lamenting some enforced chastity.
    Tie up my love's tongue, bring him silently. [*Exeunt.*

But to return to Hermia, who made her escape out of her father's house that night, to avoid the death she was doomed to for refusing to marry Demetrius. When she entered the wood, she found her dear Lysander waiting for her, to conduct her to his aunt's house; but before they had passed half through the wood, Hermia was so much fatigued, that Lysander, who was very careful of this dear lady, who had proved her affection for him even by hazarding her life for his sake, persuaded her to rest till morning on a bank of soft moss, and lying down himself on the ground at some little distance, they soon fell fast asleep. Here they were found by Puck, who, seeing a handsome young man asleep, and perceiving that his clothes were made in the Athenian fashion, and that a pretty lady was sleeping near him, concluded that this must be the Athenian maid and her disdainful lover whom Oberon had sent him to seek; and he naturally enough conjectured that, as they were alone together, she must be the first thing he would see when he awoke; so, without more ado, he proceeded to pour some of the juice of the little purple flower into his eyes. But it so fell out, that Helena came that way, and, instead of Hermia, was the first object Lysander beheld when he opened his eyes; and strange to relate, so powerful was the love-charm, all his love for Hermia vanished away, and Lysander fell in love with Helena.

Had he first seen Hermia when he awoke, the blunder Puck committed would have been of no consequence, for he could not love that faithful lady too well; but for poor Lysander to be forced by a fairy love-charm to forget his own true Hermia, and to run after another lady, and leave Hermia asleep quite alone in a wood at midnight, was a sad chance indeed.

Thus this misfortune happened. Helena, as has been before related, endeavoured to keep pace with Demetrius when he ran away so rudely from her; but she could not continue this unequal race long, men being always better runners in a long race than ladies. Helena soon lost sight of Demetrius; and as she was wandering about, dejected and forlorn, she arrived at the place where Lysander was sleeping. "Ah!" said she, "this is Lysander lying on the ground: is he dead or asleep?" Then, gently touching him, she said, "Good sir, if you are alive, awake." Upon this Lysander opened his eyes, and (the love-charm beginning to work) immediately addressed her in terms of extravagant love and admiration; telling her she as much excelled Hermia in beauty as a dove does a raven, and that he would run through fire for her sweet sake; and many more such lover-like speeches. Helena, knowing Lysander was her friend Hermia's lover, and that he was solemnly engaged to marry her, was in the utmost rage when she heard herself addressed in this manner; for she thought (as well she might) that Lysander was making a jest of her. "Oh!" said she, "why was I born to be mocked and scorned by every one? Is it not enough, is it not enough, young man, that I can never get a sweet look or a kind word from Demetrius; but you, sir, must pretend in this disdainful manner to court me? I thought, Lysander, you were a lord of more true gentleness." Saying these words in great anger, she ran away; and Lysander followed her, quite forgetful of his own Hermia, who was still asleep.

When Hermia awoke, she was in a sad fright at finding herself alone. She wandered about the wood, not knowing what was become of Lysander, or which way to go to seek for him. In the meantime Demetrius not being able to find Hermia and his rival Lysander, and fatigued with his fruitless search, was observed by Oberon fast asleep. Oberon had learnt by some questions he had asked of Puck, that he had applied the love-charm to the wrong person's eyes; and now having found the person first intended, he touched the eyelids of the sleeping Demetrius with the love-juice, and he instantly awoke; and the first thing he saw being Helena, he, as Lysander had done before, began to address love-speeches to her; and just at that moment Lysander, followed by Hermia (for through Puck's unlucky mistake it was now become Hermia's turn to run after her lover), made his appearance; and then Lysander and Demetrius, both speaking together, made love to Helena, they being each one under the influence of the same potent charm.

The astonished Helena thought that Demetrius, Lysander, and her once dear friend Hermia, were all in a plot together to make a jest of her.

Hermia was as much surprised as Helena: she knew not why Lysander and Demetrius, who both before loved her, were now become the lovers of Helena; and to Hermia the matter seemed to be no jest.

The ladies, who before had always been the dearest of friends, now fell to high words together.

"Unkind Hermia," said Helena, "it is you have set Lysander on to vex me with mock praises; and your other lover Demetrius, who used almost to spurn me with his foot, have you not bid him call me Goddess, Nymph, rare, precious, and celestial? He would not speak thus to me, whom he hates, if you did not set him on to make a jest of me. Unkind Hermia, to join with men in scorning your poor friend. Have you forgot our school-day friendship? How often, Hermia, have we two, sitting on one cushion, both singing one song, with our needles working the same flower, both on the same sampler wrought; growing up together in fashion of a double cherry, scarcely seeming parted? Hermia, it is not friendly in you, it is not maidenly to join with men in scorning your poor friend."

"I am amazed at your passionate words," said Hermia: "I scorn you not; it seems you scorn me." "Ay, do," returned Helena, "persevere; counterfeit serious looks, and make mouths at me when I turn my back; then wink at each other, and hold the sweet jest up. If you had any pity, grace, or manners, you would not use me thus."

While Helena and Hermia were speaking these angry words to each other, Demetrius and Lysander left them, to fight together in the wood for the love of Helena.

When they found the gentlemen had left them, they

departed, and once more wandered weary in the wood in search of their lovers.

As soon as they were gone, the fairy king, who with little Puck had been listening to their quarrels, said to him, "This is your negligence, Puck; or did you do this wilfully?"

Tales from Shakespeare

SCENE: *The wood.*

OBERON. This is thy negligence: still thou mistak'st,
Or else committ'st thy knaveries wilfully.

PUCK. Believe me, king of shadows, I mistook.
Did you not tell me I should know the man
By the Athenian garments he had on?
And so far blameless proves my enterprise,
That I have 'nointed an Athenian's eyes;
And so far am I glad it so did sort,
As this their jangling I esteem a sport.

OBERON. Thou see'st these lovers seek a place to fight:
Hie therefore, Robin, overcast the night;
The starry welkin cover thou anon
With drooping fog as black as Acheron;
And lead these testy rivals so astray
As one come not within another's way.
Like to Lysander sometime frame thy tongue,
Then stir Demetrius up with bitter wrong;
And sometime rail thou like Demetrius;
And from each other look thou lead them thus,
Till o'er their brows death-counterfeiting sleep
With leaden legs and batty wings doth creep:
Then crush this herb into Lysander's eye;
Whose liquor hath this virtuous property,
To take from thence all error with his might,
And make his eyeballs roll with wonted sight.
When they next wake, all this derision
Shall seem a dream and fruitless vision;

And back to Athens shall the lovers wend,
With league whose date till death shall never end.
Whiles I in this affair do thee employ,
I'll to my queen and beg her Indian boy;
And then I will her charmed eye release
From monster's view, and all things shall be peace.

PUCK. My fairy lord, this must be done with haste,
For night's swift dragons cut the clouds full fast,
And yonder shines Aurora's harbinger;
At whose approach, ghosts, wandering here and there,
Troop home to churchyards: damned spirits all,
That in crossways and floods have burial,
Already to their wormy beds are gone;
For fear lest day should look their shames upon,
They wilfully themselves exile from light,
And must for aye consort with black-brow'd night.

OBERON. But we are spirits of another sort.
I with the morning's love have oft made sport;
And, like a forester, the groves may tread,
Even till the eastern gate, all fiery-red,
Opening on Neptune with fair-blessed beams,
Turns into yellow gold his salt-green streams.
But, notwithstanding, haste; make no delay:
We may effect this business yet ere day.   [*Exit.*

PUCK. Up and down, up and down,
    I will lead them up and down:
    I am fear'd in field and town:
    Goblin, lead them up and down.
Here comes one.

Re-enter LYSANDER.

LYSANDER. Where art thou, proud Demetrius? speak
thou now.

PUCK. Here, villain; drawn and ready. Where art thou?

LYSANDER. I will be with thee straight.

PUCK.   Follow me, then,
To plainer ground.   [*Exit* LYSANDER, *as following the voice.*

Re-enter DEMETRIUS.

DEMETRIUS. Lysander! speak again:
Thou runaway, thou coward, art thou fled?
Speak! in some bush? where dost thou hide thy head?
  PUCK. Thou coward, art thou bragging to the stars,
Telling the bushes that thou look'st for wars,
And wilt not come? Come, recreant; come, thou
    child;
I'll whip thee with a rod: he is defil'd
That draws a sword on thee.
  DEMETRIUS.   Yea, art thou there?
  PUCK. Follow my voice; we'll try no manhood here.
                                                    [*Exeunt.*
              Re-enter LYSANDER.

LYSANDER. He goes before me and still dares me on;
When I come where he calls, then he is gone.
The villain is much lighter-heel'd than I:
I follow'd fast, but faster he did fly;
That fallen am I in dark uneven way,
And here will rest me. [*Lies down.*] Come, thou gentle
    day!
For, if but once thou show me thy grey light,
I'll find Demetrius and revenge this spite.   [*Sleeps.*
            Re-enter PUCK *and* DEMETRIUS.

  PUCK. Ho, ho, ho! Coward, why comest thou not?
  DEMETRIUS. Abide me, if thou dar'st; for well I wot
Thou runn'st before me, shifting every place,
And dar'st not stand, nor look me in the face.
Where art thou now?
  PUCK.   Come hither: I am here.
  DEMETRIUS. Nay, then thou mock'st me. Thou shalt buy
    this dear,
If ever I thy face by daylight see;
Now, go thy way. Faintness constraineth me
To measure out my length on this cold bed.
By day's approach look to be visited. [*Lies down and sleeps.*

Re-enter HELENA.

HELENA. O weary night, O long and tedious night,
  Abate thy hours! Shine comforts from the east,
That I may back to Athens by daylight,
  From these that my poor company detest:
And sleep, that sometimes shuts up sorrow's eye,
Steal me awhile from mine own company.

[Lies down and sleeps.

PUCK.   Yet but three? Come one more;
  Two of both kinds makes up four.
  Here she comes, curst and sad:
  Cupid is a knavish lad,
  Thus to make poor females mad.

Re-enter HERMIA.

HERMIA. Never so weary, never so in woe,
  Bedabbled with the dew, and torn with briers,
I can no further crawl, no further go;
  My legs can keep no pace with my desires.
Here will I rest me till the break of day.
Heavens shield Lysander, if they mean a fray!

[Lies down and sleeps.

PUCK.   On the ground
  Sleep sound:
  I'll apply
  To your eye,
Gentle lover, remedy.

[Squeezing the juice on LYSANDER's *eyes.*

  When thou wak'st,
  Thou tak'st
  True delight
  In the sight
Of thy former lady's eye:
And the country proverb known,
That every man should take his own,
In your waking shall be shown:
  Jack shall have Jill;

Nought shall go ill;
The man shall have his mare again, and all shall be well.

[*Exit.*

SCENE: *The same.* LYSANDER, DEMETRIUS, HELENA,
and HERMIA, *lying asleep.*

Enter TITANIA *and* BOTTOM; PEASEBLOSSOM, COBWEB, MOTH,
MUSTARDSEED, *and other* FAIRIES *attending;* OBERON *behind
unseen.*

TITANIA. Come, sit thee down upon this flowery bed,
While I thy amiable cheeks do coy,
And stick musk-roses in thy sleek smooth head,
And kiss thy fair large ears, my gentle joy.

BOTTOM. Where's Peaseblossom?

PEASEBLOSSOM. Ready.

BOTTOM. Scratch my head, Peaseblossom. Where's
Mounsieur Cobweb?

COBWEB. Ready.

BOTTOM. Mounsieur Cobweb, good mounsieur, get you
your weapons in your hand, and kill me a red-hipp'd
humble-bee on the top of a thistle; and, good mounsieur,
bring me the honey-bag. Do not fret yourself too much in
the action, mounsieur; and, good mounsieur, have a care
the honey-bag break not; I would be loth to have you
overflown with a honey-bag, signior. Where's Mounsieur
Mustardseed?

MUSTARDSEED. Ready.

BOTTOM. Give me your neaf, Mounsieur Mustardseed.
Pray you, leave your courtesy, good mounsieur.

MUSTARDSEED. What's your will?

BOTTOM. Nothing, good mounsieur, but to help Cavalery
Cobweb to scratch. I must to the barber's, mounsieur;
for methinks I am marvellous hairy about the face; and
I am such a tender ass, if my hair do but tickle me, I must
scratch.

TITANIA. What, wilt thou hear some music, my sweet
love?

BOTTOM. I have a reasonable good ear in music. Let's have the tongs and the bones.

TITANIA. Or say, sweet love, what thou desirest to eat.

BOTTOM. Truly, a peck of provender: I could munch your good dry oats. Methinks I have a great desire to a bottle of hay: good hay, sweet hay, hath no fellow.

TITANIA I have a venturous fairy that shall seek
The squirrel's hoard, and fetch thee new nuts.

BOTTOM. I had rather have a handful or two of dried peas. But, I pray you, let none of your people stir me: I have an exposition of sleep come upon me.

TITANIA. Sleep thou, and I will wind thee in my arms. Fairies, be gone, and be all ways away.   [*Exeunt* FAIRIES.
So doth the woodbine the sweet honeysuckle
Gently entwist; the female ivy so
Enrings the barky fingers of the elm.
O, how I love thee! how I dote on thee!   [*They sleep*.

Enter PUCK.

OBERON [*advancing*]. Welcome, good Robin. See'st thou
    this sweet sight?
Her dotage now I do begin to pity:
For, meeting her of late behind the wood,
Seeking sweet favours for this hateful fool,
I did upbraid her, and fall out with her;
For she his hairy temples then had rounded
With coronet of fresh and fragrant flowers;
And that same dew, which sometime on the buds
Was wont to swell like round and orient pearls,
Stood now within the pretty flowerets' eyes
Like tears that did their own disgrace bewail.
When I had at my pleasure taunted her
And she in mild terms begg'd my patience,
I then did ask of her her changeling child;
Which straight she gave me, and her fairy sent

To bear him to my bower in fairy-land.
And now I have the boy, I will undo
This hateful imperfection of her eyes:
And, gentle Puck, take this transformed scalp
From off the head of this Athenian swain;
That he, awaking when the other do,
May all to Athens back again repair,
And think no more of this night's accidents
But as the fierce vexation of a dream.
But first I will release the fairy queen.

        Be as thou wast wont to be;
        See as thou wast wont to see:
        Dian's bud o'er Cupid's flower
        Hath such force and blessed power.

Now, my Titania; wake you, my sweet queen.

TITANIA. My Oberon! what visions have I seen!
Methought I was enamour'd of an ass.

OBERON. There lies your love.

TITANIA.   How came these things to pass?
O, how mine eyes do loathe his visage now!

OBERON. Silence awhile. Robin, take off this head.
Titania, music call; and strike more dead
Than common sleep of all these five the sense.

TITANIA. Music, ho! music, such as charmeth sleep!

                         [*Music, still.*

PUCK. Now, when thou wak'st, with thine own fool's
    eyes peep.

OBERON. Sound, music! Come, my queen, take hands
    with me,
And rock the ground whereon these sleepers be.
Now thou and I are new in amity
And will to-morrow midnight solemnly
Dance in Duke Theseus' house triumphantly,
And bless it to all fair posterity:
There shall the pairs of faithful lovers be
Wedded, with Theseus, all in jollity.

PUCK.   Fairy king, attend, and mark;
           I do hear the morning lark.
OBERON.   Then, my queen, in silence sad,
           Trip we after the night's shade;
           We the globe can compass soon,
           Swifter than the wandering moon.
TITANIA.   Come, my lord; and in our flight
           Tell me how it came this night
           That I sleeping here was found
           With these mortals on the ground.   [*Exeunt.*
                                    [*Horns winded within.*

    Enter THESEUS, HIPPOLYTA, EGEUS, *and train.*

  THESEUS. Go, one of you, find out the forester;
For now our observation is perform'd;
And since we have the vaward of the day,
My love shall hear the music of my hounds.
Uncouple in the western valley; let them go:
Dispatch, I say, and find the forester. [*Exit an* ATTENDANT.
We will, fair queen, up to the mountain's top,
And mark the musical confusion
Of hounds and echo in conjunction.

  HIPPOLYTA. I was with Hercules and Cadmus once,
When in a wood of Crete they bay'd the bear
With hounds of Sparta: never did I hear
Such gallant chiding; for, besides the groves,
The skies, the fountains, every region near
Seem'd all one mutual cry. I never heard
So musical a discord, such sweet thunder.

  THESEUS. My hounds are bred out of the Spartan kind,
So flew'd, so sanded; and their heads are hung
With ears that sweep away the morning dew;
Crook-knee'd, and dew-lapp'd like Thessalian bulls;
Slow in pursuit, but match'd in mouth like bells,
Each under each. A cry more tuneable
Was never holla'd to, nor cheer'd with horn,
In Crete, in Sparta, nor in Thessaly:

Judge when you hear. But, soft! what nymphs are these?

EGEUS. My lord, this is my daughter here asleep;
And this, Lysander; this Demetrius is;
This Helena, old Nedar's Helena:
I wonder of their being here together.

THESEUS. No doubt they rose up early to observe
The rite of May, and, hearing our intent,
Came here in grace of our solemnity.
But speak, Egeus; is not this the day
That Hermia should give answer of her choice?

EGEUS. It is, my lord.

THESEUS. Go, bid the huntsmen wake them with their
  horns. [*Horns and shouts within.* LYSANDER, DEMETRIUS,
        HELENA, *and* HERMIA *wake and start up.*
Good morrow, friends. Saint Valentine is past;
Begin these wood-birds but to couple now?

LYSANDER. Pardon, my lord.

THESEUS. I pray you all, stand up.
I know you two are rival enemies:
How comes this gentle concord in the world,
That hatred is so far from jealousy,
To sleep by hate, and fear no enmity?

LYSANDER. My lord, I shall reply amazedly,
Half sleep, half waking: but as yet, I swear,
I cannot truly say how I came here;
But, as I think,—for truly would I speak,
And now I do bethink me, so it is—
I came with Hermia hither: our intent
Was to be gone from Athens, where we might,
Without the peril of the Athenian law——

EGEUS. Enough, enough, my lord; you have enough:
I beg the law, the law, upon his head.
They would have stol'n away; they would, Demetrius,
Thereby to have defeated you and me,
You of your wife, and me of my consent,
Of my consent that she should be your wife.

DEMETRIUS. My lord, fair Helen told me of their stealth,
Of this their purpose hither to this wood;
And I in fury hither follow'd them,
Fair Helena in fancy following me.
But, my good lord, I wot not by what power—
But by some power it is,—my love to Hermia,
Melted as the snow, seems to me now
As the remembrance of an idle gaud,
Which in my childhood I did dote upon;
And all the faith, the virtue of my heart,
The object, and the pleasure of mine eye,
Is only Helena. To her, my lord,
Was I betroth'd ere I saw Hermia:
But, like in sickness, did I loathe this food;
But, as in health, come to my natural taste,
Now do I wish it, love it, long for it,
And will for evermore be true to it.

THESEUS. Fair lovers, you are fortunately met:
Of this discourse we more will hear anon.
Egeus, I will overbear your will;
For in the temple, by and by, with us,
These couples shall eternally be knit:
And, for the morning now is something worn,
Our purposed hunting shall be set aside.
Away with us to Athens; three and three,
We'll hold a feast in great solemnity.
Come, Hippolyta.

[*Exeunt* THESEUS, HIPPOLYTA, EGEUS, *and train.*
DEMETRIUS. These things seem small and undistinguish-
able,
Like far-off mountains turned into clouds.

HERMIA. Methinks I see these things with parted eye,
When every thing seems double.

HELENA. So methinks:
And I have found Demetrius like a jewel,
Mine own, and not mine own.

DEMETRIUS.   Are you sure
That we are awake? It seems to me
That yet we sleep, we dream. Do not you think
The duke was here, and bid us follow him?

HERMIA. Yea; and my father.

HELENA.   And Hippolyta.

LYSANDER. And he did bid us follow to the temple.

DEMETRIUS. Why, then we are awake. Let's follow him;
And by the way let us recount our dreams.   [*Exeunt.*

BOTTOM [*awaking*]. When my cue comes, call me, and
I will answer: my next is, 'Most fair Pyramus.' Heigh-ho!
Peter Quince! Flute, the bellows-mender! Snout, the
tinker! Starveling! God's my life, stolen hence, and left
me asleep! I have had a most rare vision. I have had a
dream, past the wit of man to say what dream it was:
man is but an ass, if he go about to expound this dream.
Methought I was—there is no man can tell what. Methought I was, and methought I had, but man is but a
patch'd fool, if he will offer to say what methought I had.
The eye of man hath not heard, the ear of man hath not
seen, man's hand is not able to taste, his tongue to conceive,
nor his heart to report, what my dream was. I will get
Peter Quince to write a ballad of this dream: it shall be
called Bottom's Dream, because it hath no bottom; and
I will sing it in the latter end of a play, before the duke:
peradventure, to make it the more gracious, I shall sing
it at her death.   [*Exit.*

While these events were taking place in the wood,
there was much concern at Athens among Bottom's
companions because he had not returned home.
Great was the joy of the actors when he arrived with
the news that they were to prepare to present their
play before Theseus.

SCENE: *Athens.* QUINCE's *house.*

Enter QUINCE, FLUTE, SNOUT, *and* STARVELING.

QUINCE. Have you sent to Bottom's house? is he come home yet?

STARVELING. He cannot be heard of. Out of doubt he is transported.

FLUTE. If he come not, then the play is marr'd: it goes not forward, doth it?

QUINCE. It is not possible: you have not a man in all Athens able to discharge Pyramus but he.

FLUTE. No, he hath simply the best wit of any handicraft man in Athens.

QUINCE. Yea, and the best person too; and he is a very paramour for a sweet voice.

FLUTE. You must say 'paragon': a paramour is, God bless us, a thing of naught.

Enter SNUG.

SNUG. Masters, the duke is coming from the temple, and there is two or three lords and ladies more married: if our sport had gone forward, we had all been made men.

FLUTE. O sweet bully Bottom! Thus hath he lost sixpence a day during his life; he could not have 'scaped sixpence a day: and the duke had not given him sixpence a day for playing Pyramus, I'll be hang'd; he would have deserv'd it: sixpence a day in Pyramus, or nothing.

Enter BOTTOM.

BOTTOM. Where are these lads? where are these hearts?

QUINCE. Bottom! O most courageous day! O most happy hour!

BOTTOM. Masters, I am to discourse wonders: but ask me not what; for if I tell you, I am no true Athenian. I will tell you every thing, right as it fell out.

QUINCE. Let us hear, sweet Bottom.

BOTTOM. Not a word of me. All that I will tell you is, that the duke hath din'd. Get your apparel together, good strings to your beards, new ribbons to your pumps; meet presently at the palace; every man look o'er his part; for the short and the long is, our play is preferr'd. In any case, let Thisby have clean linen; and let not him that plays the lion pare his nails, for they shall hang out for the lion's claws. And, most dear actors, eat no onions nor garlic, for we are to utter sweet breath; and I do not doubt but to hear them say, it is a sweet comedy. No more words: away! go, away!

[*Exeunt.*

After Theseus had been married to Hippolyta, he asked Philostrate, his master of the revels, what entertainments had been prepared to celebrate the occasion. From the list Philostrate presented to him he chose

A tedious brief scene of young Pyramus
And his love Thisbe; very tragical mirth.

But he was somewhat puzzled by this description, and asked Philostrate about the play.

SCENE: *Athens. The palace of* THESEUS.

THESEUS. Merry and tragical! tedious and brief!
That is, hot ice and wondrous strange snow.
How shall we find the concord of this discord?

PHILOSTRATE. A play there is, my lord, some ten words long,
Which is as brief as I have known a play;
But by ten words, my lord, it is too long,
Which makes it tedious; for in all the play
There is not one word apt, one player fitted.
And tragical, my noble lord, it is;
For Pyramus therein doth kill himself.
Which, when I saw rehears'd, I must confess,
Made mine eyes water; but more merry tears
The passion of loud laughter never shed.

THESEUS. What are they that do play it?

PHILOSTRATE. Hard-handed men that work in Athens
  here,
Which never labour'd in their minds till now,
And now have toil'd their unbreath'd memories
With this same play, against your nuptial.
    THESEUS. And we will hear it.
    PHILOSTRATE.   No, my noble lord;
It is not for you: I have heard it over,
And it is nothing, nothing in the world;
Unless you can find sport in their intents,
Extremely stretch'd and conn'd with cruel pain,
To do you service.
    THESEUS.   I will hear that play;
For never anything can be amiss,
When simpleness and duty tender it.
Go, bring them in: and take your places, ladies.
                        [*Exit* PHILOSTRATE.
    HIPPOLYTA. I love not to see wretchedness o'ercharged
And duty in his service perishing.
    THESEUS. Why, gentle sweet, you shall see no such thing.
    HIPPOLYTA. He says they can do nothing in this kind.
    THESEUS. The kinder we, to give them thanks for nothing.
Our sport shall be to take what they mistake:
And what poor duty cannot do, noble respect
Takes it in might, not merit.
Where I have come, great clerks have purposed
To greet me with premeditated welcomes;
Where I have seen them shiver and look pale,
Make periods in the midst of sentences,
Throttle their practis'd accent in their fears,
And in conclusion dumbly have broke off,
Not paying me a welcome. Trust me, sweet,
Out of this silence yet I pick'd a welcome;
And in the modesty of fearful duty
I read as much as from the rattling tongue
Of saucy and audacious eloquence.

Love, therefore, and tongue-tied simplicity,
In least speak most, to my capacity.

Re-enter PHILOSTRATE.

PHILOSTRATE.   So please your grace, the Prologue is
address'd.

THESEUS.   Let him approach.   [*Flourish of trumpets.*
Enter QUINCE, *for the Prologue.*

PROLOGUE.   If we offend, it is with our good will.
That you should think, we come not to offend,
But with good will.   To show our simple skill,
That is the true beginning of our end.
Consider then we come but in despite.
We do not come as minding to content you,
Our true intent is.   All for your delight,
We are not here.   That you should here repent you,
The actors are at hand;   and, by their show,
You shall know all that you are like to know.

THESEUS.   This fellow doth not stand upon points.

LYSANDER.   He hath rid his prologue like a rough colt;
he knows not the stop.   A good moral, my lord: it is not
enough to speak, but to speak true.

HIPPOLYTA.   Indeed he hath play'd on his prologue like
a child on a recorder;   a sound, but not in government.

THESEUS.   His speech was like a tangled chain;   nothing
impaired, but all disordered.   Who is next?

Enter with a trumpet before them PYRAMUS *and* THISBE,
WALL, MOONSHINE, *and* LION.

PROLOGUE.   Gentles, perchance you wonder at this show;
But wonder on, till truth make all things plain.
This man is Pyramus, if you would know;
This beauteous lady Thisby is certain.
This man, with lime and rough-cast, doth present
Wall, that vile Wall which did these lovers sunder;

And through Wall's chink, pour souls, they are content
   To whisper. At the which let no man wonder.
This man, with lantern, dog, and bush of thorn,
   Presenteth Moonshine; for, if you will know,
By moonshine did these lovers think no scorn
   To meet at Ninus' tomb, there, there to woo.
This grisly beast, which Lion hight by name,
The trusty Thisby, coming first by night,
Did scare away, or rather did affright;
And, as she fled, her mantle she did fall,
   Which Lion vile with bloody mouth did stain.
Anon comes Pyramus, sweet youth and tall,
   And finds his trusty Thisby's mantle slain:
Whereat, with blade, with bloody blameful blade.
   He bravely broach'd his boiling bloody breast;
And Thisby, tarrying in mulberry shade,
   His dagger drew, and died. For all the rest,
Let Lion, Moonshine, Wall, and lovers twain
At large discourse, while here they do remain.

> [*Exeunt* PROLOGUE, PYRAMUS, THISBE, LION, *and*
> MOONSHINE.

THESEUS. I wonder if the lion be to speak.

DEMETRIUS. No wonder, my lord: one lion may, when
   many asses do.

WALL. In this same interlude it doth befall
That I, one Snout by name, present a wall;
And such a wall, as I would have you think,
That had in it a crannied hole or chink,
Through which the lovers, Pyramus and Thisby,
Did whisper often very secretly.
This loam, this rough-cast, and this stone, doth show
That I am that same wall; the truth is so:
And this the cranny is, right and sinister,
Through which the fearful lovers are to whisper.

THESEUS. Would you desire lime and hair to speak better?

DEMETRIUS. It is the wittiest partition that ever I heard discourse, my lord.

THESEUS. Pyramus draws near the wall: silence!

Re-enter PYRAMUS.

PYRAMUS. O grim-look'd night! O night with hue so
     black!
   O night, which ever art when day is not!
O night, O night! alack, alack, alack,
   I fear my Thisby's promise is forgot!
And thou, O wall, O sweet, O lovely wall,
   That stand'st between her father's ground and mine!
Thou wall, O wall, O sweet and lovely wall,
   Show me thy chink, to blink through with mine eyne!
                         [WALL *holds up his fingers.*
Thanks, courteous wall: Jove shield thee well for this!
   But what see I? No Thisby do I see.
O wicked wall, through whom I see no bliss!
   Curs'd be thy stones for thus deceiving me!

THESEUS. The wall, methinks, being sensible, should curse again.

PYRAMUS. No, in truth, sir, he should not. 'Deceiving me' is Thisby's cue: she is to enter now, and I am to spy her through the wall. You shall see, it will fall pat as I told you. Yonder she comes.

Re-enter THISBE.

THISBE. O wall, full often hast thou heard my moans,
   For parting my fair Pyramus and me!
My cherry lips have often kiss'd thy stones,
   Thy stones with lime and hair knit up in thee.

PYRAMUS. I see a voice: now will I to the chink,
   To spy an I can hear my Thisby's face.
Thisby!

THISBE. My love thou art, my love I think.

PYRAMUS. Think what thou wilt, I am thy lover's grace;
And, like Limander, am I trusty still.

THISBE. And I like Helen, till the Fates me kill.

PYRAMUS. Not Shafalus to Procrus was so true.

THISBE. As Shafalus to Procrus, I to you.

PYRAMUS. O, kiss me through the hole of this vile wall!

THISBE. I kiss the wall's hole, not your lips at all.

PYRAMUS. Wilt thou at Ninny's tomb meet me straight-way?

THISBE. 'Tide life, 'tide death, I come without delay.

[*Exeunt* PYRAMUS *and* THISBE.

WALL. Thus have I, Wall, my part discharged so;
And, being done, thus Wall away doth go.   [*Exit.*

THESEUS. Now is the mural down between the two neighbours.

DEMETRIUS. No remedy, my lord, when walls are so wilful to hear without warning.

HIPPOLYTA. This is the silliest stuff that e'er I heard.

THESEUS. The best in this kind are but shadows; and the worst are no worse, if imagination amend them.

HIPPOLYTA. It must be your imagination then, and not theirs.

THESEUS. If we imagine no worse of them than they of themselves, they may pass for excellent men. Here come two noble beasts in, a man and a lion.

Re-enter LION *and* MOONSHINE.

LION. You, ladies, you, whose gentle hearts do fear
   The smallest monstrous mouse that creeps on floor,
May now perchance both quake and tremble here,
   When lion rough in wildest rage doth roar.
Then know that I, one Snug the joiner, am
A lion fell, nor else no lion's dam;
For, if I should as lion come in strife
Into this place, 't were pity on my life.

THESEUS. A very gentle beast, and of a good conscience.

DEMETRIUS. The very best at a beast, my lord, that e'er I saw.

LYSANDER. This lion is a very fox for his valour.

THESEUS. True; and a goose for his discretion.

DEMETRIUS. Not so, my lord; for his valour cannot carry his discretion; and the fox carries the goose.

THESEUS. His discretion, I am sure, cannot carry his valour; for the goose carries not the fox. It is well: leave it to his discretion, and let us listen to the moon.

MOON. This lanthorn doth the horned moon present;
Myself the man i' the moon do seem to be.

THESEUS. This is the greatest error of all the rest: the man should be put into the lanthorn. How is it else the man i' the moon?

DEMETRIUS. He dares not come there for the candle; for, you see, it is already in snuff.

HIPPOLYTA. I am aweary of this moon: would he would change!

THESEUS. It appears, by his small light of discretion, that he is in the wane; but yet, in courtesy, in all reason, we must stay the time.

LYSANDER. Proceed, Moon.

MOON. All that I have to say, is, to tell you that the lanthorn is the moon; I, the man i' the moon; this thorn-bush, my thorn-bush; and this dog, my dog.

DEMETRIUS. Why, all these should be in the lanthorn; for all these are in the moon. But, silence! here comes Thisbe.

Re-enter THISBE.

THISBE. This is old Ninny's tomb. Where is my love?

LION [*roaring*]. Oh——   [THISBE *runs off*.

DEMETRIUS. Well roar'd, Lion.

THESEUS. Well run, Thisbe.

HIPPOLYTA. Well shone, Moon. Truly, the moon shines with a good grace.

[*The* LION *shakes* THISBE's *mantle, and exit.*

THESEUS. Well mous'd, Lion.

LYSANDER. And so the lion vanish'd.

DEMETRIUS. And then came Pyramus.

Re-enter PYRAMUS.

PYRAMUS. Sweet Moon, I thank thee for thy sunny beams,
   I thank thee, Moon, for shining now so bright;
For, by thy gracious, golden, glittering gleams,
   I trust to take of truest Thisby sight.
         But stay, O spite!
         But mark, poor knight,
   What dreadful dole is here!
         Eyes, do you see?
         How can it be?
   O dainty duck! O dear!
         Thy mantle good,
         What, stain'd with blood!
   Approach, ye Furies fell!
         O Fates, come, come,
         Cut thread and thrum;
   Quail, crush, conclude, and quell!

THESEUS. This passion, and the death of a dear friend,
would go near to make a man look sad.

HIPPOLYTA. Beshrew my heart, but I pity the man.

PYRAMUS. O wherefore, Nature, didst thou lions frame?
   Since lion vile hath here deflower'd my dear:
Which is—no, no—which was the fairest dame
   That liv'd, that lov'd, that lik'd, that look'd with cheer.
         Come, tears, confound;
         Out, sword, and wound
   The pap of Pyramus;
         Ay, that left pap,
         Where heart doth hop: [*Stabs himself.*
   Thus die I, thus, thus, thus.
         Now am I dead,
         Now am I fled;

My soul is in the sky:
Tongue, lose thy light;
Moon, take thy flight: [*Exit* MOONSHINE.
Now die, die, die, die, die.   [*Dies.*

DEMETRIUS.   No die, but an ace, for him; for he is but one.

LYSANDER.   Less than an ace, man; for he is dead; he is nothing.

THESEUS.   With the help of a surgeon he might yet recover, and prove an ass.

HIPPOLYTA.   How chance Moonshine is gone before Thisbe comes back and finds her lover?

THESEUS.   She will find him by starlight. Here she comes; and her passion ends the play.

Re-enter THISBE.

HIPPOLYTA.   Methinks she should not use a long one for such a Pyramus: I hope she will be brief.

DEMETRIUS.   A mote will turn the balance, which Pyramus, which Thisbe, is the better; he for a man, God warrant us; she for a woman, God bless us.

LYSANDER.   She hath spied him already with those sweet eyes.

DEMETRIUS.   And thus she means, videlicet:

THISBE.   Asleep, my love?
What, dead, my dove?
O Pyramus, arise!
Speak, speak. Quite dumb?
Dead, dead? A tomb
Must cover thy sweet eyes.
These lily lips,
This cherry nose,
These yellow cowslip cheeks,
Are gone, are gone:
Lovers, make moan.

His eyes were green as leeks.
  O Sisters Three,
  Come, come to me,
With hands as pale as milk;
  Lay them in gore,
  Since you have shore
With shears his thread of silk.
  Tongue, not a word:
  Come, trusty sword;
Come, blade, my breast imbrue:

                                       [Stabs herself.

  And, farewell, friends;
  Thus Thisbe ends:
Adieu, adieu, adieu.   *[Dies.*

THESEUS. Moonshine and Lion are left to bury the dead.
DEMETRIUS. Ay, and Wall too.

BOTTOM [*starting up*]. No, I assure you; the wall is down that parted their fathers. Will it please you to see the epilogue, or to hear a Bergomask dance between two of our company?

THESEUS. No epilogue, I pray you; for your play needs no excuse. Never excuse; for when the players are all dead, there need none to be blam'd. Marry, if he that writ it had play'd Pyramus and hang'd himself in Thisbe's garter, it would have been a fine tragedy; and so it is, truly; and very notably discharg'd.
But, come, your Bergomask: let your epilogue alone.

                                       [A dance.

The iron tongue of midnight hath told twelve:
Lovers, to bed; 'tis almost fairy-time.
I fear we shall out-sleep the coming morn
As much as we this night have overwatch'd.
This palpable-gross play hath well beguil'd
The heavy gait of night. Sweet friends, to bed.
A fortnight hold we this solemnity,
In nightly revels and new jollity.   *[Exeunt.*

MACBETH
Characters

MACBETH ⎱ *Scottish generals*
BANQUO ⎰

MALCOLM ⎱ *the King's sons*
DONALBAIN ⎰

MACDUFF
LENNOX
ROSS
MENTEITH ⎬ *Scottish noblemen*
ANGUS
CAITHNESS

SIWARD, EARL OF NORTHUMBERLAND
YOUNG SIWARD, *his son*
SEYTON, *Macbeth's servant*
A PORTER
A DOCTOR
LADY MACBETH
A GENTLEWOMAN
HECATE
THREE WITCHES
APPARITIONS

WHEN Duncan the Meek reigned king of Scotland, there
lived a great thane, or lord, called Macbeth. This Macbeth was a near kinsman to the king, and in great esteem at court for his valour and conduct in the wars; an
example of which he had lately given, in defeating a
rebel army assisted by the troops of Norway in terrible
numbers.

The two Scottish generals, Macbeth and Banquo, returning victorious from this great battle, their way lay over a blasted heath, where they were stopped by the strange appearance of three figures like women, except that they had beards, and their withered skins and wild attire made them look not like any earthly creatures.

Tales from Shakespeare

SCENE: *A heath.*

Thunder. Enter the three WITCHES.

FIRST WITCH.   Where hast thou been, sister?

SECOND WITCH. Killing swine.

THIRD WITCH. Sister, where thou?

FIRST WITCH. A sailor's wife had chestnuts in her lap,
And munch'd, and munch'd, and munch'd: 'Give me,' quoth I:
'Aroint thee, witch!' the rump-fed ronyon cries.
Her husband's to Aleppo gone, master o' the *Tiger*:
But in a sieve I'll thither sail,
And, like a rat without a tail,
I'll do, I'll do, and I'll do.

SECOND WITCH. I'll give thee a wind.

FIRST WITCH. Thou'rt kind.

THIRD WITCH. And I another.

FIRST WITCH. I myself have all the other;
And the very ports they blow,
All the quarters that they know
I' the shipman's card.
I will drain him dry as hay:
Sleep shall neither night nor day
Hang upon his pent-house lid;
He shall live a man forbid:
Weary se'nnights nine times nine
Shall he dwindle, peak and pine:
Though his bark cannot be lost,
Yet it shall be tempest-tost.
Look what I have.

SECOND WITCH. Show me, show me.

FIRST WITCH.   Here I have a pilot's thumb,
                    Wreck'd as homeward he did come.
                                        [*Drum within.*

THIRD WITCH.   A drum, a drum!
                    Macbeth doth come.

ALL.   The weird sisters, hand in hand,
                    Posters of the sea and land,
                    Thus do go about, about:
                    Thrice to thine, and thrice to mine,
                    And thrice again, to make up nine.
                    Peace! the charm's wound up.

            Enter MACBETH *and* BANQUO.

MACBETH. So foul and fair a day I have not seen.

BANQUO. How far is't call'd to Forres? What are these
So wither'd and so wild in their attire,
That look not like the inhabitants o' the earth,
And yet are on't? Live you? or are you aught
That man may question? You seem to understand me,
By each at once her choppy finger laying
Upon her skinny lips: you should be women,
And yet your beards forbid me to interpret
That you are so.

    MACBETH. Speak, if you can: what are you?

    FIRST WITCH. All hail, Macbeth! hail to thee, thane of
        Glamis!

    SECOND WITCH. All hail, Macbeth! hail to thee, thane
        of Cawdor!

    THIRD WITCH. All hail, Macbeth, that shalt be king
        hereafter!

BANQUO. Good sir, why do you start, and seem to fear
Things that do sound so fair? I' the name of truth,
Are ye fantastical, or that indeed
Which outwardly ye show? My noble partner
You greet with present grace and great prediction
Of noble having and of royal hope,

That he seems rapt withal: to me you speak not.
If you can look into the seeds of time,
And say which grain will grow and which will not,
Speak then to me, who neither beg nor fear
Your favours nor your hate.

FIRST WITCH. Hail!

SECOND WITCH. Hail!

THIRD WITCH. Hail!

FIRST WITCH. Lesser than Macbeth, and greater.

SECOND WITCH. Not so happy, yet much happier.

THIRD WITCH. Thou shalt get kings, though thou be
    none:

So all hail, Macbeth and Banquo!

FIRST WITCH. Banquo and Macbeth, all hail!

MACBETH. Stay, you imperfect speakers, tell me more:
By Sinel's death I know I am thane of Glamis;
But how of Cawdor? the thane of Cawdor lives,
A prosperous gentleman; and to be king
Stands not within the prospect of belief
No more than to be Cawdor. Say from whence
You owe this strange intelligence? or why
Upon this blasted heath you stop our way
With such prophetic greeting? Speak, I charge you.

[WITCHES *vanish.*

BANQUO. The earth hath bubbles, as the water has,
And these are of them. Whither are they vanish'd?

MACBETH. Into the air; and what seem'd corporal
    melted
As breath into the wind. Would they had stay'd!

BANQUO. Were such things here as we do speak about?
Or have we eaten on the insane root
That takes the reason prisoner?

MACBETH. Your children shall be kings.

BANQUO. You shall be king.

MACBETH. And thane of Cawdor, too: went it not so?

BANQUO. To the selfsame tune and words. Who's here?

While they stood pondering on the strangeness of this adventure, there arrived certain messengers from the king, who were empowered by him to confer upon Macbeth the dignity of thane of Cawdor: an event so miraculously corresponding with the prediction of the witches astonished Macbeth, and he stood wrapped in amazement, unable to make reply to the messengers; and in that point of time swelling hopes arose in his mind that the prediction of the third witch might in like manner have its accomplishment, and that he should one day reign king in Scotland.

Turning to Banquo, he said, "Do you not hope that your children shall be kings, when what the witches promised to me has so wonderfully come to pass?" "That hope," answered the general, "might enkindle you to aim at the throne; but oftentimes these ministers of darkness tell us truths in little things, to betray us into deeds of greatest consequence."

But the wicked suggestions of the witches had sunk too deep into the mind of Macbeth to allow him to attend to the warnings of the good Banquo. From that time he bent all his thoughts how to compass the throne of Scotland.

Macbeth had a wife, to whom he communicated the strange prediction of the weird sisters, and its partial accomplishment. She was a bad, ambitious woman, and so as her husband and herself could arrive at greatness, she cared not much by what means. She spurred on the reluctant purpose of Macbeth, who felt compunction at the thoughts of blood, and did not cease to represent the murder of the king as a step absolutely necessary to the fulfilment of the flattering prophecy.

It happened at this time that the king, who out of his royal condescension would oftentimes visit his principal nobility upon gracious terms, came to Macbeth's house, attended by his two sons, Malcolm and Donalbain, and a numerous train of thanes and attendants, the more to honour Macbeth for the triumphal success of his wars.

The castle of Macbeth was pleasantly situated, and the air about it was sweet and wholesome, which appeared by the nests which the martlet, or swallow, had built under all the jutting friezes and buttresses of the building, wherever it found a place of advantage; for where those birds most breed and haunt, the air is observed to be delicate. The king entered well-pleased with the place, and not less so with the attentions and respect of his honoured hostess, Lady Macbeth, who had the art of covering treacherous purposes with smiles; and could look like the innocent flower, while she was indeed the serpent under it.

The king being tired with his journey, went early to bed, and in his state-room two grooms of his chamber (as was the custom) slept beside him. He had been unusually pleased with his reception, and had made presents before he retired to his principal officers; and among the rest, had sent a rich diamond to Lady Macbeth, greeting her by the name of his most kind hostess.

Now was the middle of night, when over half the world nature seems dead, and wicked dreams abuse men's minds asleep, and none but the wolf and the murderer is abroad. This was the time when Lady Macbeth waked to plot the murder of the king. She would not have undertaken a deed so abhorrent to her sex, but that she feared her husband's nature, that it was too full of the milk of human kindness, to do a contrived murder. She knew him to be ambitious, but withal to be scrupulous, and not yet prepared for that height of crime which commonly in the end accompanies inordinate ambition. She had won him to consent to the murder, but she doubted his resolution; and she feared that the natural tenderness of his disposition (more humane than her own) would come between, and defeat the purpose. So with her own hands armed with a dagger, she approached the king's bed; having taken care to ply the grooms of his chamber so with wine, that they slept intoxicated, and careless of their charge. There lay Duncan in a sound sleep after the fatigues of his journey, and as she viewed him earnestly, there was something in his face, as he slept, which resembled her own father; and she had not the courage to proceed.

She returned to confer with her husband. His resolution had begun to stagger. He considered that there were strong reasons against the deed. In the first place, he was not only a subject, but a near kinsman to the king; and he had been his host and entertainer that day, whose duty, by the laws of hospitality, it was to shut the door against his murderers, not bear the knife himself. Then he considered how just and merciful a king this Duncan had been, how clear of offence to his subjects, how loving to his nobility, and in particular to him; that such kings are the peculiar care of Heaven, and their subjects doubly bound to revenge their deaths. Besides, by the favours of the king, Macbeth stood high in the opinion of all sorts of men, and how would those honours be stained by the reputation of so foul a murder!

In these conflicts of the mind Lady Macbeth found her husband inclining to the better part, and resolving to proceed no further. But she being a woman not easily shaken from her evil purpose, began to pour in at his ears words which infused a portion of her own spirit into his mind, assigning reason upon reason why he should not shrink from what he had undertaken; how easy the deed was; how soon it would be over; and how the action of one short night would give to all their nights and days to come sovereign sway and royalty! Then she threw contempt on his change of purpose, and accused him of fickleness and cowardice. Then she added, how practicable it was to lay the guilt of the deed upon the drunken, sleepy grooms. And with the valour of her tongue she so chastised his sluggish resolutions, that he once more summoned up courage to the bloody business.

So, taking the dagger in his hand, he softly stole in the

dark to the room where Duncan lay; and as he went, he thought he saw another dagger in the air, with the handle towards him, and on the blade and at the point of it drops of blood; but when he tried to grasp at it, it was nothing but air, a mere phantasm proceeding from his own hot and oppressed brain and the business he had in hand.

Getting rid of this fear, he entered the king's room, whom he despatched with one stroke of his dagger.

Tales from Shakespeare

SCENE: *Inverness. Court of* MACBETH'S *castle.*

Enter LADY MACBETH.

LADY MACBETH. That which hath made them drunk
    hath made me bold;
What hath quench'd them hath given me fire. Hark!
    Peace!
It was the owl that shriek'd, the fatal bellman,
Which gives the stern'st good-night. He is about it:
The doors are open; and the surfeited grooms
Do mock their charge with snores: I have drugg'd their
    possets,
That death and nature do contend about them,
Whether they live or die.

    MACBETH [*within*]. Who's there, what, ho!

    LADY MACBETH. Alack, I am afraid they have awak'd,
And 'tis not done. The attempt and not the deed
Confounds us. Hark! I laid their daggers ready;
He could not miss 'em. Had he not resembled
My father as he slept, I had done't. [*Enter* MACBETH.] My
    husband!

    MACBETH. I have done the deed. Didst thou not hear a
    noise?

    LADY MACBETH. I heard the owl scream and the crickets
    cry.
Did not you speak?

MACBETH.   When?

LADY MACBETH.   Now.

MACBETH.   As I descended?

LADY MACBETH. Ay.

MACBETH. Hark!

Who lies i' the second chamber?

LADY MACBETH. Donalbain.

MACBETH. This is a sorry sight.   [*Looking on his hands.*

LADY MACBETH. A foolish thought, to say a sorry sight.

MACBETH. There's one did laugh in's sleep, and one
    cried 'Murder!'

That they did wake each other: I stood and heard them:
But they did say their prayers, and address'd them
Again to sleep.

LADY MACBETH. There are two lodg'd together.

MACBETH. One cried 'God bless us!' and 'Amen' the
    other;

As they had seen me with these hangman's hands.
Listening their fear, I could not say 'Amen,'
When they did say 'God bless us!'

LADY MACBETH. Consider it not so deeply.

MACBETH. But wherefore could I not pronounce 'Amen'?
I had most need of blessing, and 'Amen'
Stuck in my throat.

LADY MACBETH. These deeds must not be thought
After these ways; so, it will make us mad.

MACBETH. Methought I heard a voice cry 'Sleep no
more!

Macbeth does murder sleep,' the innocent sleep,
Sleep that knits up the ravell'd sleave of care,
The death of each day's life, sore labour's bath,
Balm of hurt minds, great nature's second course,
Chief nourisher in life's feast,—

LADY MACBETH. What do you mean?

MACBETH. Still it cried 'Sleep no more!' to all the
    house:

'Glamis hath murder'd sleep, and therefore Cawdor
Shall sleep no more; Macbeth shall sleep no more!'
    LADY MACBETH. Who was it that thus cried? Why,
    worthy thane,
You do unbend your noble strength, to think
So brainsickly of things. Go get some water,
And wash this filthy witness from your hand.
Why did you bring these daggers from the place?
They must lie there: go carry them; and smear
The sleepy grooms with blood.
    MACBETH. I'll go no more:
I am afraid to think what I have done;
Look on't again I dare not.
    LADY MACBETH. Infirm of purpose!
Give me the daggers: the sleeping and the dead
Are but as pictures; 'tis the eye of childhood
That fears a painted devil. If he do bleed,
I'll gild the faces of the grooms withal;
For it must seem their guilt.   [*Exit. Knocking within.*
    MACBETH. Whence is that knocking?
How is't with me, when every noise appals me?
What hands are here? ha! they pluck out mine eyes.
Will all great Neptune's ocean wash this blood
Clean from my hand? No, this my hand will rather
The multitudinous seas incarnadine,
Making the green one red.
        Re-enter LADY MACBETH.
    LADY MACBETH. My hands are of your colour, but I
    shame
To wear a heart so white. [*Knocking within.*] I hear a
    knocking
At the south entry: retire we to our chamber:
A little water clears us of this deed:
How easy is it, then! Your constancy
Hath left you unattended. [*Knocking within.*] Hark! more
    knocking.

Get on your night-gown, lest occasion call us,
And show us to be watchers. Be not lost
So poorly in your thoughts.

    MACBETH. To know my deed, 'twere best not know
    myself.

                           [Knocking within.
Wake Duncan with thy knocking! I would thou couldst!
                               [Exeunt.

SCENE: *The same.*

Enter a PORTER. *Knocking within.*

    PORTER. Here's a knocking indeed! If a man were
porter of hell-gate, he should have old turning the key.
                               [Knocking.
Knock, knock, knock! Who's there, i' the name of
Beelzebub? Here's a farmer, that hang'd himself on the
expectation of plenty: come in time; have napkins enough
about you; here you'll sweat for't.   *[Knocking.*
Knock, knock! Who's there, in the other devil's name?
Faith, here's an equivocator, that could swear in both the
scales against either scale; who committed treason enough
for God's sake, yet could not equivocate to heaven: O,
come in, equivocator.   *[Knocking.*
Knock, knock, knock! Who's there? Faith, here's an
English tailor come hither for stealing out of a French hose.
Come in, tailor; here you may roast your goose.
                               [Knocking.
Knock, knock; never at quiet! What are you? But this
place is too cold for hell. I'll devil-porter it no further: I
had thought to have let in some of all professions, that go
the primrose way to the everlasting bonfire. *[Knocking.*
Anon, anon! I pray you, remember the porter.
                           [Opens the gate.

Enter MACDUFF *and* LENNOX.

    MACDUFF. Was it so late, friend, ere you went to bed,
That you do lie so late?

PORTER.   Faith, sir, we were carousing till the second cock.

MACDUFF.   I believe drink gave thee the lie last night.

PORTER.   That it did, sir, i' the very throat on me: but I requited him for his lie; and, I think, being too strong for him, though he took up my legs sometime, yet I made a shift to cast him.

Enter MACBETH.

MACDUFF.   Is thy master stirring?

Our knocking has awak'd him; here he comes.

LENNOX.   Good morrow, noble sir.

MACBETH.   Good morrow, both.

MACDUFF.   Is the king stirring, worthy thane?

MACBETH.   Not yet.

MACDUFF.   He did command me to call timely on him: I have almost slipp'd the hour.

MACBETH.   I'll bring you to him.

MACDUFF.   I know this is a joyful trouble to you; But yet 'tis one.

MACBETH.   The labour we delight in physics pain. This is the door.

MACDUFF.   I'll make so bold to call, For 'tis my limited service.   [*Exit.*

LENNOX.   Goes the king hence to-day?

MACBETH.   He does: he did appoint so.

LENNOX.   The night has been unruly: where we lay, Our chimneys were blown down; and, as they say, Lamentings heard i' the air; strange screams of death, And prophesying with accents terrible Of dire combustion and confus'd events New hatch'd to the woeful time: the obscure bird Clamour'd the livelong night: some say, the earth Was feverous and did shake.

MACBETH.   'Twas a rough night.

LENNOX.   My young remembrance cannot parallel A fellow to it.

Re-enter MACDUFF.

MACDUFF. O horror, horror, horror! Tongue nor heart
Cannot conceive nor name thee!

MACBETH.⎫
LENNOX. ⎭ What's the matter?

MACDUFF. Confusion now hath made his masterpiece!
Most sacrilegious murder hath broke ope
The Lord's anointed temple, and stole thence
The life o' the building.

MACBETH. What is't you say? the life?

LENNOX. Mean you his majesty?

MACDUFF. Approach the chamber, and destroy your sight
With a new Gorgon: do not bid me speak;
See, and then speak yourselves.

[*Exeunt* MACBETH *and* LENNOX.

Awake, awake!

Ring the alarum-bell. Murder and treason!
Banquo and Donalbain! Malcolm! awake!
Shake off this downy sleep, death's counterfeit,
And look on death itself! up, up, and see
The great doom's image! Malcolm! Banquo!
As from your graves rise up, and walk like sprites
To countenance this horror. Ring the bell.   [*Bell rings.*

Enter LADY MACBETH.

LADY MACBETH. What's the business,
That such a hideous trumpet calls to parley
The sleepers of the house? speak, speak!

MACDUFF. O gentle lady,
'Tis not for you to hear what I can speak:
The repetition, in a woman's ear,
Would murder as it fell.

Enter BANQUO.

O Banquo, Banquo,
Our royal master's murder'd!

LADY MACBETH.   Woe, alas!
What, in our house?

BANQUO.   Too cruel any where.
Dear Duff, I prithee, contradict thyself,
And say it is not so.

   Re-enter MACBETH *and* LENNOX, *with* ROSS.

 MACBETH. Had I but died an hour before this chance,
I had liv'd a blessed time; for, from this instant,
There's nothing serious in mortality:
All is but toys; renown and grace is dead;
The wine of life is drawn, and the mere lees
Is left this vault to brag of.

   Enter MALCOLM *and* DONALBAIN.

 DONALBAIN. What is amiss?
 MACBETH.   You are, and do not know't?
The spring, the head, the fountain of your blood
Is stopp'd; the very source of it is stopp'd.
 MACDUFF. Your royal father's murder'd.
 MALCOLM.   O! by whom?
 LENNOX. Those of his chamber, as it seem'd, had done't:
Their hands and faces were all badg'd with blood;
So were their daggers, which unwip'd we found
Upon their pillows:
They star'd, and were distracted; no man's life
Was to be trusted with them.
 MACBETH. O, yet I do repent me of my fury,
That I did kill them.
 MACDUFF. Wherefore did you so?
 MACBETH. Who can be wise, amaz'd, temperate and
  furious,
Loyal and neutral, in a moment? No man:
The expedition of my violent love
Outrun the pauser, reason. Here lay Duncan,
His silver skin lac'd with his golden blood;
And his gash'd stabs look'd like a breach in nature
For ruin's wasteful entrance: there, the murderers,
Steep'd in the colours of their trade, their daggers
Unmannerly breech'd with gore: who could refrain,

That had a heart to love, and in that heart
Courage to make's love known?

    LADY MACBETH. Help me hence, ho!

    MACDUFF. Look to the lady.

    MALCOLM [*aside to* DONALBAIN]. Why do we hold our tongues,

That most may claim this argument for ours?

    DONALBAIN [*aside to* MALCOLM]. What should be spoken here, where our fate,

Hid in an auger-hole, may rush, and seize us?
Let's away:
Our tears are not yet brew'd.

    MALCOLM [*aside to* DONALBAIN]. Nor our strong sorrow
Upon the foot of motion.

    BANQUO. Look to the lady;

                      [LADY MACBETH *is carried out.*

And when we have our naked frailties hid,
That suffer in exposure, let us meet,
And question this most bloody piece of work,
To know it further. Fears and scruples shake us:
In the great hand of God I stand, and thence
Against the undivulg'd pretence I fight
Of treasonous malice.

    MACDUFF.   And so do I.

    ALL.   So all.

    MACBETH. Let's briefly put on manly readiness,
And meet i' the hall together.

    ALL. Well contented.

            [*Exeunt all but* MALCOLM *and* DONALBAIN.

    MALCOLM. What will you do? Let's not consort with them:

To show an unfelt sorrow is an office
Which the false man does easy. I'll to England.

    DONALBAIN. To Ireland, I; our separated fortune
Shall keep us both the safer: where we are,
There's daggers in men's smiles: the near in blood,
The nearer bloody.

MALCOLM. This murderous shaft that's shot
Hath not yet lighted; and our safest way
Is to avoid the aim. Therefore, to horse;
And let us not be dainty of leave-taking,
But shift away: there's warrant in that theft
Which steals itself, when there's no mercy left.   [*Exeunt.*

The king's sons, who should have succeeded him, having
thus vacated the throne, Macbeth as next heir was crowned
king, and thus the prediction of the weird sisters was
literally accomplished.

Though placed so high, Macbeth and his queen could
not forget the prophecy of the weird sisters, that, though
Macbeth should be king, yet not his children, but the
children of Banquo, should be kings after him. The thought
of this, and that they had defiled their hands with blood,
and done so great crimes, only to place the posterity of
Banquo upon the throne, so rankled within them, that
they determined to put to death both Banquo and his son,
to make void the predictions of the weird sisters, which in
their own case had been so remarkably brought to pass.

For this purpose they made a great supper, to which they
invited all the chief thanes; and, among the rest, with
marks of particular respect, Banquo and his son Fleance
were invited. The way by which Banquo was to pass to
the palace at night was beset by murderers appointed by
Macbeth, who stabbed Banquo; but in the scuffle Fleance
escaped. From that Fleance descended a race of monarchs
who afterwards filled the Scottish throne, ending with
James the Sixth of Scotland and the First of England,
under whom the two crowns of England and Scotland
were united.

At supper, the queen, whose manners were in the highest
degree affable and royal, played the hostess with a grace-
fulness and attention which conciliated every one present,
and Macbeth discoursed freely with his thanes and nobles,

saying, that all that was honourable in the country was under his roof, if he had but his good friend Banquo present.

Tales from Shakespeare

SCENE: *Hall in the palace.*

A banquet prepared. Enter MACBETH, LADY MACBETH, ROSS, LENNOX, LORDS, *and* ATTENDANTS.

MACBETH. You know your own degrees; sit down: at first
And last the hearty welcome.

LORDS. Thanks to your majesty.

MACBETH. Ourself will mingle with society.
And play the humble host.
Our hostess keeps her state, but in best time
We will require her welcome.

LADY MACBETH. Pronounce it for me, sir, to all our friends;
For my heart speaks they are welcome.

[*First* MURDERER *appears at the door.*

MACBETH. See, they encounter thee with their hearts' thanks.
Both sides are even: here I'll sit i' the midst:
Be large in mirth; anon we'll drink a measure
The table round. [*Goes to the door*] There's blood upon thy face.

MURDERER. 'Tis Banquo's then.

MACBETH. 'Tis better thee without than he within.
Is he dispatch'd?

MURDERER. My lord, his throat is cut; that I did for him.

MACBETH. Thou art the best o' the cut-throats; yet he's good
That did the like for Fleance: if thou didst it,
Thou art the nonpareil.

MURDERER.   Most royal sir,
Fleance is 'scap'd.

MACBETH. Then comes my fit again: I had else been
    perfect,
Whole as the marble, founded as the rock,
As broad and general as the casing air:
But now I am cabin'd, cribb'd, confin'd, bound in
To saucy doubts and fears. But Banquo's safe?

MURDERER. Ay, my good lord; safe in a ditch he bides,
With twenty trenched gashes on his head;
The least a death to nature.

MACBETH.   Thanks for that.
There the grown serpent lies; the worm that's fled
Hath nature that in time will venom breed,
No teeth for the present. Get thee gone: to-morrow
We'll hear, ourselves, again.   [*Exit* MURDERER.

LADY MACBETH. My royal lord,
You do not give the cheer: the feast is sold
That is not often vouch'd, while 'tis a-making,
'Tis given with welcome: to feed were best at home;
From thence the sauce to meat is ceremony;
Meeting were bare without it.

MACBETH.   Sweet remembrancer!
Now, good digestion wait on appetite,
And health on both!

LENNOX. May't please your highness sit.

    Enter the Ghost *of* BANQUO, *and sits in* MACBETH's *place.*

MACBETH. Here had we now our country's honour
    roof'd,
Were the grac'd person of our Banquo present;
Who may I rather challenge for unkindness
Than pity for mischance.

ROSS.   His absence, sir,
Lays blame upon his promise. Please't your highness
To grace us with your royal company.

MACBETH. The table's full.

LENNOX.   Here is a place reserv'd, sir.

MACBETH. Where?

LENNOX. Here, my good lord. What is't that moves your highness?

MACBETH Which of you have done this?

LORDS.   What, my good lord?

MACBETH. Thou canst not say I did it: never shake
Thy gory locks at me.

ROSS. Gentlemen, rise; his highness is not well.

LADY MACBETH. Sit, worthy friends: my lord is often thus,
And hath been from his youth: pray you, keep seat;
The fit is momentary; upon a thought
He will again be well: if much you note him,
You shall offend him, and extend his passion:
Feed, and regard him not. [*Aside to* MACBETH] Are you a man?

MACBETH. Ay, and a bold one, that dare look on that
Which might appal the devil.

LADY MACBETH [*aside to* MACBETH]. O proper stuff!
This is the very painting of your fear:
This is the air-drawn dagger which, you said,
Led you to Duncan. O, these flaws and starts,
Impostors to true fear, would well become
A woman's story at a winter's fire,
Authoriz'd by her grandam. Shame itself!
Why do you make such faces? When all's done,
You look but on a stool.

MACBETH. Prithee, see there! behold! look! lo! how say you?
Why, what care I? If thou canst nod, speak too.
If charnel-houses and our graves must send
Those that we bury back, our monuments
Shall be the maws of kites.   [GHOST *vanishes.*

LADY MACBETH [*aside to* MACBETH]. What, quite un-
mann'd in folly?

MACBETH. If I stand here, I saw him!

LADY MACBETH [*aside to* MACBETH]. Fie, for shame!

MACBETH. Blood hath been shed ere now, i' the olden
    time,

Ere humane statute purg'd the gentle weal;
Ay, and since too, murders have been perform'd
Too terrible for the ear: the time has been,
That, when the brains were out, the man would die,
And there an end; but now they rise again,
With twenty mortal murders on their crowns,
And push us from our stools: this is more strange
Than such a murder is.

LADY MACBETH. My worthy lord,
Your noble friends do lack you.

MACBETH.   I do forget.

Do not muse at me, my most worthy friends;
I have a strange infirmity, which is nothing
To those that know me. Come, love and health to all;
Then I'll sit down. Give me some wine; fill full.
I drink to the general joy o' the whole table,
And to our dear friend Banquo, whom we miss;
Would he were here! to all, and him, we thirst,
And all to all.

LORDS. Our duties, and the pledge.

Re-enter GHOST.

MACBETH. Avaunt! and quit my sight! let the earth
    hide thee!

Thy bones are marrowless, thy blood is cold;
Thou hast no speculation in those eyes
Which thou dost glare with!

LADY MACBETH. Think of this, good peers,
But as a thing of custom: 'tis no other;
Only it spoils the pleasure of the time.

MACBETH. What man dare, I dare:
Approach thou like the rugged Russian bear,
The arm'd rhinoceros, or the Hyrcan tiger;

Take any shape but that, and my firm nerves
Shall never tremble: or be alive again,
And dare me to the desert with thy sword;
If trembling I inhabit then, protest me
The baby of a girl. Hence, horrible shadow!
Unreal mockery, hence!   [GHOST *vanishes*.
                    Why, so: being gone,
I am a man again. Pray, you, sit still.

    LADY MACBETH. You have displac'd the mirth, broke
the good meeting,
With most admir'd disorder.

    MACBETH. Can such things be,
And overcome us like a summer's cloud,
Without our special wonder? You make me strange
Even to the disposition that I owe,
When now I think you can behold such sights,
And keep the natural ruby of your cheeks,
When mine is blanch'd with fear.

    ROSS.   What sights, my lord?

    LADY MACBETH. I pray you, speak not; he grows worse
and worse;
Question enrages him. At once, good night:
Stand not upon the order of your going,
But go at once.

    LENNOX. Good night; and better health
Attend his majesty!

    LADY MACBETH. A kind good night to all!

                [*Exeunt all but* MACBETH *and* LADY MACBETH.

    MACBETH. It will have blood; they say blood will have
    blood:
Stones have been known to move and trees to speak;
Augurs and understood relations have
By magot-pies and choughs and rooks brought forth
The secret'st man of blood. What is the night?

    LADY MACBETH. Almost at odds with morning, which is
    which.

MACBETH. How say'st thou, that Macduff denies his person
At our great bidding?

LADY MACBETH.   Did you send to him, sir?

MACBETH. I hear it by the way; but I will send:
There's not a one of them but in his house
I keep a servant fee'd. I will to-morrow,
And betimes I will, to the weird sisters:
More shall they speak; for now I am bent to know,
By the worst means, the worst. For mine own good
All causes shall give way: I am in blood
Stepp'd in so far that, should I wade no more,
Returning were as tedious as go o'er:
Strange things I have in head that will to hand,
Which must be acted ere they may be scann'd.

LADY MACBETH. You lack the season of all natures, sleep.

MACBETH. Come, we'll to sleep. My strange and self-abuse
Is the initiate fear that wants hard use:
We are yet but young in deed.   [*Exeunt.*

To such dreadful fancies Macbeth was subject. His queen and he had their sleeps afflicted with terrible dreams, and the blood of Banquo troubled them not more than the escape of Fleance, whom now they looked upon as father to a line of kings who should keep their posterity out of the throne. With these miserable thoughts they found no peace, and Macbeth determined once more to seek out the weird sisters, and know from them the worst.

He sought them in a cave upon the heath, where they, who knew by foresight of his coming, were engaged in preparing their dreadful charms, by which they conjured up infernal spirits to reveal to them futurity.

Tales from Shakespeare

Scene: *A cavern. In the middle, a boiling cauldron.*
Thunder. Enter the three WITCHES.

FIRST WITCH.	Thrice the brinded cat hath mew'd.
SECOND WITCH.	Thrice and once the hedge-pig whin'd.
THIRD WITCH.	Harpier cries; 'tis time, 'tis time.
FIRST WITCH.	Round about the cauldron go;
	In the poison'd entrails throw.
	Toad, that under cold stone
	Days and nights has thirty-one
	Swelter'd venom sleeping got,
	Boil thou first i' the charmed pot.
ALL.	Double, double toil and trouble;
	Fire burn and cauldron bubble.
SECOND WITCH.	Fillet of a fenny snake,
	In the cauldron boil and bake;
	Eye of newt and toe of frog,
	Wool of bat and tongue of dog,
	Adder's fork and blind-worm's sting,
	Lizard's leg and howlet's wing,
	For a charm of powerful trouble,
	Like a hell-broth boil and bubble.
ALL.	Double, double toil and trouble;
	Fire burn and cauldron bubble.
THIRD WITCH.	Scale of dragon, tooth of wolf,
	Witches' mummy, maw and gulf
	Of the ravin'd salt-sea shark;
	Root of hemlock digg'd i' the dark,
	Liver of blaspheming Jew,
	Gall of goat, and slips of yew
	Sliver'd in the moon's eclipse,
	Nose of Turk and Tartar's lips,
	Make the gruel thick and slab:
	Add thereto a tiger's chaudron,
	For the ingredients of our cauldron.

ALL.   Double, double toil and trouble;
        Fire burn and cauldron bubble.

SECOND WITCH   Cool it with a baboon's blood,
        Then the charm is firm and good.

Enter HECATE *to the other three* WITCHES.

HECATE.   O, well done ! I commend your pains;
        And every one shall share i' the gains:
        And now about the cauldron sing,
        Like elves and fairies in a ring,
        Enchanting all that you put in.
        [*Music, and a Song,* 'Black spirits,' *etc.*
                                    [*Exit* HECATE.

SECOND WITCH.   By the pricking of my thumbs,
        Something wicked this way comes.
        Open, locks,
        Whoever knocks !

Enter MACBETH.

MACBETH.   How now, you secret, black, and midnight
hags !
What is't you do?
ALL.   A deed without a name.

MACBETH.   I conjure you, by that which you profess,
Howe'er you come to know it, answer me:
Though you untie the winds and let them fight
Against the churches; though the yesty waves
Confound and swallow navigation up;
Though bladed corn be lodg'd and trees blown down;
Though castles topple on their warders' heads;
Though palaces and pyramids do slope
Their heads to their foundations; though the treasure
Of nature's germens tumble all together,
Even till destruction sicken; answer me
To what I ask you.

FIRST WITCH.   Speak.

SECOND WITCH.   Demand.

THIRD WITCH.   We'll answer.

FIRST WITCH. Say, if thou'dst rather hear it from our mouths,
Or from our masters?

MACBETH.   Call 'em; let me see 'em.

FIRST WITCH.   Pour in sow's blood, that hath eaten
Her nine farrow; grease that's sweaten
From the murderer's gibbet throw
Into the flame.

ALL.   Come, high or low;
Thyself and office deftly show!

Thunder. First APPARITION, *an armed Head.*

MACBETH. Tell me, thou unknown power,—

FIRST WITCH.   He knows thy thought:
Hear his speech, but say thou nought.

FIRST APPARITION. Macbeth! Macbeth! Macbeth!
beware Macduff;
Beware the thane of Fife. Dismiss me: enough.

                                              [*Descends.*

MACBETH. Whate'er thou art, for thy good caution, thanks;
Thou hast harp'd my fear aright: but one word more,——

FIRST WITCH. He will not be commanded: here's another,
More potent than the first.

Thunder. Second APPARITION, *a bloody Child.*

SECOND APPARITION. Macbeth! Macbeth! Macbeth!

MACBETH. Had I three ears, I'ld hear thee.

SECOND APPARITION. Be bloody, bold, and resolute;
laugh to scorn
The power of man, for none of woman born
Shall harm Macbeth.   [*Descends.*

MACBETH. Then live, Macduff: what need I fear of thee?
But yet I'll make assurance double sure,
And take a bond of fate: thou shalt not live;
That I may tell pale-hearted fear it lies,
And sleep in spite of thunder.

Thunder. Third APPARITION, *a Child crowned, with a*
tree in his hand.

                              What is this,
That rises like the issue of a king,
And wears upon his baby brow the round
And top of sovereignty?

    ALL.   Listen, but speak not to't.

    THIRD APPARITION Be lion-mettl'd, proud; and take no
care
Who chafes, who frets, or where conspirers are:
Macbeth shall never vanquish'd be until
Great Birnam wood to high Dunsinane hill
Shall come against him.   [*Descends.*

    MACBETH.   That will never be:
Who can impress the forest, bid the tree
Unfix his earth-bound root? Sweet bodements! good!
Rebellion's head, rise never till the wood
Of Birnam rise, and our high-plac'd Macbeth
Shall live the lease of nature, pay his breath
To time and mortal custom. Yet my heart
Throbs to know one thing: tell me, if your art
Can tell so much: shall Banquo's issue ever
Reign in this kingdom?

    ALL.   Seek to know no more.

    MACBETH. I will be satisfied: deny me this,
And an eternal curse fall on you! Let me know:
Why sinks that cauldron? and what noise is this?

                                        [*Hautboys.*

    FIRST WITCH.   Show!
    SECOND WITCH.   Show!
    THIRD WITCH.   Show!
    ALL.   Show his eyes, and grieve his heart;
                Come like shadows, so depart!

A show of eight Kings, *the last with a glass in his hand;*
    BANQUO's Ghost *following.*

MACBETH. Thou art too like the spirit of Banquo; down!
Thy crown does sear mine eye-balls. And thy hair,
Thou other gold-bound brow, is like the first:
A third is like the former. Filthy hags!
Why do you show me this? A fourth! Start, eyes!
What, will the line stretch out to the crack of doom?
Another yet! A seventh! I'll see no more:
And yet the eighth appears, who bears a glass
Which shows me many more; and some I see
That twofold balls and treble sceptres carry:
Horrible sight! Now I see 'tis true;
For the blood-bolter'd Banquo smiles upon me,
And points at them for his. What, is this so?

FIRST WITCH.   Ay, sir, all this is so; but why
                         Stands Macbeth thus amazedly?
                         Come, sisters, cheer we up his sprites,
                         And show the best of our delights:
                         I'll charm the air to give a sound,
                         While you perform your antic round;
                         That this great king may kindly say
                         Our duties did his welcome pay.

[*Music. The* WITCHES *dance, and vanish with* HECATE.
MACBETH. Where are they? Gone? Let this pernicious hour
Stand aye accursed in the calendar!

The first thing Macbeth heard when he got out of the
witches' cave, was that Macduff, thane of Fife, had fled
to England, to join the army which was forming against
him under Malcolm, the eldest son of the late king, with
intent to displace Macbeth, and set Malcolm, the right
heir, upon the throne. Macbeth, stung with rage, set
upon the castle of Macduff, and put his wife and children,
whom the thane had left behind, to the sword, and extended
the slaughter to all who claimed the least relationship to
Macduff.

These and such-like deeds alienated the minds of all his chief nobility from him. Such as could, fled to join with Malcolm and Macduff, who were now approaching with a powerful army, which they had raised in England; and the rest secretly wished success to their arms, though for fear of Macbeth they could take no active part. His recruits went on slowly. Everybody hated the tyrant; nobody loved or honoured him; but all suspected him, and he began to envy the condition of Duncan, whom he had murdered, who slept soundly in his grave, against whom treason had done its worst: steel nor poison, domestic malice nor foreign levies, could hurt him no longer.

Tales from Shakespeare

Although she had helped in only one of the murders, Lady Macbeth was as unhappy and as sorely troubled in mind as her husband was. Even in her sleep she was haunted by remorseful thoughts of the terrible crimes which had been committed.

SCENE: *Dunsinane. Ante-room in the castle.*

Enter a DOCTOR *of* Physic, *and a* WAITING-GENTLEWOMAN.

DOCTOR. I have two nights watch'd with you, but can perceive no truth in your report. When was it she last walk'd?

GENTLEWOMAN. Since his majesty went into the field, I have seen her rise from her bed, throw her night-gown upon her, unlock her closet, take forth paper, fold it, write upon't, read it, afterwards seal it and again return to bed; yet all this while in a most fast sleep.

DOCTOR. A great perturbation in nature, to receive at once the benefit of sleep, and do the effects of watching! In this slumbery agitation, besides her walking and other actual performances, what, at any time, have you heard her say?

GENTLEWOMAN. That, sir, which I will not report after her.

DOCTOR. You may to me; and 'tis most meet you should.

GENTLEWOMAN. Neither to you nor any one; having no witness to confirm my speech.

Enter LADY MACBETH, *with a taper.*

Lo you, here she comes! This is her very guise; and, upon my life, fast asleep. Observe her; stand close.

DOCTOR. How came she by that light?

GENTLEWOMAN. Why, it stood by her: she has light by her continually; 'tis her command.

DOCTOR. You see, her eyes are open.

GENTLEWOMAN. Ay, but their sense is shut.

DOCTOR. What is it she does now? Look, how she rubs her hands.

GENTLEWOMAN. It is an accustom'd action with her, to seem thus washing her hands: I have known her continue in this a quarter of an hour.

LADY MACBETH. Yet here's a spot.

DOCTOR. Hark! she speaks; I will set down what comes from her, to satisfy my remembrance the more strongly.

LADY MACBETH. Out, damned spot! out, I say!—One; two: why, then 'tis time to do't.—Hell is murky!—Fie, my lord, fie! a soldier, and afeard? What need we fear who knows it, when none can call our power to account? —Yet who would have thought the old man to have had so much blood in him?

DOCTOR. Do you mark that?

LADY MACBETH. The thane of Fife had a wife; where is she now?—What, will these hands ne'er be clean?— No more o' that, my lord, no more o' that: you mar all with this starting.

DOCTOR. Go to, go to; you have known what you should not.

GENTLEWOMAN. She has spoke what she should not, I am sure of that: heaven knows what she has known.

LADY MACBETH. Here's the smell of blood still: all the perfumes of Arabia will not sweeten this little hand. Oh, oh, oh !

DOCTOR. What a sigh is there ! The heart is sorely charg'd.

GENTLEWOMAN. I would not have such a heart in my bosom for the dignity of the whole body.

DOCTOR. Well, well, well,——

GENTLEWOMAN. Pray God it be, sir.

DOCTOR. This disease is beyond my practice: yet I have known those which have walk'd in their sleep who have died holily in their beds.

LADY MACBETH. Wash your hands, put on your night-gown; look not so pale. I tell you yet again, Banquo's buried; he cannot come out on's grave.

DOCTOR. Even so?

LADY MACBETH. To bed, to bed; there's knocking at the gate: come, come, come, come, give me your hand: what's done cannot be undone. To bed, to bed, to bed.

[*Exit.*

DOCTOR. Will she go now to bed?

GENTLEWOMAN. Directly.

DOCTOR. Foul whisperings are abroad: unnatural deeds
Do breed unnatural troubles: infected minds
To their deaf pillows will discharge their secrets:
More needs she the divine than the physician.
God, God forgive us all ! Look after her;
Remove from her the means of all annoyance,
And still keep eyes upon her. So, good night:
My mind she has mated, and amaz'd my sight.
I think, but dare not speak.

GENTLEWOMAN.   Good night, good doctor.

[*Exeunt.*

Macbeth grew careless of life, and wished for death; but the near approach of Malcolm's army roused in him what remained of his ancient courage, and he determined to die (as he expressed it) "with armour on his back." Besides this, the hollow promises of the witches had filled him with a false confidence, and he remembered the sayings of the spirits, that none of woman born was to hurt him, and that he was never to be vanquished till Birnam wood should come to Dunsinane, which he thought could never be. So he shut himself up in his castle, whose impregnable strength was such as defied a siege: here he sullenly waited the approach of Malcolm.

Tales from Shakespeare

SCENE: *Dunsinane. A room in the castle.*

Enter MACBETH, *the* DOCTOR, *and* Attendants.

MACBETH. Bring me no more reports; let them fly all:
Till Birnam wood remove to Dunsinane
I cannot taint with fear. What's the boy Malcolm?
Was he not born of woman? The spirits that know
All mortal consequences have pronounc'd me thus:
'Fear not, Macbeth; no man that's born of woman
Shall e'er have power upon thee.' Then fly, false thanes,
And mingle with the English epicures:
The mind I sway by and the heart I bear
Shall never sag with doubt nor shake with fear.

Enter a SERVANT.

The devil damn thee black, thou cream-fac'd loon!
Where got'st thou that goose look?

SERVANT. There is ten thousand——

MACBETH.   Geese, villain?

SERVANT.   Soldiers, sir.

MACBETH. Go, prick thy face, and over-red thy fear,
Thou lily-liver'd boy. What soldiers, patch?
Death of thy soul! those linen cheeks of thine
Are counsellors to fear. What soldiers, whey-face?

SERVANT. The English force, so please you.

MACBETH. Take thy face hence.   [*Exit* SERVANT.
              Seyton!—I am sick at heart,
When I behold—Seyton, I say!—This push
Will cheer me ever, or disseat me now.
I have liv'd long enough: my way of life
Is fall'n into the sear, the yellow leaf;
And that which should accompany old age,
As honour, love, obedience, troops of friends,
I must not look to have; but, in their stead,
Curses, not loud but deep, mouth-honour, breath,
Which the poor heart would fain deny, and dare not.
Seyton!

Enter SEYTON.

SEYTON.   What is your gracious pleasure?
MACBETH.   What news more?
SEYTON.   All is confirm'd, my lord, which was
   reported.
MACBETH.   I'll fight till from my bones my flesh be hack'd.
Give me my armour.
SEYTON.   'Tis not needed yet.
MACBETH.   I'll put it on.
Send out more horses; skirr the country round;
Hang those that talk of fear. Give me mine armour.
How does your patient, doctor?
DOCTOR.   Not so sick, my lord,
As she is troubled with thick-coming fancies,
That keep her from her rest.
MACBETH.   Cure her of that.
Canst thou not minister to a mind diseas'd,
Pluck from the memory a rooted sorrow,
Raze out the written troubles of the brain,
And with some sweet oblivious antidote
Cleanse the stuff'd bosom of that perilous stuff
Which weighs upon the heart?
DOCTOR.   Therein the patient
Must minister to himself.

MACBETH. Throw physic to the dogs; I'll none of it.
Come, put mine armour on; give me my staff.
Seyton, send out. Doctor, the thanes fly from me.
Come, sir, dispatch. If thou couldst, doctor, cast
The water of my land, find her disease,
And purge it to a sound and pristine health,
I would applaud thee to the very echo,
That should applaud again. Pull 't off, I say.
What rhubarb, senna, or what purgative drug,
Would scour these English hence? Hear'st thou of them?

DOCTOR. Ay, my good lord; your royal preparation
Makes us hear something.

MACBETH.   Bring it after me.
I will not be afraid of death and bane,
Till Birnam forest come to Dunsinane.

DOCTOR [aside]. Were I from Dunsinane away and clear,
Profit again should hardly draw me here.   [Exeunt.

SCENE: *Country near Birnam wood.*

Drum and colours. Enter MALCOLM, *old* SIWARD *and his* SON,
MACDUFF, MENTEITH, CAITHNESS, ANGUS, LENNOX, ROSS, *and*
SOLDIERS, *marching.*

MALCOLM. Cousins, I hope the days are near at hand
That chambers will be safe.

MENTEITH.   We doubt it nothing.

SIWARD. What wood is this before us?

MENTEITH.   The wood of Birnam.

MALCOLM. Let every soldier hew him down a bough,
And bear't before him: thereby shall we shadow
The numbers of our host, and make discovery
Err in report of us.

SOLDIERS.   It shall be done.

SIWARD. We learn no other but the confident tyrant
Keeps still in Dunsinane, and will endure
Our setting down before 't.

MALCOLM. 'Tis his main hope:
For where there is advantage to be given,
Both more and less have given him the revolt
And none serve with him but constrained things
Whose hearts are absent too.

MACDUFF. Let our just censures
Attend the true event, and put we on
Industrious soldiership.

SIWARD. The time approaches
That will with due decision make us know
What we shall say we have and what we owe.
Thoughts speculative their unsure hopes relate,
But certain issues strokes must arbitrate;
Towards which advance the war. [*Exeunt, marching.*

SCENE: *Dunsinane. The castle.*

Enter MACBETH, SEYTON, *and* Soldiers, *with drum
and colours.*

MACBETH. Hang out our banners on the outward walls;
The cry is still, 'They come.' Our castle's strength
Will laugh a siege to scorn; here let them lie
Till famine and the ague eat them up.
Were they not forc'd with those that should be ours,
We might have met them dareful, beard to beard,
And beat them backward home. [*A cry of women within.*
What is that noise?

SEYTON. It is the cry of women, my good lord. [*Exit.*

MACBETH. I have almost forgot the taste of fears:
The time has been, my senses would have cool'd
To hear a night-shriek, and my fell of hair
Would at a dismal treatise rouse and stir
As life were in't: I have supp'd full with horrors;
Direness, familiar to my slaughterous thoughts,
Cannot once start me.

Re-enter SEYTON.

Wherefore was that cry?

SEYTON. The queen, my lord, is dead.

MACBETH. She should have died hereafter;
There would have been a time for such a word.
To-morrow, and to-morrow, and to-morrow,
Creeps in this petty pace from day to day,
To the last syllable of recorded time;
And all our yesterdays have lighted fools
The way to dusty death. Out, out, brief candle !
Life's but a walking shadow, a poor player
That struts and frets his hour upon the stage
And then is heard no more: it is a tale
Told by an idiot, full of sound and fury,
Signifying nothing.

Enter a MESSENGER.

Thou com'st to use thy tongue; thy story quickly.

MESSENGER. Gracious my lord,
I should report that which I say I saw,
But know not how to do it.

MACBETH.   Well, say, sir.

MESSENGER. As I did stand my watch upon the hill,
I look'd toward Birnam, and anon, methought,
The wood began to move.

MACBETH.   Liar and slave !

MESSENGER. Let me endure your wrath, if't be not so:
Within this three mile may you see it coming;
I say, a moving grove.

MACBETH.   If thou speak'st false,
Upon the next tree shalt thou hang alive,
Till famine cling thee: if thy speech be sooth,
I care not if thou dost for me as much.
I pull in resolution, and begin
To doubt the equivocation of the fiend
That lies like truth: 'Fear not, till Birnam wood
Do come to Dunsinane'; and now a wood

Comes toward Dunsinane. Arm, arm and out!
If this which he avouches does appear,
There is nor flying hence nor tarrying here.
I 'gin to be aweary of the sun,
And wish the estate o' the world were now undone.
Ring the alarum-bell! Blow, wind! come, wrack!
At least we'll die with harness on our back.   [*Exeunt.*

SCENE: *Dunsinane. Before the castle.*

Drum and colours. Enter MALCOLM, *old* SIWARD, MACDUFF,
and their Army, *with boughs.*

MALCOLM. Now near enough: your leavy screens throw
   down,
And show like those you are. You, worthy uncle,
Shall, with my cousin, your right-noble son,
Lead our first battle: worthy Macduff and we
Shall take upon's what else remains to do,
According to our order.
   SIWARD.   Fare you well.
Do we but find the tyrant's power to-night,
Let us be beaten, if we cannot fight.
   MACDUFF. Make all our trumpets speak; give them all
      breath,
Those clamorous harbingers of blood and death.   [*Exeunt.*
                                           [*Alarums continued.*

SCENE: *Another part of the field.*

Enter MACBETH.

MACBETH. They have tied me to a stake; I cannot fly,
But, bear-like, I must fight the course. What's he
That was not born of woman? Such a one
Am I to fear, or none.
            Enter young SIWARD.
YOUNG SIWARD. What is thy name?
MACBETH. Thou'lt be afraid to hear it.

YOUNG SIWARD. No; though thou call'st thyself a hotter name
Than any is in hell.

MACBETH.   My name's Macbeth.

YOUNG SIWARD. The devil himself could not pronounce a title
More hateful to mine ear.

MACBETH.   No, nor more fearful.

YOUNG SIWARD. Thou liest, abhorred tyrant; with my sword
I'll prove the lie thou speak'st.

            [*They fight, and young* SIWARD *is slain.*

MACBETH. Thou wast born of woman.
But swords I smile at, weapons laugh to scorn,
Brandish'd by man that's of a woman born.   [*Exit.*

            Alarums. Enter MACDUFF.

MACDUFF. That way the noise is. Tyrant, show thy face!
If thou be'st slain, and with no stroke of mine,
My wife and children's ghosts will haunt me still.
I cannot strike at wretched kerns, whose arms
Are hir'd to bear their staves: either thou, Macbeth,
Or else my sword with an unbatter'd edge
I sheathe again undeeded. There thou shouldst be;
By this great clatter, one of greatest note
Seems bruited. Let me find him, fortune!
And more I beg not.   [*Exit. Alarums.*

            Enter MALCOLM *and old* SIWARD.

SIWARD. This way, my lord; the castle's gently render'd:
The tyrant's people on both sides do fight;
The noble thanes do bravely in the war;
The day almost itself professes yours,
And little is to do.

MALCOLM.   We have met with foes
That strike beside us.

SIWARD.   Enter, sir, the castle.
            [*Exeunt. Alarums.*

SCENE: *Another part of the field.*

Enter MACBETH.

MACBETH. Why should I play the Roman fool, and die
On mine own sword? whiles I see lives, the gashes
Do better upon them.

Enter MACDUFF.

MACDUFF.   Turn, hell-hound, turn!

MACBETH. Of all men else I have avoided thee:
But get thee back; my soul is too much charg'd
With blood of thine already.

MACDUFF.   I have no words;
My voice is in my sword; thou bloodier villain
Than terms can give thee out!   [*They fight.*

MACBETH.   Thou losest labour:
As easy mayst thou the intrenchant air
With thy keen sword impress as make me bleed:
Let fall thy blade on vulnerable crests;
I bear a charmed life, which must not yield
To one of woman born.

MACDUFF.   Despair thy charm;
And let the angel whom thou still hast serv'd
Tell thee, Macduff was from his mother's womb
Untimely ripp'd.

MACBETH. Accursed be that tongue that tells me so,
For it hath cow'd my better part of man!
And be these juggling fiends no more believ'd,
That palter with us in a double sense;
That keep the word of promise to our ear,
And break it to our hope. I'll not fight with thee.

MACDUFF. Then yield thee, coward,
And live to be the show and gaze o' the time:
We'll have thee, as our rarer monsters are,
Painted upon a pole, and underwrit,
'Here may you see the tyrant.'

MACBETH.   I will not yield,
To kiss the ground before young Malcolm's feet,
And to be baited with the rabble's curse.
Though Birnam wood be come to Dunsinane,
And thou oppos'd, being of no woman born,
Yet will I try the last: before my body
I throw my warlike shield. Lay on, Macduff,,
And damn'd be him that first cries, 'Hold, enough!'
                         [*Exeunt, fighting. Alarums.*
Retreat. Flourish. Enter with drum and colours, MALCOLM.
    old SIWARD, ROSS, *the other thanes and soldiers.*

MALCOLM. I would the friends we miss were safe arriv'd.

SIWARD. Some must go off; and yet, by these I see,
So great a day as this is cheaply bought.

MALCOLM. Macduff is missing, and your noble son.

ROSS. Your son, my lord, has paid a soldier's debt:
He only liv'd but till he was a man;
The which no sooner had his prowess confirm'd
In the unshrinking station where he fought,
But like a man he died.

SIWARD.   Then he is dead?

ROSS. Ay, and brought off the field: your cause of
    sorrow
Must not be measur'd by his worth, for then
It hath no end.

SIWARD.   Had he his hurts before?

ROSS. Ay, on the front.

SIWARD.   Why then, God's soldier be he!
Had I as many sons as I have hairs,
I would not wish them to a fairer death:
And so his knell is knoll'd.

MALCOLM.   He's worth more sorrow,
And that I'll spend for him.

SIWARD.   He's worth no more:
They say he parted well, and paid his score:
And so, God be with him! Here comes newer comfort.

Re-enter MACDUFF, *with* MACBETH's *head.*

MACDUFF. Hail, king! for so thou art: behold, where
    stands
The usurper's cursed head: the time is free:
I see thee compass'd with thy kingdom's pearl,
That speak my salutation in their minds;
Whose voices I desire aloud with mine:
Hail, King of Scotland!

   ALL. Hail, King of Scotland!   [*Flourish.*

   MALCOLM. We shall not spend a large expense of time
Before we reckon with your several loves,
And make us even with you. My thanes and kinsmen,
Henceforth be earls, the first that ever Scotland
In such an honour nam'd. What's more to do,
Which would be planted newly with the time,
As calling home our exil'd friends abroad
That fled the snares of watchful tyranny;
Producing forth the cruel ministers
Of this dead butcher and his fiend-like queen,
Who, as 'tis thought, by self and violent hands
Took off her life; this, and what needful else
That calls upon us, by the grace of Grace,
We will perform in measure, time, and place:
So, thanks to all at once and to each one,
Whom we invite to see us crown'd at Scone.

                              [*Flourish. Exeunt.*

PART THREE
A PICTURE OF AN ELIZABETHAN
PLAYHOUSE
SCENES FROM
"THE KNIGHT OF THE BURNING PESTLE"

BY

FRANCIS BEAUMONT AND JOHN FLETCHER

THE play from which these scenes are taken was written
early in the seventeenth century, when Shakespeare was
nearing the end of his career. It gives an excellent picture
of the theatre as it was at that time. Those of you who
have read the story of Don Quixote, which had been
written a few years earlier, will be reminded by the action
of the play of the adventures of that amusing knight.

You will remember that, when you were reading about
the Elizabethan playhouse, you learned that the seats
behind the stage were considered the best. Sometimes the
young gallants of the court—and apparently the London
citizens also—paid sixpence extra to have stools on the
stage itself, and then interrupted the play by making
criticisms and suggestions. The dramatists resented this,
and *The Knight of the Burning Pestle* was probably an attempt
to put a stop to the practice by ridiculing the interrupters.
This may explain why the play, when first produced, was
not well received.

Characters

SPEAKER OF THE PROLOGUE
A CITIZEN
HIS WIFE
RALPH, *his apprentice*
TIM
GEORGE } *apprentices*

HOST
BARBER
THREE MEN, *supposed captives*

INDUCTION

Several Gentlemen *sitting on stools upon the stage. The*
CITIZEN, *his* WIFE, *and* RALPH *sitting below among the*
audience.

Enter SPEAKER OF THE PROLOGUE.

SPEAKER OF THE PROLOGUE. "From all that's near the
    court, from all that's great,
Within the compass of the city-walls,
We now have brought our scene——"
                        CITIZEN [*leaps on the stage*].

CITIZEN. Hold your peace, goodman boy!

SPEAKER OF THE PROLOGUE. What do you mean, sir?

CITIZEN. That you have no good meaning: this seven
years there hath been plays at this house, I have observed
it, you have still girds at citizens; and now you call your
play *The London Merchant*. Down with your title, boy!
down with your title!

SPEAKER OF THE PROLOGUE. Are you a member of the
noble city?

CITIZEN. I am.

SPEAKER OF THE PROLOGUE. And a freeman?

CITIZEN. Yea, and a grocer.

SPEAKER OF THE PROLOGUE. So, grocer, then, by your
sweet favour, we intend no abuse to the city.

CITIZEN. No, sir! yes, sir. If you were not resolved to
play the Jacks, what need you study for new subjects,
purposely to abuse your betters? Why could you not be
contented, as well as others, with *The Legend of Whittington*,
or *The Life and Death of Sir Thomas Gresham, with the building
of the Royal Exchange*, or *The story of Queen Eleanor, with the
rearing of London Bridge upon woolsacks*?

SPEAKER OF THE PROLOGUE   You seem to be an understanding man: what would you have us do, sir?

CITIZEN. Why, present something notably in honour of the commons of the city.

SPEAKER OF THE PROLOGUE. Why, what do you say to *The Life and Death of fat Drake*?

CITIZEN. I do not like that; but I will have a citizen, and he shall be of my own trade.

SPEAKER OF THE PROLOGUE   Oh, you should have told us your mind a month since: our play is ready to begin now.

CITIZEN. 'Tis all one for that; I will have a grocer, and he shall do admirable things.

SPEAKER OF THE PROLOGUE. What will you have him do?

CITIZEN. Marry, I will have him——

WIFE [*below*]. Husband, husband!

RALPH [*below*]. Peace, mistress.

WIFE [*below*]. Hold thy peace, Ralph; I know what I do, I warrant ye. Husband, husband!

CITIZEN. What sayest thou, cony?

WIFE [*below*]. Let him kill a lion with a pestle, husband! Let him kill a lion with a pestle!

CITIZEN   So he shall.—I'll have him kill a lion with a pestle.

WIFE [*below*]. Husband! shall I come up, husband?

CITIZEN. Ay, cony.—Ralph, help your mistress this way. —Pray, gentlemen, make her a little room.—I pray you, sir, lend me your hand to help up my wife: I thank you, sir.—So.   [WIFE *comes on the stage.*

WIFE. By your leave, gentlemen all; I'm something troublesome. I'm a stranger here; I was ne'er at one of these plays, as they say, before; but I should have seen *Jane Shore* once; and my husband hath promised me, any time this twelvemonth, to carry me to *The Bold Beauchamps*, but in truth he did not. I pray you, bear with me.

CITIZEN. Boy, let my wife and I have a couple of stools and then begin; and let the grocer do rare things.

[*Stools are brought.*

SPEAKER OF THE PROLOGUE. But, sir, we have never a boy to play him; every one hath a part already.

WIFE. Husband, husband, for God's sake, let Ralph play him! Beshrew me, if I do not think he will go beyond them all.

CITIZEN. Well remembered, wife.—Come up, Ralph.— I'll tell you, gentlemen; let them but lend him a suit of reparel and necessaries.   [RALPH *comes on the stage.*

WIFE. I pray you, youth, let him have a suit of reparel! —I'll be sworn, gentlemen, my husband tells you true. He will act you sometimes at our house, that all the neighbours cry out on him; he will fetch you up a couraging part so in the garret, that we are all as feared, I warrant you, that we quake again: we'll fear our children with him; if they be never so unruly, do but cry, "Ralph comes, Ralph comes!" to them, and they'll be as quiet as lambs.—Hold up thy head, Ralph; speak a huffing part; I warrant you, the gentlemen will accept of it.

CITIZEN. Do, Ralph, do.

RALPH. "By Heaven, methinks, it were an easy leap
To pluck bright honour from the pale-faced moon;
Or dive into the bottom of the sea,
Where never fathom-line touched any ground,
And pluck up drowned honour from the lake of hell."

CITIZEN. How say you, gentlemen, is it not as I told you?

WIFE. Nay, gentlemen, he hath played before, my husband says, "Mucedorus," before the wardens of our company.

CITIZEN. Ay, and he should have played Jeronimo with a shoemaker for a wager.

SPEAKER OF THE PROLOGUE. He shall have a suit of apparel, if he will go in.

CITIZEN. In, Ralph, in, Ralph; and set out the grocery in their kind, if thou lovest me.   [*Exit* RALPH.

WIFE. I warrant, our Ralph will look finely when he's dressed.

SPEAKER OF THE PROLOGUE. But what will you have it called?

CITIZEN. "The Grocer's Honour."

SPEAKER OF THE PROLOGUE. Methinks "The Knight o' the Burning Pestle" were better.

WIFE. I'll be sworn, husband, that's as good a name as can be.

CITIZEN. Let it be so.—Begin, begin; my wife and I will sit down.

SPEAKER OF THE PROLOGUE. I pray you, do.

CITIZEN. What stately music have you? You have shawms?

SPEAKER OF THE PROLOGUE. Shawms? No.

CITIZEN. No! I'm a thief, if my mind did not give me so. Ralph plays a stately part, and he must needs have shawms. I'll be at the charge of them myself, rather than we'll be without them.

SPEAKER OF THE PROLOGUE. So you are like to be.

CITIZEN. Why, and so I will be: there's two shillings, —[*Gives money*]—let's have the waits of Southwark; they are as rare fellows as any are in England; and that will fetch them all o'er the water with a vengeance, as if they were mad.

SPEAKER OF THE PROLOGUE. You shall have them. Will you sit down, then?

CITIZEN. Ay.—Come, wife.

WIFE. Sit you merry all, gentlemen; I'm bold to sit amongst you for my ease.   [CITIZEN *and* WIFE *sit down.*

SPEAKER OF THE PROLOGUE. "From all that's near the court, from all that's great,

Within the compass of the city-walls,

We now have brought our scene. Fly far from hence

All private taxes, immodest phrases,
Whatever may but show like vicious!
For wicked mirth never true pleasure brings,
But honest minds are pleased with honest things."—
Thus much for that we do; but for Ralph's part you must
answer for yourself.

CITIZEN. Take you no care for Ralph; he'll discharge
himself, I warrant you.   [*Exit* SPEAKER OF THE PROLOGUE.

WIFE. I' faith, gentlemen, I'll give my word for Ralph.

SCENE: *A grocer's shop.*

Enter RALPH, *as a grocer, reading "Palmerin of England,"*
with TIM *and* GEORGE.

[WIFE. Oh, husband, husband, now, now! there's
Ralph, there's Ralph.

CITIZEN. Peace, fool! let Ralph alone.—Hark you,
Ralph; do not strain yourself too much at the first.—
Peace!—Begin, Ralph.]

RALPH [*reads*]. Then Palmerin and Trineus, snatching
their lances from their dwarfs, and clasping their helmets,
gallopt amain after the giant; and Palmerin, having
gotten a sight of him, came posting amain, saying, "Stay,
traitorous thief! for thou mayst not so carry away her,
that is worth the greatest lord in the world"; and, with
these words, gave him a blow on the shoulder, that he
struck him besides his elephant. And Trineus, coming to
the knight that had Agricola behind him, set him soon
besides his horse, with his neck broken in the fall; so that
the princess, getting out of the throng, between joy and
grief, said, "All happy knight, the mirror of all such as
follow arms, now may I be well assured of the love thou
bearest me." I wonder why the kings do not raise an army
of fourteen or fifteen hundred thousand men, as big as
the army that the Prince of Portigo brought against

Rosicleer, and destroy these giants; they do much hurt to wandering damsels, that go in quest of their knights.

[WIFE. Faith, husband, and Ralph says true; for they say the King of Portugal cannot sit at his meat, but the giants and the ettins will come and snatch it from him.

CITIZEN. Hold thy tongue.—On, Ralph!]

RALPH. And certainly those knights are much to be commended, who, neglecting their possessions, wander with a squire and a dwarf through the deserts to relieve poor ladies.

[WIFE. Ay, by my faith, are they, Ralph; let 'em say what they will, they are indeed. Our knights neglect their possessions well enough, but they do not the rest.]

RALPH. There are no such courteous and fair well-spoken knights in this age. But what brave spirit could be content to sit in his shop, with a flappet of wood, and a blue apron before him, selling mithridatum and dragon's-water to visited houses, that might pursue feats of arms, and, through his noble achievements, procure such a famous history to be written of his heroic prowess?

[CITIZEN. Well said, Ralph; some more of those words, Ralph!

WIFE. They go finely, by my troth.]

RALPH. Why should not I, then, pursue this course, both for the credit of myself and our company? for amongst all the worthy books of achievements, I do not call to mind that I yet read of a grocer-errant. I will be the said knight. Have you heard of any that hath wandered unfurnished of his squire and dwarf? My elder prentice Tim shall be my trusty squire, and little George my dwarf. Hence, my blue apron! Yet, in remembrance of my former trade, upon my shield shall be portrayed a Burning Pestle, and I will be called the Knight of the Burning Pestle.

[WIFE. Nay, I dare swear thou wilt not forget thy old trade; thou wert ever meek.]

RALPH. Tim!

TIM. Anon.

RALPH. My beloved squire, and George my dwarf, I charge you that from henceforth you never call me by any other name but "the right courteous and valiant Knight of the Burning Pestle"; and that you never call any female by the name of a woman or wench, but "fair lady," if she have her desires, if not, "distressed damsel": that you call all forests and heaths "deserts," and all horses "palfreys."

[WIFE. This is very fine, faith.—Do the gentlemen like Ralph, think you, husband?

CITIZEN. Ay, I warrant thee; the players would give all the shoes in their shop for him.]

RALPH. My beloved squire Tim, stand out. Admit this were a desert, and over it a knight-errant pricking, and I should bid you inquire of his intents, what would you say?

TIM. Sir, my master sent me to know whither you are riding?

RALPH. No, thus: "Fair sir, the right courteous and valiant Knight of the Burning Pestle commanded me to inquire upon what adventure you are bound, whether to relieve some distressed damsels, or otherwise."

[CITIZEN. Blockhead, cannot remember!

WIFE. I' faith, and Ralph told him on't before: all the gentlemen heard him.—Did he not, gentlemen? did not Ralph tell him on't?]

GEORGE. Right courteous and valiant Knight of the Burning Pestle, here is a distressed damsel to have a halfpenny-worth of pepper.

[WIFE. That's a good boy! See, the little boy can hit it; by my troth, it's a fine child.]

RALPH. Relieve her, with all courteous language. Now shut up shop; no more my prentices, but my trusty squire and dwarf. I must bespeak my shield and arming pestle

[*Exeunt* TIM *and* GEORGE.

[CITIZEN. Go thy ways, Ralph! As I'm a true man, thou art the best on 'em all.

WIFE. Ralph, Ralph!

RALPH. What say you, mistress?

WIFE. I prithee, come again quickly, sweèt Ralph.

RALPH. By and by.]   [*Exit.*

SCENE: *Before a barber's shop, Waltham.*

Enter RALPH, HOST, TIM, *and* GEORGE.

[WIFE. Oh, Ralph's here, George! God send thee good luck, Ralph!]

HOST. Puissant knight, yonder his mansion is.
Lo, where the spear and copper basin are!
Behold that string, on which hangs many a tooth,
Drawn from the gentle jaw of wandering knights!
I dare not stay to sound; he will appear.   [*Exit.*

RALPH. Oh, faint not, heart! Susan, my lady dear,
The cobbler's maid in Milk-street, for whose sake
I take these arms, oh, let the thought of thee
Carry thy knight through all adventurous deeds;
And, in the honour of thy beauteous self,
May I destroy this monster Barbaroso!—
Knock, squire, upon the basin, till it break
With the shrill strokes, or till the giant speak.
                        [TIM *knocks upon the basin.*
                    Enter BARBER.

[WIFE. Oh, George, the giant, the giant!—Now, Ralph, for thy life!]

BARBER. What fond unknowing wight is this, that dares
So rudely knock at Barbaroso's cell,
Where no man comes but leaves his fleece behind?

RALPH. I, traitorous caitiff, who am sent by fate
To punish all the sad enormities
Thou hast committed against ladies gent
And errant knights. Traitor to God and men,

Prepare thyself! This is the dismal hour
Appointed for thee to give strict account
Of all thy beastly treacherous villanies.

BARBER. Fool-hardy knight, full soon thou shalt aby
This fond reproach: thy body will I bang;

[Takes down his pole.

And, lo, upon that string thy teeth shall hang!
Prepare thyself, for dead soon shalt thou be.

RALPH. Saint George for me!   *[They fight.*

BARBER. Gargantua for me!

[WIFE. To him, Ralph, to him! hold up the giant; set
out thy leg before, Ralph!

CITIZEN. Falsify a blow, Ralph, falsify a blow! the giant
lies open on the left side.

WIFE. Bear't off, bear't off still! there, boy!—
Oh! Ralph's almost down, Ralph's almost down!]

RALPH. Susan, inspire me! Now have up again.

[WIFE. Up, up, up, up, up! so, Ralph! down with him,
down with him, Ralph!

CITIZEN. Fetch him o'er the hip, boy!

[RALPH knocks down the BARBER.

WIFE. There, boy! kill, kill, kill, kill, kill, Ralph!

CITIZEN. No, Ralph; get all out of him first.]

RALPH. Presumptuous man, see to what desperate end
Thy treachery hath brought thee! The just gods,
Who never prosper those that do despise them,
For all the villanies which thou hast done
To knights and ladies, now have paid thee home
By my stiff arm, a knight adventurous.
But say, vile wretch, before I send thy soul
To sad Avernus, (whither it must go),
What captives holdst thou in thy sable cave?

BARBER. Go in, and free them all; thou hast the day.

RALPH. Go, squire and dwarf, search in this dreadful cave,
And free the wretched prisoners from their bonds.

[Exeunt TIM *and* GEORGE.

BARBER. I crave for mercy, as thou art a knight,
And scorn'st to spill the blood of those that beg.

RALPH. Thou show'd'st no mercy, nor shalt thou have any;
Prepare thyself, for thou shalt surely die.

Re-enter TIM *leading a* MAN *winking, with a basin under his chin.*

TIM. Behold, brave knight, here is one prisoner,
Whom this vile man hath used as you see.

[WIFE. This is the first wise word I heard the squire speak.]

RALPH. Speak what thou art, and how thou hast been used,
That I may give him condign punishment.

MAN. I am a knight that took my journey post
Northward from London; and in courteous wise
This giant trained me to his loathsome den,
Under pretence of killing of the itch;
And all my body with a powder strewed,
That smarts and stings; and cut away my beard,
And my curled locks wherein were ribands tied;
And with a water washed my tender eyes,
(Whilst up and down about me still he skipt,)
Whose virtue is, that, till my eyes be wiped
With a dry cloth, for this my foul disgrace,
I shall not dare to look a dog i' the face.

[WIFE. Alas, poor knight!—Relieve him,
Ralph; relieve poor knights, whilst you live.]

RALPH. My trusty squire, convey him to the town,
Where he may find relief.—Adieu, fair knight.

[*Exeunt* MAN *with* TIM, *who presently re-enters.*
Re-enter GEORGE, *leading a second* MAN, *with a patch over his nose.*

GEORGE. Puissant Knight, of the Burning Pestle hight,
See here another wretch, whom this foul beast
Hath scotched and scored in this inhuman wise.

RALPH. Speak me thy name, and eke thy place of birth
And what hath been thy usage in this cave.

SECOND MAN. I am a knight,
And by my birth I am a Londoner,
Free by my copy, but my ancestors
Were Frenchmen all; and riding hard this way
Upon a trotting horse, my bones did ache;
And I, faint knight, to easy my weary limbs,
Light at this cave; when straight this furious fiend,
With sharpest instrument of purest steel,
Did cut the gristle of my nose away,
And in the place this velvet plaster stands.
Relieve me, gentle knight, out of his hands!

[WIFE. Good Ralph, relieve him, and send him away.]

RALPH. Convey him straight after the other knight.

SECOND MAN. Kind sir, good night.

> [*Exit with* GEORGE, *who presently enters.*
> *Cries within.*

THIRD MAN [*within*]. Deliver us!

WOMAN [*within*]. Deliver us!

[WIFE. Hark, George, what a woeful cry there is!]

THIRD MAN [*within*]. Deliver us!

WOMAN [*within*]. Deliver us!

RALPH. What ghastly noise is this? Speak, Barbaroso,
Or, by this blazing steel, thy head goes off!

BARBER. Prisoners of mine, whom I in diet keep.
Send lower down into the cave,
There may they find them, and deliver them.

RALPH. Run, squire and dwarf; deliver them with
speed.   [*Exeunt* TIM *and* GEORGE.

[WIFE. But will not Ralph kill this giant? Surely I am
afeard, if he let him go, he will do as much hurt as ever
he did.

CITIZEN. Not so, mouse, neither, if he could convert
him.

WIFE. Ay, George, if he could convert him; but a giant

is not so soon converted as one of us ordinary people.
There's a pretty tale of a witch, that had the devil's mark
about her, (God bless us!) that had a giant to her son,
that was called Lob-lie-by-the-fire; didst never hear it,
George?

    CITIZEN. Peace, Nell, here comes the prisoners.]

    Re-enter TIM, *leading a third* MAN, *with a glass of lotion in*
    his hand, and GEORGE *leading a* WOMAN, *with diet-bread*
    and drink in her hand.

    GEORGE. Here be these pinèd wretches, manful knight,
That for this six weeks have not seen a wight.

    RALPH. Deliver what you are, and how you came
To this sad cave, and what your usage was?

    THIRD MAN. I am an errant knight that followed
arms
With spear and shield; and in my tender years
I stricken was with Cupid's fiery shaft,
And fell in love with this my lady dear,
And stole her from her friends in Turnbull-street,
And bore her up and down from town to town,
Where we did eat and drink, and music hear;
Till at the length of this unhappy town
We did arrive, and coming to this cave,
This beast us caught, and put us in a tub,
Where we this two months sweat, and should have done
Another month, if you had not relieved us.

    WOMAN. This bread and water hath our diet been,
Together with a rib cut from a neck
Of burned mutton; hard hath been our fare.
Release us from this ugly giant's snare!

    THIRD MAN. This hath been all the food we have re-
ceived;
But only twice a-day, for novelty,
He gave a spoonful of this hearty broth
To each of us, through this same slender squill.

                        [Pulls out a syringe.

RALPH. From this infernal monster you shall go,
That useth knights and gentle ladies so !
Convey them hence.

> [*Third* MAN *and* WOMAN *are led off by* TIM *and*
>   GEORGE, *who presently re-enter.*

[CITIZEN. Cony, I can tell thee, the gentlemen like Ralph.

WIFE. Ay, George, I see it well enough.—Gentlemen, I
thank you all heartily for gracing my man Ralph; and I
promise you, you shall see him oftener.]

BARBER. Mercy, great knight ! I do recant my ill,
And henceforth never gentle blood will spill.

RALPH. I give thee mercy; but yet shalt thou swear
Upon my Burning Pestle, to perform
Thy promise uttered.

BARBER. I swear and kiss.   [*Kisses the pestle.*

RALPH. Depart, then, and amend.   [*Exit* BARBER.
Come, squire and dwarf; the sun grows towards his set,
And we have many more adventures yet.   [*Exeunt.*

[CITIZEN. Now Ralph is in this humour, I know he
would ha' beaten all the boys in the house, if they had
been set on him.

WIFE. Ay, George, but it is well as it is: I warrant you,
the gentlemen do consider what it is to overthrow a giant.]

PART FOUR
TWO MODERN VIEWS OF SHAKESPEARE AND HIS TIMES

THREE EXTRACTS FROM "SHAKESPEARE'S CHRISTMAS"

BY
A. T. QUILLER-COUCH

THESE extracts will help you to form a still clearer idea of the Elizabethan playhouse. They are taken from a story which tells how The Theatre, built by James Burbage and owned after his death by his sons, was taken down and carried across the Thames, to be re-erected as the Globe Theatre.

THE LAST PERFORMANCE AT THE THEATRE

AT the theatre in Shoreditch, on Christmas Eve, 1598, the Lord Chamberlain's servants presented a new comedy. Never had the Burbages played to such a house. It cheered every speech—good, bad, or indifferent. To be sure, some of the *dramatis personæ*—Prince Hal and Falstaff, Bardolph and Mistress Quickly—were old friends, but this alone would not account for such a welcome. A cutpurse in the twopenny gallery who had been paid to lead the applause gave up toiling in the wake of it, and leaned back with a puzzled grin.

"Bravo, master!" said he to his left-hand neighbour, a burly, red-faced countryman well past middle age, whose laughter kept the bench rocking. "But have a care, lest they mistake you for the author!"

"The author? Ho-ho!"—but here he broke off to leap to his feet and lead another round of applause.

"The author?" he repeated, dropping back and glancing an eye sidelong from under his handkerchief while he mopped his brow. "You shoot better than you know, my friend: the bolt grazes. But a miss, they say, is as good as a mile."

The cutpurse kept his furtive grin, but was evidently mystified. A while before it had been the countryman who showed signs of bewilderment. Until the drawing of the curtains he had fidgeted nervously, then, as now, mopping his forehead in despite of the raw December air. The first shouts of applause had seemed to astonish as well as delight him. When, for example, a player stepped forward and flung an arm impressively towards heaven while he recited—

> When we mean to build,
> We first survey the plot, then draw the model—

and so paused with a smile, his voice drowned in thunder from every side of the house, our friend had rubbed his eyes and gazed around in amiable protest, as who should say, "Come, come, . . . but let us discriminate!" By-and-by, however, as the indifferent applause grew warmer, he warmed with it. At the entrance of Falstaff he let out a bellowing laugh worthy of Olympian Jove, and from that moment led the house. The fops on the sixpenny stools began to mimic, the pit and lower gallery to crane necks for a sight of their fugleman; a few serious playgoers called to have him pitched out; but the mass of the audience backed him with shouts of encouragement. Some wag hailed him as "Burbage's Landlord," and apparently there was meaning, if not merit, in the jest. Without understanding it he played up to it royally, leaning forward for each tally-ho! and afterwards waving his hat as a huntsman laying on his hounds.

The pace of the performance (it had begun at one o'clock) dragged sensibly with all this, and midway in Act IV, as the edge of a grey river-fog overlapped and settled gradually upon the well of the unroofed theatre, voices began to cough and call for lanterns. Two lackeys ran with a dozen. Some they hung from the balcony at the back, others they disposed along both sides of the stage, in front of the sixpenny stools, the audience all the while chaffing them by their Christian names and affectionately pelting them with nuts. Still the fog gathered, until the lantern-rays criss-crossed the stage in separate shafts, and among them the actors moved through Act V in a luminous haze, their figures looming large, their voices muffled and incredibly remote.

An idle apprentice, seated on the right of the cutpurse, began for a game to stop and unstop his ears. This gave the cutpurse an opportunity to search his pockets. *Cantat vacuus*: the apprentice felt him at it and went on with his game. Whenever he stopped his ears the steaming breath of the players reminded him of the painted figures he had seen carried in my Lord Mayor's Show, with labels issuing from their mouths.

He had stopped his ears during the scene of King Henry's reconciliation with Chief Justice Gascoigne, and unstopped them eagerly again when his old friends reappeared— Falstaff and Bardolph and Pistol, all agog and hurrying, hot-foot, boot-and-saddle, to salute the rising sun of favour. "Welcome these pleasant days!" He stamped and clapped, following his neighbours' lead, and also because his feet and hands were cold.

THE END OF THE THEATRE

Play, epilogue, dance, all were over; the curtains drawn, the lanterns hidden behind them. The cutpurse had slipped away, and the countryman and apprentice found themselves side by side waiting while the gallery dissolved its crowd into the fog. . . . The countryman gazed down into the well of the theatre as if seeking an acquaintance among the figures below. "But what are they doing?

What a plague means this hammering? A man cannot hear himself speak for it."

"'Tis the play."

"The play?"

"The true play—the play you applauded: and writ by the same Will Shakespeare, they tell me—some share of it at least. Cometh he not, by the way, from your part of the world?"

The countryman's eyes glistened in their turn: almost in the dusk they appeared to shine with tears.

"Ay, I knew him, down in Warwickshire: a good lad he was, though his mother wept over him for a wild one. Hast ever seen a hen when her duckling takes to water? So it is with woman when, haply, she has hatched out genius."

The apprentice slapped his leg. "I could have sworn it!"

"Hey?"

"Nay, question me not, master, for I cannot bring it to words. You tell me that you knew him: and I—on the instant I clapped eyes on you it seemed that somehow you were part of his world and somehow had belonged to him. Nearer I cannot get, unless you tell me more."

"I knew him: to be sure, down in Warwickshire: but he has gone somedel beyond my ken, living in London, you see."

"He goes beyond any man's kenning: he that has taught us to ken the world with new eyes. I tell you, master,"—the apprentice stretched out a hand,—"I go seeking him like one seeking a father who has begotten him into a new world, seeking him with eyes derived from him. Tell me——"

But the countryman was leaning over the gallery-rail and scanning the pit again. He seemed a trifle bored by a conversation if not of less, then certainly of other, wit than he had bargained for. Somebody had drawn the curtains back from the stage, where the two lackeys who had decked the balcony with lanterns were busy now with crowbars, levering its wooden supports from their sockets.

"Sure," said he, musing, "they don't lift and pack away the stage every night, do they? Or is this some new law to harass players?" He brought his attention back to the apprentice with an effort. "If you feel that way towards him, lad," he answered, "why not accost him? He walks London streets; and he has, if I remember, a courteous, easy manner."

"If the man and his secret were one! But they are not, and there lies the fear—that by finding one I shall miss the other and recover it never. I cannot dare either risk: I want them both. You saw, this afternoon, how, when the secret came within grasp, the man slipped away; how, having taught us to know Falstaff as a foot its old shoe, he left us wondering on a sudden why we laughed! And yet 'twas not sudden, but bred in the play from the beginning; no, nor cruel, but merely right: only he had persuaded us to forget it."

The countryman put up a hand to hide a yawn: and the yawn ended in a slow chuckle.

"Eh? that rogue Falstaff was served out handsomely: though, to tell the truth, I paid no great heed to the last scene, my midriff being sore with laughing."

The apprentice sighed.

"But what is happening below?" the other went on impatiently. "Are they taking the whole theatre to pieces?"

"That is part of the play."

"A whole regiment of workmen!"

"And no stage-army, neither. Yet they come into the play—not the play you saw without understanding, but the play you understood without seeing. They call it *The Phoenix*. Be seated, master, while I unfold the plot: this hammering deafens me The Burbages, you must know——"

"I knew old James, the father. He brought me down a

company of players to our town the year I was High
Bailiff; the first that ever played in our Guildhall. Though
a countryman, I have loved the arts—even to the length
of losing much money by them. A boon fellow, old James!
and yet dignified as any alderman. He died—let me see
—was it two year agone? The news kept me sad for a
week."

"A good player, too,"—the apprentice nodded,—
"though not a patch upon his son Richard. Cuthbert will
serve, in ripe sententious parts that need gravity and a
good memory for the lines. But Richard bears the bell
of the Burbages. Well, Sir, old James being dead, and
suddenly, and (as you say) these two years come February,
his sons must go suing to the ground landlord, the theatre
being leased upon their dad's life. You follow me?"

The countryman nodded in his turn.

"Very well. The landlord, being a skinflint, was willing
to renew the lease, but must raise the rent. If they refuse
to pay it, the playhouse fell to him. You may fancy how
the Burbages called gods and men to witness. Being
acquainted with players, you must know how little they
enjoy affliction until the whole town shares it. Never so
rang Jerusalem with all the woes of Jeremy as did City
and suburb,—from north beyond Bishopsgate to south
along the river, with the cursings of this landlord, who—
to cap the humour of it—is a precisian, and never goes
near a playhouse. Nevertheless, he patched up a truce
for two years ending to-night, raising the rent a little, but
not to the stretch of his demands. To-morrow—or, rather,
the day after, since to-morrow is Christmas—the word is
pay or quit. But in yielding this he yielded our friends the
counterstroke. They have bought a plot across the water,
in the Clink Liberty: and to-morrow, should he pass this
way to church, no theatre will be here for him to smack
his Puritan lips over. But for this hammering and the
deep slush outside you might even now hear the rumbling

of wagons; for wagons there be, a dozen of them, ready to cart the Muses over the bridge before midnight. 'Tis the proper vehicle of Thespis. See those dozen stout rascals lifting the proscenium——"

The countryman smote his great hands together, flung back his head, and let his lungs open in shout after shout of laughter.

"But, master——"

"Oh—oh—oh! Hold my sides, lad, or I start a rib. . . . Nay, if you keep st-staring at me with that s-sol-ol-ol-emn face. Don't—oh, *don't*!"

"Now I know," murmured the apprentice, "what kind of jest goes down in the country: and, by'r Lady, it goes deep!"

But an instant later the man had heaved himself upon his feet; his eyes expanded from their creases into great O's; his whole body towered and distended itself in gigantic indignation. "The villain! The nipcheese curmudgeonly villain! And we tarry here, talking, while such things are done in England! A Nabal, I say. Give me a hammer!" He heaved up an enormous thigh and bestrode the gallery-rail.

"Have a care, master: the rail——"

"A hammer! Below there. A hammer!" He leaned over, bellowing. The gang of workmen lifting the proscenium stared up open-mouthed into the foggy gloom—a ring of ghostly faces upturned in a luminous haze.

Already the man's legs dangled over the void. Twelve, fifteen feet perhaps, beneath him projected a lower gallery, empty but for three tiers of disordered benches. Plumb as a gannet he dropped, and an eloquent crash of timber reported his arrival below. The apprentice, craning over, saw him regain his feet, scramble over the second rail, and vanish. Followed an instant's silence, a dull thud, a cry from workmen in the area. The apprentice ran for the gallery stairs and leapt down them, three steps at a time.

It took him, maybe, forty seconds to reach the area. There already, stripped to the shirt, in a whirl of dust and voices, stood his friend waving a hammer and shouting down the loudest. The man was possessed, transformed, a Boanerges; his hammer, a hammer of Thor! He had caught it from the hand of a douce, sober-looking man in a plum-coloured doublet, who stood watching but taking no active share in the work.

"By your leave, Sir!"

"With or without my leave, good Sir, since you are determined to have it," said the quiet man, surrendering the hammer.

The countryman snatched and thrust it between his knees while he stripped. Then, having spat on both hands, he grasped the hammer and tried its poise.

The Removal

"Tom! What, Tom! Where be the others? I tell thee, Tom, there have been doings . . . ."

"Is that Dick Burbage?" A frail, thin windlestraw of a man came coughing across the foggy courtyard with a stable-lantern, holding it high. Its rays wavered on his own face, which was young but extraordinarily haggard, and on the piles of timber between and over which he picked his way—timbers heaped pell-mell in the slush of the yard or stacked against the boundary wall, some daubed with paint, others gilded wholly or in part, and twinkling as the lantern swung. "Dick Burbage already? Has it miscarried, then?"

"Miscarried? What in the world was there to miscarry? I tell thee, Tom—but where be the others?"

The frail man jerked a thumb at the darkness behind his shoulder. "Hark to them, back yonder, stacking the beams! Where should they be? and what doing but at work like galley-slaves, by the pace you have kept us going? Look around. I tell you from the first 'twas busy-all to get the yard clear between the wagons' coming, and at the fifth load we gave it up. My shirt clings like a dish-clout; a chill on this will be the death o' me. What a plague! How many scoundrels did you hire, that they take a house to pieces and cart it across Thames faster than we can unload it?"

"That's the kernel of the story, lad. I hired the two-score rogues agreed on, neither more nor less: but one descended out of heaven and raised the number to twelve-score. Ten-score extra, as I am a sinner; and yet but one man, for I counted him. His name, he told me, was Legion."

"Dick," said the other sadly, "when a sober man gives way to drinking—I don't blame you: and your pocket will be the loser more than all the rest if you've boggled to-night's work; but poor Cuthbert will take it to heart."

"There was a man, I tell you——"

"Tut, tut, pull yourself together and run back across bridge. Or let me go: take my arm now, before the others see you. You shall tell me on the way what's wrong at Shoreditch."

"There is naught wrong with Shoreditch, forby that it has lost a theatre: and I am not drunk, Tom Nashe — no, not by one-tenth as drunk as I deserve to be, seeing that the house is down, every stick of it, and the bells scarce yet tolling midnight. 'Twas all this man, I tell you!"

"Down? The Theatre down? Oh, go back, Dick Burbage!"

"Level with the ground, I tell you—his site a habitation for the satyr. *Cecidit, cecidit Babylon illa magna!* and the last remains of it, more by token, following close on my heels in six wagons. Hist, then, my Thomas, my Didymus, my doubting one!—Canst not hear the rumble of their wheels? and—and—oh, good Lord!" Burbage caught his friend by the arm and leaned against him heavily. "*He's* there, and following!"

The wagons came rolling over the cobbles of the Clink along the roadway outside the high boundary-wall of the yard: and as they came, clear above their rumble and the slow clatter of hoofs a voice like a trumpet declaimed into the night—

"Above all ryvers thy Ryver hath renowne,
　　Whose beryall streamys, pleasaunt and preclare,
Under thy lusty wallys renneth downe,
　　Where many a swan doth swymme with wyngis fair,
Where many a barge doth sail and row with are—

We had done better—a murrain on their cobbles!—we had done better, lad, to step around by Paul's Wharf and take boat. . . . This jolting ill agrees with a man of my weight. . . .

　　Where many a barge doth sail and row with are—

Gr-r-r! Did I not warn thee beware, master wagoner, of the kerbstones at the corners? We had done better by water, what though it be dark. . . . Lights of Bankside on the water . . . no such sight in Europe, they tell me. . . . My Lord of Surrey took boat one night from Westminster and fired into their windows with a stone-bow, breaking much glass . . . drove all the longshore queans screaming into the streets in their night-rails. . . . He went to the Fleet for it . . . a Privy Council matter. . . . I forgive the lad, for my part: for only think of it—all those windows aflame on the river, and no such river in Europe!—

　　Where many a barge doth sail and row with are;
　　　Where many a ship doth rest with top-royall.
　　O towne of townes! patrone and not compare,
　　　London, thou art the flow'r of Cities all!

Who-oop!"

"In the name of——" stammered Nashe, as he listened, Burbage all the while clutching his arm.

"He dropped from the top gallery, I tell you—clean into the pit from the top gallery—and he weighs eighteen stone if an ounce. 'Your servant, Sir, and of all the Muses,' he says, picking himself up; and with that takes the hammer from my hand and plays Pyrrhus in Troy— Pyrrhus with all the ravening Danai behind him: for those hired scoundrels of mine took fire, and started ripping out the bowels of the poor old theatre as though it had been the Fleet and lodged all their cronies within! It went down before my eyes like a sand-castle before the tide. Within three hours they had wiped the earth of it. The Lord be praised that Philip Gosson had ne'er such an arm, nor could command such! Oh, but he's a portent! Troy's horse and Bankes's bay gelding together are a fool to him: he would harness them as Samson did the little foxes, and fire brushwood under their tails. . . ."

"Of a certainty you are drunk, Dick."

"Drunk? I?" Burbage gripped the other's thin arm hysterically. "If you want to see a man drunk come to the gate. Nay, then, stay where you are: for there's no escaping him."

Nor was there. Between them and the wagoners' lanterns at the gate a huge shadow thrust itself, the owner of it rolling like a ship in a seaway, while he yet recited—

"Strong be thy wallis that about thee standis,

(meaning the Clink, my son),

Wise be the people that within thee dwellis,

(which you may take for the inhabitants thereof),

Fresh is thy ryver with his lusty strandis,
Blith be thy chirches, wele sowning be thy bellis."

"Well sounding is my belly, master, any way," put in a high, thin voice; "and it calls on a gentleman of Warwickshire to redeem his promise."

"He shall, he shall, lad—in the fullness of time: 'but

before dining ring at the bell,' says the proverb. Grope, lad, feel along the gate-posts if this yard, this courtlage, this base-court, hath any such thing as bell or knocker."

[While Burbage and Nashe were talking with the countryman and the apprentice somebody was seen approaching across the yard with another lantern.]

"Tom Nashe! Tom Nashe!" called a voice, clear and strong and masculine, from the darkness behind the advancing lantern.

"Anon, anon, Sir," quoted Nashe, swinging his own lantern about and mimicking.

"Don't tell me there be yet more wagons arrived?" asked the voice.

"Six, lad—six, as I hope for mercy: and outside the gate at this moment."

"There they must tarry, then, till our fellows take breath to unload 'em. But—six? How is it managed, think you? Has Dick Burbage called out the train-bands to help him? Why, hullo, Dick! What means——" The newcomer's eyes, round with wonder as they rested a moment on Burbage, grew rounder yet as they travelled past him to the countryman. "Father?" he stammered, incredulous.

"Good evening, Will! Give ye good evening, my son! Set down that lantern and embrace me, like a good boy: a good boy, albeit a man of fame. Didst not see me, then, in the theatre this afternoon? Yet was I to the fore there, methinks, and proud to be called John Shakespeare."

"Nay, I was not there; having other fish to fry."

"Shouldst have heard the applause, lad; it warmed your old father's heart. Yet 'twas no more than the play deserved. A very neat, pretty drollery—upon my faith, no man's son could have written a neater!"

"But what hath fetched you to London?"

"Business, business: a touch, too, maybe, of the old homesickness: but business first. Dick Quiney—but pass me the lantern, my son, that I may take a look at thee. Ay, thou hast sobered, thou hast solidified: thy beard hath ta'en the right citizen's cut—'twould ha' been a cordial to thy poor mother to see thee wear so staid a beard. Rest her soul! There's nothing like property for filling out a man's frame, firming his eye, his frame, bearing, footstep. Talking of property, I have been none so idle a steward for thee. New Place I have made habitable—the house at least; patched up the roof, taken down and rebuilt the west chimney that was overleaning the road, repaired the launders, enlarged the parlour-window, run out the kitchen passage to a new back-entrance. The garden I cropped with peas this summer, and have set lettuce and winter-kale between the young apple-trees, whereof the whole are doing well, and the mulberry likewise I look for to thrive. . . ."

A heavy tread approached from the gateway.

"Are we to bide here all night, and on Christmas morn, too?" a gruff voice demanded. "Unpack, and pay us our wage, or we tip the whole load of it into Thames." Here the wagoner's shin encountered in the darkness with a plank, and he cursed violently.

"Go you back to your horses, my friend," answered Burbage. "The unloading shall begin anon. As for your wage, your master will tell you I settled it at the time I bargained for his wagons—ay, and paid. I hold his receipt."

"For tenpence a man—mowers' wages," growled the wagoner.

"I asked him his price and he fixed it. 'Tis the current rate, I understand, and a trifle over."

"Depends on the job. I've been talkin' with my mates, and we don't like it. We're decent labouring men, and shifting a lot of play-actors' baggage don't come in our day's work. I'd as lief wash dirty linen for my part. Therefore," the fellow wound up lucidly, "you'll make it twelvepence a head, master. We don't take a groat less."

"I see," said Burbage blandly: "twopence for salving your conscience, hey? And so, being a decent man, you don't stomach players?"

"No, nor the Bankside at this hour o' night. I live clean, I tell you."

"'Tis a godless neighbourhood and a violent." Burbage drew a silver whistle from his doublet and eyed it. "Listen a moment, master wagoner, and tell me what you hear."

"I hear music o' sorts No Christmas carols, I warrant."

"Aught else?"

"Ay: a sound like a noise of dogs baying over yonder."

"Right again: it comes from the kennels by the Bear Pit. Have you a wish, my friend, to make nearer acquaintance with these dogs? No? With the bears, then? Say the word, and inside of a minute I can whistle up your two-pennyworth."

The wagoner with a dropping jaw stared from one to another of the ring of faces in the lantern-light. They were quiet, determined. Only the apprentice stood with ears pricked, as it were, and shivered at the distant baying.

"No offence, Sir; I meant no offence, you'll understand," the wagoner stammered.

"Nay, call your mates, man!" spoke up William Shakespeare, sudden and sharp, and with a scornful ring in his voice which caused our apprentice to jump. "Call them in and let us hear you expound Master Burbage's proposal. I am curious to see how they treat you—having an opinion of my own on crowds and their leaders."

But the wagoner had swung about surlily on his heel.

"I'll not risk disputing it," he growled. "'Tis your own dung-hill, and I must e'en take your word that 'tis worse than e'er a man thought. But one thing I'll not take back. You're a muck of play-actors, and a man that touches ye should charge for his washing. Gr-r!" he spat—"ye're worse than Patty Ward's sow, and *she* was no lavender!"

THE REHEARSAL

BY

MAURICE BARING

In Part One of this book you read a description of an
Elizabethan playhouse, and the difficulties and absurdities
of play-production in the sixteenth and seventeenth centuries were pointed out to you. In Part Two you read many
scenes from Shakespeare's tragedy *Macbeth*. In the very
amusing burlesque which follows a modern writer gives
his impression of what a rehearsal of *Macbeth* must have
been like when the play was first produced.

Characters

Mr William Shakespeare
The Producer
The Stage Manager
Mr Burbage (*Macbeth*)
Mr Hughes (*Lady Macbeth*)
Mr Kydd (*Banquo*)
Mr Foote (*Macduff*)
Mr Thomas (*The Doctor*)
Mr Lyle (*First Witch*)
Second Witch
Third Witch

Scene: *The Globe Theatre*, 1606. *On the stage the*
author, *the* producer, *and the* stage manager *are
standing. A rehearsal of "Macbeth" is about to begin.
Waiting in the wings are the actors who are playing the*
witches, banquo, macduff, *etc. They are all men.*

the stage manager. We'd better begin with the last act.

THE PRODUCER. I think we'll begin with the first act. We've never done it all through yet.

THE STAGE MANAGER. Mr Colman isn't here. It's no good doing the first act without Duncan.

THE PRODUCER. Where is Mr Colman? Did you let him know about rehearsal?

THE STAGE MANAGER. I sent a messenger to his house in Gray's Inn.

THE FIRST WITCH. Mr Colman is playing Psyche in a masque at Kenilworth. He won't be back until the day after to-morrow.

THE PRODUCER. That settles it. We'll begin with the fifth act.

THE FIRST WITCH. Then I suppose I can go.

THE SECOND WITCH.⎫
THE THIRD WITCH. ⎬And I suppose we needn't wait.

THE STAGE MANAGER. Certainly not. We're going on to the fourth act as soon as we've done the fifth.

BANQUO. But I suppose you don't want me.

THE STAGE MANAGER. And what about your ghost entrance in Act Four? We must get the business right this time; besides, we'll do the second act if we've time. Now, Act Five, Mr Thomas and Mr Bowles, please.

THE FIRST WITCH. Mr Bowles can't come to-day. He told me to tell you. He's having a tooth pulled out.

THE STAGE MANAGER. Then will you read the waiting gentlewoman's part, Mr Lyle. You can take this scrip.

[*The* FIRST WITCH *takes the scrip.*
Where is Mr Thomas?

THE FIRST WITCH. He said he was coming.

THE STAGE MANAGER. We can't wait. I'll read his part. We'll leave out the beginning and just give Mr Hughes his cue.

THE FIRST WITCH [*reading*]. "Having no witness to confirm my speech."

THE STAGE MANAGER. Mr Hughes.

THE FIRST WITCH. He was here a moment ago.

THE STAGE MANAGER [*louder*]. Mr Hughes.

Enter LADY MACBETH (MR HUGHES, *a young man about twenty-four.*)

LADY MACBETH. Sorry.

[*He comes on down some steps L.C.*

THE PRODUCER. That will never do, Mr Hughes; there's no necessity to sway as if you were intoxicated, and you mustn't look at your feet.

LADY MACBETH. It's the steps. They're so rickety.

THE PRODUCER. We'll begin again from "speech."

[LADY MACBETH *comes on again. He looks straight in front of him and falls heavily on to the ground.*

I said those steps were to be mended yesterday.

[*The* FIRST WITCH *is convulsed with laughter.*

LADY MACBETH. There's nothing to laugh at.

THE PRODUCER. Are you hurt, Mr Hughes?

LADY MACBETH. Not much.

[*The steps are replaced by two supers.*

THE PRODUCER. Now from "speech."

[MR HUGHES *comes on again.*

THE PRODUCER. You must not hold the taper upside down.

LADY MACBETH. How can I rub my hands and hold a taper too? What's the use of the taper?

THE PRODUCER. You can rub the back of your hand. You needn't wash your hands in the air. That's better.

GENTLEWOMAN. "Neither to you nor anyone; having no witness to confirm my speech. Lo you, here she comes!"

Enter LADY MACBETH.

GENTLEWOMAN. "This is her very guise; and, upon my life, fast asleep. Observe her! stand close."

THE DOCTOR. "How came she by that light?"

GENTLEWOMAN. "Why, it stood by her: she has light by her continually; 'tis her command."

THE DOCTOR. "You see, her eyes are open."

GENTLEWOMAN. "Ay, but their sense is shut."

THE DOCTOR. "What is it she does now? Look, how she rubs her hands."

GENTLEWOMAN. "It is an accustomed action with her to seem thus washing her hands: I have known her continue in this a quarter of an hour."

Enter the DOCTOR (MR THOMAS). *He waits* R.

LADY MACBETH. "Here's a damned spot."

THE STAGE MANAGER. No, no, Mr Hughes, "Yet here's a spot."

THE PRODUCER. Begin again from "hands."

GENTLEWOMAN. "It is an accustomed action with her to seem thus washing her hands. I've known her to continue in this three-quarters of an hour."

LADY MACBETH. "Yet here's a damned spot."

THE STAGE MANAGER. It's not "damned" at all. That comes later.

LADY MACBETH. It's catchy. Couldn't I say "mark" instead of "spot" in the first line?

THE DOCTOR [*coming forward*]. That would entirely spoil the effect of my "Hark." You see "mark" rhymes with "Hark." It's impossible.

THE PRODUCER. Oh! It's you, Mr Thomas. Will you go straight on. We'll do the whole scene over presently. Now from "hour."

LADY MACBETH. "Yes, here's a spot."

THE STAGE MANAGER. It's not "Yes," but "Yet," Mr Hughes.

LADY MACBETH. "Yet here's a spot."

THE DOCTOR [*at the top of his voice*]. "Hark!"

THE PRODUCER. Not so loud, Mr Thomas, that would wake her up.

THE DOCTOR [*in a high falsetto*]. "Har-r-rk! She spe-e-e-aks. I will . . . set . . . down."

THE PRODUCER. You needn't bleat that "speaks," Mr Thomas, and the second part of that line is cut.

THE DOCTOR. It's not cut in my part. "Hark, she speaks."

LADY MACBETH. "Yet here's a spot."

THE STAGE MANAGER. No, Mr Hughes; "out, damned spot."

LADY MACBETH. Sorry.

THE PRODUCER. We must get that right. Now from "hour."

LADY MACBETH. "Yet here's a spot."

THE DOCTOR. "Hark! she speaks."

LADY MACBETH. "Get out, damned spot! Get out, I say! One, two, three, four: why there's plenty of time to do't. Oh! Hell! Fie, fie, my Lord! a soldier and a beard! What have we got to fear when none can call our murky power to swift account withal? You'd never have thought the old man had so much blood in him!"

THE AUTHOR. I don't think you've got those lines quite right yet, Mr Hughes.

LADY MACBETH. What's wrong?

THE STAGE MANAGER. There's no "get." It's "one; two": and not "one, two, three, four." Then it's "Hell is murky." And there's no "plenty." And it's "a soldier and *afeared*," and not "a soldier and a *beard*."

THE AUTHOR. And after that you made two lines into rhymed verse.

MR HUGHES. Yes, I know I did. I thought it wanted it.

THE PRODUCER. Please try to speak your lines as they are written, Mr Hughes.

Enter MR BURBAGE, *who plays* MACBETH.

MR BURBAGE. That scene doesn't go. Now don't you think Macbeth had better walk in his sleep instead of Lady Macbeth?

THE STAGE MANAGER. That's an idea.

THE PRODUCER. I think the whole scene might be cut. It's quite unnecessary.

LADY MACBETH. Then I shan't come on in the whole of the fifth act. If that scene's cut I shan't play at all.

THE STAGE MANAGER. We're thinking of transferring the scene to Macbeth. [*To the* AUTHOR] It wouldn't need much altering. Would you mind rewriting that scene, Mr Shakespeare? It wouldn't want much alteration. You'd have to change that line about Arabia. Instead of "this little hand," you might say: "All the perfumes of Arabia will not sweeten this horny hand." I'm not sure it isn't more effective.

THE AUTHOR. I'm afraid it might get a laugh.

MR BURBAGE. Not if I play it.

THE AUTHOR. I think it's more likely that Lady Macbeth would walk in her sleep, but——

MR BURBAGE. That doesn't signify. I can make a great hit in that scene.

LADY MACBETH. If you take that scene from me, I shan't play Juliet to-night.

THE STAGE MANAGER [*aside to* PRODUCER]. We can't possibly get another Juliet.

THE PRODUCER. On the whole, I think we must leave the scene as it is.

MR BURBAGE. I've got nothing to do in the last act. What's the use of my coming to rehearsal when there's nothing for me to rehearse?

THE PRODUCER. Very well, Mr Burbage. We'll go on to the Third Scene at once. We'll go through your scene again later, Mr Hughes.

MR BURBAGE. Before we do this scene there's a point I wish to settle. In Scene Five, when Seyton tells me the Queen's dead, I say: "She should have died hereafter; there would have been a time for such a word"; and then the messenger enters. I should like a soliloquy here, about twenty or thirty lines, if possible in rhyme, in any case ending with a tag. I should like it to be about Lady Macbeth. Macbeth might have something touching to say about their happy domestic life, and the early days of their marriage. He might refer to their courtship. I must have something to make Macbeth sympathetic, otherwise the public won't stand it. He might say his better-half had left him, and then he might refer to her beauty. The speech might begin:

> O dearest chuck, it is unkind indeed
> To leave me in the midst of my sore need.

Or something of the kind. In any case it ought to rhyme. Could I have that written at once, and then we could rehearse it?

THE PRODUCER. Certainly, certainly, Mr Burbage. Will you write it yourself, Mr Shakespeare, or shall we get some one else to do it?

THE AUTHOR. I'll do it myself if some one will read my part

THE PRODUCER. Let me see; I forget what is your part.

THE STAGE MANAGER. Mr Shakespeare is playing Seyton. [*Aside*] We cast him for Duncan, but he wasn't up to it.

THE PRODUCER. Mr Kydd, will you read Mr Shakespeare's part?

BANQUO. Certainly.

THE PRODUCER. Please let us have that speech, Mr Shakespeare, as quickly as possible. [*Aside*] Don't make it too long. Ten lines at the most.

THE AUTHOR [*aside*]. Is it absolutely necessary that it should rhyme?

THE PRODUCER [*aside*]. No, of course not; that's Burbage's fad.   [*Exit the* AUTHOR *into the wings.*

MR BURBAGE. I should like to go through the fight first.

THE PRODUCER. Very well, Mr Burbage.

THE STAGE MANAGER. Macduff—Mr Foote——

MACDUFF I'm here.

MR BURBAGE. I'll give you the cue:

"Why should I play the fool and like a Roman

Die on my sword: while there is life, there's hope,
The gashes are for them."

MACDUFF. "Turn, hell-hound, turn."

MR BURBAGE. I don't think Macduff ought to call Macbeth a hell-hound.

THE PRODUCER. What do you suggest?

MR BURBAGE. I should suggest: "False monarch, turn." It's more dignified.

MACDUFF. I would rather say "hell-hound."

THE PRODUCER. Supposing we made it "King of Hell."

MR BURBAGE. I don't think that would do.

THE PRODUCER. Then we must leave it for the present.

MACDUFF. "Turn, hell-hound, turn."

[*They begin to fight with wooden swords.*

THE STAGE MANAGER. You don't begin to fight till Macduff says "Give thee out."

MR BURBAGE. I think we might run those two speeches into one, and I might say:
"Of all men I would have avoided thee,
But come on now, although my soul is charged
With blood of thine, I'll have no further words.
My voice is in my sword."
Then Macduff could say:
"O bloodier villain than terms can well express."

THE PRODUCER. We must consult the author about that.

MR BURBAGE. We'll do the fencing without words first.

[*They begin to fight again.* MACDUFF *gives* MR BURBAGE
a tremendous blow on the shoulder.

MR BURBAGE. Oh! Oh! That's my rheumatic shoulder. Please be a little more careful, Mr Foote. You know I've got no padding. I can't go on rehearsing now. I am very seriously hurt indeed.

MACDUFF. I'm sure I'm very sorry It was entirely an accident.

MR BURBAGE. I'm afraid I must go home. I don't feel up to it.

THE STAGE MANAGER. I'll send for some ointment. Please be more careful, Mr Foote. Couldn't you possibly see your way to take Scene Three, Mr Burbage?

MR BURBAGE. I know Scene Three backwards. However, I'll just run through my speech.

THE STAGE MANAGER. What? "This push will cheer me ever?"

MR BURBAGE [*peevishly*]. No, not that one. You know that's all right. That tricky speech about the medicine. Give me the cue.

THE STAGE MANAGER. "That keep her from her rest."

MR BURBAGE.   "Cure her of that:
Canst thou not minister to a sickly mind,
Pull from the memory a booted sorrow,
Rub out the troubles of the busy brain,
And with a sweet and soothing antidote
Clean the stiff bosom of that dangerous poison
Which weighs upon the heart?"
There, you see, word-perfect. What did I say?

THE STAGE MANAGER. No, no, Mr Burbage. It's not a booted sorrow, but a *rooted* sorrow. It's not a stiff bosom but a *stuff* bosom—but here's Mr Shakespeare.

THE AUTHOR. I've written that speech. Shall I read it?

THE PRODUCER. Please.

MR SHAKESPEARE [*reads*]. "To-morrow, and to-morrow, and to-morrow,
Creeps in this petty pace from day to day,
To the last syllable of recorded time;
And all our yesterdays have lighted fools
The way to dusty death. Out, out, brief candle!
Life's but a walking shadow, a poor player
That struts and frets his hour upon the stage,
And then is heard no more: it is a tale
Told by an idiot, full of sound and fury,
Signifying nothing."

MR BURBAGE. Well, you don't expect me to say that, I

suppose. It's a third too short. There's not a single rhyme in it. It's got nothing to do with the situation, and it's an insult to the stage. "Struts and frets" indeed! I see there's nothing left for me but to throw up the part. You can get any one you please to play Macbeth. One thing is quite certain, I won't.

[*Exit* MR BURBAGE *in a passion.*

THE STAGE MANAGER [*to the* AUTHOR]. Now you've done it.

THE AUTHOR [*to the* PRODUCER]. You said it needn't rhyme.

THE PRODUCER. It's Macduff. It was all your fault, Mr Foote.

LADY MACBETH. Am I to wear a fair wig or a dark wig?

THE PRODUCER. Oh! I don't know.

THE AUTHOR. Dark, if you please. People are always saying I'm making portraits. So, if you're dark, nobody can say I meant the character for the Queen or for Mistress Mary Fytton.

THE STAGE MANAGER. It's no good going on now. It's all up—it's all up.

CURTAIN